The Preschool Calendar

Monthly Teaching Resources from *The Preschool Papers*

Edited by
Sherrill B. Flora

Cover illustration by
Linda Hohag

Inside illustrations by
Julie Anderson

Published by Instructional Fair • TS Denison
an imprint of

 McGraw-Hill
Children's Publishing

Credits
Author: Sherrill B. Flora
Cover Illustration: Linda Hohag
Inside Illustrations: Julie Anderson
Project Director: Sherrill B. Flora
Editor: Karen Seberg
Cover Art Direction: Darcy Bell-Myers
Graphic Layout: Deborah Hanson McNiff

McGraw-Hill
Children's Publishing
A Division of The **McGraw·Hill** Companies

Published by Instructional Fair • TS Denison
An imprint of McGraw-Hill Children's Publishing
Copyright © 2000 McGraw-Hill Children's Publishing

Send all inquiries to:
McGraw-Hill Children's Publishing
3195 Wilson Drive NW
Grand Rapids, Michigan 49544

The Preschool Calendar
ISBN: 1-56822-999-2

ᗗᗗᗗ Introduction ᗗᗗᗗ

The Preschool Calendar consists of three complete years of T.S. Denison's monthly early childhood publication, *The Preschool Papers*. The years included in this book are September 1984 through summer 1987. All the issues have been reorganized and bound in book form to provide early childhood teachers with a wealth of material to be used year after year.

The Preschool Calendar offers teachers instructional units, organized by the month and subject area. The practical activities and timeless teaching suggestions can be used as a complete early childhood curriculum, or they may be used to enrich or supplement a preexisting curriculum program. The content has been tried, tested, validated as age-appropriate, and has been well-received by early childhood educators. *The Preschool Calendar* is a book that all early childhood programs will want in their libraries and teaching resource centers.

The Preschool Calendar can provide teachers with creative ideas all year long. For each of the nine school months and a special summer section, you will find:

- Fine Motor/Art Activities
- Gross Motor/Movement Activities
- Language Activities
- Stories
- Learning Games /Experiential Activities
- Bulletin Boards/Wall Displays
- Music Activities
- Finger Plays/Poetry
- Reproducible Activity Pages

All the material that you will need for developing a creative, educational, stimulating, and "fun" early childhood program can be found in *The Preschool Calendar*.

ᴧᴧᴧᴧ Table of Contents ᴧᴧᴧᴧ

During the month of September many children are beginning their first preschool experience. Some children adjust quickly and are immediately able to join in, but for other children, those first few days of preschool can be "a little scary." Many of the activities this month are meant to help ease the child's adjustment to his/her new preschool setting.

Here are some helpful suggestions that will ease the child's transition from home to preschool:

1. At the time of enrollment, ask the parents to fill out an information sheet, including questions about a child's favorite toys and activities. It will help if you know something about the child's interests ahead of time.

2. Call parents the day before a child is to begin school. Ask if there is anything special you could do to make the child's first day more comfortable. This will make the parents feel more comfortable, too.

3. Allow children to bring a "special blanket." As children become more secure in their new situation, the need for the blanket will decrease. I believe this is especially important if a child is entering a toddler room or is beginning preschool at the age of 2½.

4. Let Mom or Dad visit on the first day for an hour or so. Children often reflect the attitudes of their parents. If the child can see that Mom or Dad thinks the preschool is a nice place, the child is more apt to think so, too.

5. Encourage parents not to look anxious when they leave the child. Good-byes should be kept cheerful, even if the child is in tears.

The preschool teacher not only has to help the child adjust, but also needs to help the parents make some adjustments. For parents, leaving a child under the care of someone else for the first time can be an upsetting experience. I am a teacher and I am also the parent of a preschooler. After all my years in the classroom, I could not believe how anxious I felt about leaving my little girl at what I knew to be a warm, responsible, and well-run preschool. I worried if she was going to be happy; would she nap well; would she eat? Both of us did adjust, but I think it took me longer than it did my daughter.

Here are some suggestions that I have found helpful to do as a teacher, and things that I have appreciated as the parent of a preschooler.

1. Daily Notes—Nap or rest time is a good time to write these notes. Daily notes will probably save you time in the long run, because you will not need to answer so many questions at the end of the day.

2. Post activities or lesson plans outside your classroom door. This will encourage parents to discuss daily activities with their child.

3. If possible, provide copies of finger plays, songs, or topics which are being taught.

4. Let parents know you are available to talk with them. Encourage appointments so parents do not disrupt your class.

Helping children make the transition from home to school is of the utmost importance. I believe that the first teacher a child has in school is probably the most important teacher he/she will ever have. That first teacher can set a child's attitude for all his/her school years. YOU are very important!

Storybook Friends

This bulletin board or wall display is started in September and added to all year long, or until the space is filled up.

Each time you read a story to your class, draw a picture of one or more of the main characters. Keep adding the characters to your bulletin board.

Children love seeing pictures of the characters that they have learned about in stories. This is also a fun technique for increasing memory skills. Periodically ask the children who all the characters are, and see who can retell all or part of the story.

Display the characters walking along a path or scattered in a forest scene.

I Am a Special Friend Because . . .

The teacher prepares a circle shape for the head, cut out of construction paper, and attaches it to a tongue depressor, for the body.

The children decorate the faces to look like themselves by adding yarn for hair and coloring in the features of the faces.

The teacher writes a short phrase on the tongue depressor that completes the sentence, "I am a Special Friend because . . ."

Welcome Back to School

On the first day of school, use an instant camera and take a picture of each child in your classroom. Mount the pictures on construction paper, with each child's name below his/her picture. Fold the corners of the construction paper to make a three-dimensional picture frame. Display the pictures around a drawing of an old-fashioned school house.

When it is time to take down this beginning-of-the-year display, you can use the photographs in other classroom displays that could be kept up all year round.

I Have a Special Friend

This bulletin board or wall display provides a daily activity. The children are challenged to guess who among the class is the teacher's special friend for that day. Children must guess from the clues given, such as color of hair, eyes, shoes, and so forth.

To make the board easy to change, make color wheels that fit behind the windows, or make color cards that can be pinned or taped up daily. Place a large sheet of paper on the bulletin board every day and use felt-tip markers to describe body parts and to draw the composite picture.

Problem-solving skills are developed through the mystery of the special friend; self-concept is enhanced through the attention to one child a day. Keep the bulletin board up until every child in the class has had an opportunity to be the teacher's special friend.

We Love School

This is a cute bulletin board or wall display when it is completed. The background of the bulletin board can be any color you choose. Each child makes a character that represents him/herself, using a tongue depressor body and a paper head. Yarn can be used for the hair. Each child can dictate a sentence about why they love school. The caption is placed under each child's self-image.

Helping Hands

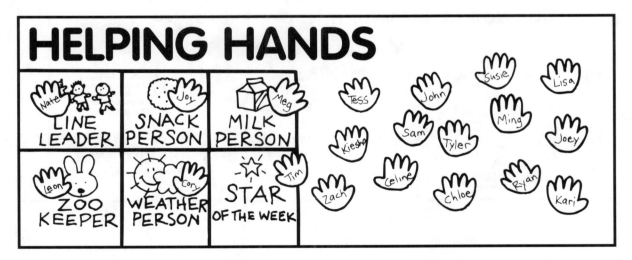

Most preschool classrooms have daily or weekly helpers. The children are assigned different jobs with which to help—classroom pet responsibilities, line leaders, someone to pass out snacks, etc.

Make a chart that lists the different responsibilities with which the children in your room assist you. Draw a picture depicting what the job is, or use photographs of the children doing the jobs.

Have each of the children trace his/her hand on heavy construction paper and cut it out. Write the child's name on the paper hand. The hands can be placed on the chart.

The Special Day

It was a beautiful, bright, sunny morning. When Michael's mother woke up, she thought to herself, "Today is Michael's special day. He will be so happy that the sun is shining for his special day." Michael's mother stretched and got out of bed to go and wake up Michael.

Michael's mother walked into his room, put the shades up, and said, "Michael, it is time to wake up. The special day you have been waiting for is here!" Michael quickly jumped out of bed and began getting ready for his special day. Michael's mother reminded him of all the things he needed to do to get ready, and then went to the kitchen to make breakfast.

Michael first put on the clothes that his mother had left out on a chair for him. He made sure that his shirt was tucked in and that the rest of his clothes were straight and neat. Next, Michael went into the bathroom, brushed his teeth, washed his hands and face, and combed his hair. Before leaving the bathroom, Michael looked into the mirror and gave himself a big smile. Michael knew that he had remembered to do everything he was supposed to do before breakfast. Michael looked very nice for his special day.

Michael walked into the kitchen, sat down at the table, and began eating the good breakfast that his mother had made. When Michael was finished eating, he washed his hands and face again. After all, he did not want to begin his special day with some of his breakfast on his hands and face.

Michael was now all ready for his special day. Michael and his mother went out of the house, got in the car, and drove to the special place where Michael's special day was going to happen.

Can you guess what Michael's special day was? Well, Michael's mother drove up to a fun-looking building. There were many happy children inside the building who were playing and singing and having so much fun.

You guessed it! Michael's special day was his first day at *(use the name of your preschool)*.

Story Activities

1. As you read the story, let the children pantomime Michael's actions; or choose two children to pantomime the actions of Michael and his mother.
2. Sequence all the things that the children in your room do when getting ready for school.
3. Let the children draw pictures of Michael or themselves getting ready for school.

Cindy Goes to School

One morning Cindy woke up very early. It was a special day. She wouldn't be staying at home today.

(put piece for Cindy on flannel board)

Cindy was afraid she would miss her mother. She was afraid she would miss her fish. She thought she might miss her crayons. She was afraid she would miss her new guitar. She was sure she would miss her teddy bear.

(put up mother)
(put up fish)
(put up crayons)
(put up guitar)
(put up bear)

Cindy's mother said, "Today is your first day of school." Cindy and her mother got ready to leave.

(take off everything but Cindy and Mother)

When they arrived at school, there were other children already there. There were toys and games that children like to play. There was a special place to look at books. In the playhouse, there were dress-up clothes. She could see a place to draw pictures. There were even goldfish in a bowl.

(put up children)
(put up book)
(put up hat)
(put up crayons)
(put up fish)

Cindy kissed her mother good-bye and felt a little sad. The teacher told Cindy that it was okay to feel sad and read her a story. As Cindy listened to the story and looked at the pictures, she felt a little better.

(take off mother)
(take off everything but Cindy)

Later she used pink and orange paint and made a special painting.

(put up painting)

When Cindy's mother arrived, Cindy gave her the picture. Then Cindy and her mother said good-bye to the teacher and went home.

(put up mother)

(take pieces off)

⋀⋀⋀ Story of the Month ⋀⋀⋀

Samantha, the Story Mouse

One fine day in the Mountainview School*, Ms. Carole Roberts and the fifteen children in her class were sitting on the rug for story time. The children's names were Jay, Kim, Jerri, Steven, Melissa, Rodney, Becky, Andrew, Mary Beth, Tim, Gina, Brian, Laura, Keith, and Kathryn. The children and their teacher loved story time, and as the children were getting settled on the rug, Ms. Roberts looked around the room and asked, "Children, do you see anything different in our story area today?"

Suddenly Jay said, "Look, there's a little house over by the corner of the rug!"

"You're absolutely right," answered Ms. Roberts. "I saw it, too. Will you bring it over to me, please, Jay?" Jay hurried to get the small house and brought it to his teacher.

Ms. Roberts held the house up for all the children to see. "What do you think this is?" she asked.

"It looks like a house for something very small," replied Jerri.

"Yes, the letters on the roof of the house say 'Samantha, the Story Mouse,'" said Ms. Roberts.

Suddenly there was a little squeak and the door to the house opened. Out hopped a small and surprised mouse. "Hello," she squeaked. "I am Samantha, the Story Mouse. And who are you?"

The children and Ms. Roberts introduced themselves to Samantha. "Why are you called a story mouse?" asked Tim.

"Because my very favorite thing of all is to listen to stories. That's why I moved here. Someone told me that you have story time every day and I decided this would be a nice place to live. Do you mind if I join you?" Samantha asked.

"Oh, yes, please live with us!" the children answered.

"I do have one special request, though," said Samantha. "When I listen to stories, I like everyone to be very quiet so I can hear every word. Is that all right with you?"

"Oh, yes, we're very quiet when we listen to stories," the children replied. "Please stay with us, and Ms. Roberts will tell us wonderful stories every day."

"Oh, thank you so much," said Samantha. "I know I'm going to be so happy here. I'll just settle down here by Ms. Roberts and we'll all listen to today's story together."

So Samantha, the Story Mouse found a new home and many new friends. Every day she came and quietly listened to the stories with the children.

Substitute the name of your school, your name, and the children's names to make the story more personal. Have your children introduce themselves to Samantha. Children love to hear about themselves as characters in the stories you tell, and they enjoy participating in the storytelling!

Use these patterns to make this into a flannel board story.

This is What I Look Like

The teacher precuts large simplified "paper doll" silhouettes of girls and boys. The figures should be about 15 inches tall. The children may personalize the figures by coloring in their hair and eye colors and the types of clothing they like.

The figures can then be mounted on the wall with the children's names displayed underneath. When the figures are on the wall it should look as if all the children are holding hands.

This activity will encourage a sense of social identity in a class group and can also be used as a language lesson. The children can name all the parts of the body and pieces of clothing.

Paint Apples

The teacher puts a large tree cut out of brown and green construction paper up on a wall.

The children paint paper plates red and paste two green paper leaves on top of each paper plate. These make wonderful apples for your apple tree.

Tape the apples on the apple tree for display.

Sand

Have the children make designs or pictures in a pan of wet sand. A large baking pan works well. Let the children get the feel of the sand, and have them make lines, circles, or impressions of their hands.

To encourage the concepts of sharing and taking turns, two children could share one large pan of sand.

Buttermilk Chalk Drawings

Brush buttermilk on manila paper. This makes a fun medium for chalk drawings.

Play Dough

Manipulating play dough is an excellent fine motor task, and a lot of fun for children. Show the children how to roll it, how to make balls, and how to use cookie cutters.

Here is a good recipe for making play dough with your children:

    1 cup salt
    2 cups sifted flour
    6 teaspoons alum
    2 tablespoons salad oil
    1 cup water

Mix together until smooth. Coloring may be added to the water before mixing. The play dough will stay soft for several weeks if kept in a plastic bag.

Popcorn Pictures

Draw an outline of an animal on paper. Fill the inside of the animal with rubber glue.
The children use popcorn to fill the inside of the animal.

A Present for My Friend

The teacher will need to prepare a sheet of paper for each child, with a picture of a large empty present. The drawing should be kept simple, a large square with a bow on top.

The teacher should explain to the children that they are each going to make a present to give to one of their friends. The children can either draw pictures, or they can look through magazines to find pictures to cut out and paste inside their presents.

When the presents are completed, the children can each choose a friend and exchange their "friendship presents."

ᴧᴧᴧᴧ Fine Motor/Art Activities ᴧᴧᴧᴧ

The Incomplete House

Give the children an outline drawing of a house. Tell the children that you would like them to draw a picture of their house. Suggest some things that they might add to the outline drawing. Let each child decide and complete the house without help.

This will give the teacher a good insight into the child's maturity and experience. There will be some children who will add everything (from trees and flowers to windows and doors), while some will show no ability to complete the house. For these children, more play activities leading to muscular development and coordination are needed.

My Mother Goose Book

Every day that you introduce a new rhyme, give a copy of the rhyme to each child. The verse should be copied on the top half of a piece of paper and the children may illustrate the rhyme on the bottom half. At the end of your nursery rhyme unit, the children will have a complete nursery rhyme book, filled with all the rhymes that were done at school.

Children really enjoy bringing home this finished project to share with their parents.

Sand Paint

Letting children paint with sand paints is tons of fun! This is how you do it:

Ingredients:

    ¼ cup paint powder
    1 cup sand
        paste

Procedure: Combine powdered paint and sand in large shakers. Shake on paper covered with paste.

This activity may also be done outside on the ground without paste.

Let's Make a "Thing"

Provide the children with scissors, paper punch, paper, yarn, string, fabric scraps, and anything else you might have on hand. Tell the children to make a "thing." No product is necessary. Young children simply have fun creating.

Leaf People

Attach real leaves to sheets of construction paper with a small amount of glue. Let the children add arms, legs, and heads. It is fun to see how many different types of people the children can make.

The Squirrel and the Nut

This is the child's first simple maze. Make a copy for each child in the room, following the example on the left.

At first, have the children trace the path with their fingers. The children are learning to go from left to right and are practicing some hand control. When the children understand how to get the squirrel to the nut, they may then use a pencil or crayon.

Shaving Cream

Let the children clean formica table tops with scented shaving cream. This is great for the senses of touch and smell. Give each child a small amount of shaving cream and let him or her spread it on the table. They may draw with fingers if they choose.

Flour and Salt Finger Paint

This finger paint has a grainy quality unlike other finger paints, providing a different sensory experience. The children will really enjoy using it.

    1 cup flour
    1½ teaspoons salt or sand
    1 cup water

Combine flour and salt. Add water.

Puppets

Puppets are a wonderful tool for helping children feel more comfortable when talking in a group. Have the children make their own puppets, and then the "puppets" can get to know each other.

Have each child color a paper bag with a heavy crayon. The fold of the bag becomes a moveable mouth. Add ears, nose, and eyes using scrap paper, fabric, or heavy yarn.

A little puppet theater is fun, too. Cut a hole in the upper half of a large piece of cardboard. This will comfortably accommodate two puppets.

My Circle

Young children enjoy creating for the sake of creating. It's not necessary that an art project look like anything real. It's the process, not the product, that's important for young children.

Give each child in your class a sheet of paper with a large circle drawn on it. Have the children decorate their circles any way that they would like. Provide lots of different materials for the children to use: crayons, markers, colored pencils, scraps of fabric or paper, foil, glitter, sequins, etc.

Making Funny Faces

Cut out eyes, noses, and mouths from the pictures of people in old magazines or catalogs. (The teacher can either prepare the facial features ahead of time, or the children can help prepare them.) Have lots of facial features from which the children may choose.

Have the children each draw a circle and paste in facial features. Hair can be added with yarn or it can be colored in. These faces look very funny and the children will have a lot of fun making them.

Classroom Apple Tree

The teacher should prepare an apple tree, using green construction paper for the leaves and brown construction paper for the trunk. Tape the tree to a wall in the classroom.

Use a real apple to make the apple prints on the tree. Cut the apple in half. Dip the apple in red paint and print on the leaves of the tree. The print will look like the shape of a real apple.

The children will also enjoy making apple print paintings of their own to bring home. Each child can put many apple prints on a white piece of paper. When the red paint dries, the children can add green stems with a crayon.

Craft Stick Drawings

Give each child a craft stick and a sheet of white construction paper. Have the children make designs on the paper by drawing around the stick with color crayons. The outline of the craft stick may be filled in with a contrasting color.

Teacher Directions: Discuss rhyme. Have children color the picture. Cut out the apples. Paste 2 *on* the tree. Paste 2 *off* the tree. Emphasize concepts of *on* and *off*.

The Apple Tree

Way up in the apple tree,
Two little apples smiled at me.
I shook that tree as hard as I could.
Down they came.
Ummmm, were they good.

— Traditional

The September Squirrel

Name _____

Mirror, Mirror on the Wall

The teacher demonstrates to the class by selecting a child as a partner. The teacher tells the class that his/her partner must pretend to be looking into a mirror. The teacher is the mirror, therefore the child must reflect exactly what the teacher does.

Use a variety of arm and leg movements. Let the children choose partners and play Mirror, Mirror on the Wall again.

Follow That Bear

The teacher prepares either cut-out paper footprints or uses tape to make the footprints. The children step on each footprint following the pattern on the floor.

Make this exciting! Tell the children that they are on a bear hunt. Place a stuffed bear at the end of the path for the children to capture.

Dancing

Preschoolers love to move and love music. Batting balloons to music can provide much fun and will help increase eye-hand coordination.

To increase listening skills, tell the children that they can only bat the balloons when the music is on. They should "freeze" when the music stops.

Follow the Leader

Follow the Leader is a wonderful group movement activity, and is always more fun when done to music. Let the children take turns being the leader.

Obstacle Course

An obstacle course should be arranged in such a way as to allow a child to go from one obstacle to the next while performing a variety of motor skills.

Equipment: Balance beams, hoola hoops, tables, boxes, tires, chairs, ropes, barrels, mats, and the teacher's imagination.

An obstacle course is also an excellent tool to help teach following directions, and to teach basic concepts such as over, under, on, through, between, next to, etc.

Wastepaper Basketball

An empty wastepaper basket on a chair provides a great basketball hoop for young children. Coffee cans work well with bean bags, too. (Encourage taking turns.)

I See Me

Standing before a full length mirror, the child is to identify body parts by pointing to the image identified in the mirror.

Other supplementary body awareness activities are:

1. Using a hand mirror, tell the child to identify parts of his/her head and face that are reflected.
2. Cover half of a large mirror with paper. Ask the child to stand directly before it and tell what part of his/her body is not reflected.

Whistle

Children really love this game. It is good for developing motor skills and for increasing listening skills.

At a given signal, children walk in any direction. When a whistle is blown, they must stop immediately. Those who do not stop on the signal are asked to sit down. Continue until only one child is left. This last player wins the game. Alternate commands you can use are: run, crawl, skate, tip toe.

This is a good game to teach at the beginning of the year. It will teach the children that when they hear a whistle, they should stop and listen to you. This will certainly make rounding up everyone on the playground a lot easier.

Follow the Path

On the floor in one part of the room, use masking tape to make a long line with several breaks in it. Give each child a turn to try hopping along the line without touching any of the breaks.

The children could pretend that they are searching for Bo Peep's lost sheep and this is the path that the sheep followed.

Bo Peep and Her Lost Sheep

This is a revised version of "Hide and Seek." One person is "it" or Bo Peep, and the rest of the children are the lost sheep. Bo Peep hides his or her eyes and the sheep run and hide. Bo Peep must find as many of the sheep as he/she can within a time period set by the teacher. Let each child have a turn playing Bo Peep (boys included).

Jack and Jill Mat Rolling

Place gymnastic mats on the floor if you have them, or use a carpeted floor. Let the children pantomime the nursery rhyme "Jack and Jill."

Encourage the children to practice many different ways to roll: forward rolls, backward rolls, somersaults, sideways rolls, etc.

Look at Me Run

This activity is very good for increasing spatial awareness. Make lines on the floor with masking tape as illustrated. Have the children stand on the end line. Make sure that the children are well spaced or you may have collisions.

Then have the children follow directions:
1. Run to the opposite end line and return.
2. Run low to the ground, touching the floor on either side alternately.
3. Run low to the ground, touching the floor with both hands.
4. Run forward, looking back over the right shoulder; return, looking over the left shoulder.
5. Run to center line, stop, and run back.
6. Run in a zigzag fashion, crossing feet in front of each other.
7. Run sideways to the center line with the right shoulder forward, stop, turn, and return to the end line running sideways with the left shoulder forward.

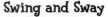

Swing and Sway

Have the children sway and trail silk streamers or parachute nylon to music. This is always a favorite activity of young children. Change the tempo or volume of the music for variety.

Learn My Way Around

Play a game where the children are asked to locate articles in the room. Use descriptive clues to help the children locate the articles. This game will help the children familiarize themselves with the new surroundings. Make this game like an adventure.

Playground Rules

Playground rules are necessary. Children need exercise for muscle development, but they must also be safe while getting the exercise. Try to lead the children in their exercise.

Say to the children: "Follow me and we will be a snake." Lead the line around and end up in a circle. Now lead the children in playing a circle game. When exercise time is over, have the children line up for a drink and "snake" back into the room.

Outdoor Game

This outdoor game is the preschool version of "Hot Potato." Put a medium-sized ball in the center of the ring. The child who is "it" pushes the ball with his/her feet, trying to get it out of the circle. The other children try to stop the ball with their feet. Once the ball is out, another leader is chosen. The ball is called the "hot potato," and the children will enjoy trying to keep it in the "oven" (circle).

Using Our Body Parts

Have the children lie on the floor, far enough apart so that their hands do not touch when outstretched. The children should lie with their feet together, looking at the ceiling, with their hands alongside their bodies. Ask the children to relax and not look at you. Then lead them in the exercises, doing them slowly.

Don't use the words "left" or "right" with preschool, kindergarten, or first grade children. Instead, use a reference point in the room, such as "the leg nearest the door," "the arm nearest the window," etc.

1. Drag right hand (substitute reference point) along ground until it is pointing above head. Return.
2. Drag left hand as above.
3. Move right leg to the right. Return.
4. Move left leg to the left. Return.
5. Drag both hands on the floor until they touch over the head. Return.
6. Move both legs apart as far as they can go. Return.
7. Move right arm and left leg. Return.
8. Move left arm and right leg. Return.
9. Raise right arm so that it points at the ceiling. Return.
10. Same with left arm. Return.
11. Raise right leg toward the ceiling as high as it can go. Return.
12. Raise left leg toward the ceiling as high as it can go. Return.
13. Raise right arm and right leg as before. Return.
14. Raise left arm and left leg as before. Return.
15. Raise right arm and left leg. Return.
16. Raise left arm and right leg. Return.

Note: When arms and legs are both moved, they should be moved together.

Our Favorite Sports

Ask the children to name as many different sports as they can. What are their favorite sports? Which sports can they play at school?

Talk about how it is now football season. How many of the children have parents that watch football? Provide the children with some footballs to throw around. Real footballs may be too much for young children, but "Nerf" footballs are wonderful. They are worth purchasing for your school.

Jack-Be-Nimble Coloring Sheet

A birthday candle may be pasted to the paper for a three-dimensional effect.

Name_____

Mr. Caterpillar

Who Lives at My House

Using a doll house and a variety of dolls, or a flannel board house and flannel board people, begin a discussion of "who lives at my house." Let each child have a turn placing all his/her family members in the house or on the flannel board. Encourage the children to name all the people and tell you something about each of them.

When you are preparing the dolls or flannel board people, do not forget to prepare grandparent figures and figures which represent pets.

You can also encourage conversation about who is the biggest, littlest, oldest, youngest, etc.

Tape Recorders

For a preschooler, hearing yourself talk on a tape recorder is almost like magic.

Interview each child in your room using a tape recorder. If the tape recorder is a new experience for your children, many of them may react by being very shy. (And of course, there will be some who will not stop talking!) Be sure to ask questions that will get a response, such as "Would you rather eat ice cream or beans?"

Let the children enjoy hearing one another. Let them try to guess who is talking.

Feelie Box

Make a mystery "feelie box." Cut an arm opening in the box. Put various objects in it and seal the cover shut.

Put in objects with interesting textures, such as cloth, paper, cellophane, plastic, rubber, sandpaper, fur, metal, wood, etc. Encourage the children to use descriptive words like smooth, soft, rough, hard, bumpy.

Alternate Activity: Place common objects in the box and let the children guess what is in the box by the way it feels.

I'm Thinking

Describe a child in the room. For example, say:

"I'm thinking about a boy."
"This boy is wearing a striped shirt."
"This boy has blue eyes."
"This boy is a good friend."

Let the children guess who you are talking about. Older preschoolers will enjoy trying to describe someone in the class.

Things We Like to Do

Make a chart titled "Things We Like to Do." The chart will list the names of all the children.

The children can then cut out pictures from magazines of things they like to do (toys, games, activities), and paste them under their names on the chart. Older preschoolers may enjoy drawing pictures of things they like.

When the chart is completed, let each child tell about his/her picture.

Telephone

If possible, borrow two telephones or make do with toy phones and the teacher's ingenuity.

Set up two "homes" or "offices" out of sight of each other (children facing away from each other, or one behind a screen).

The children can introduce themselves over the phone and guess to whom they are talking. This activity will also provide a means of teaching proper phone etiquette.

My Story

This project can be finished in one day, but you may want it to last two days.

On Day One: Have each child dictate to you a story about himself or herself. Many children will need help doing this, so ask questions to guide them. What does the child like to do at home? Who lives at his/her house? Does the child have any pets? Who is his/her best friend? The teacher will write the story out on paper.

On Day Two: The child is given his/her story and is asked to draw a picture to go with it. This is good to do in the first part of the year as a get-acquainted activity.

Mother Goose Character Poster Masks

This activity will take an extra amount of work from the teacher, but it is well worth it! Once you have made the Mother Goose Character Poster Masks, you will be able to use them for years to come, and you will save money by making them yourself.

Outline the main character for each Mother Goose rhyme on a large piece of cardboard or poster board, making holes for the child's face and hands. The children can color the character with crayon or paint.

To use the masks, have one child wear a poster mask with his/her face and hands showing through the holes. The other children can recite the rhyme as the child wearing the mask dramatizes it.

Poster masks are wonderful for language development. If you are feeling very ambitious, it is fun to make many different characters. Young children have so much fun pretending and making up their own stories when they are playing with the masks.

Up/Down

The positional concepts of up and down are two of the very easiest. Children experiment with these concepts from the time that they are very little, for example, "Pick me up," or "Put me down." Climbing up and down on furniture and playground equipment also helps children understand the concepts.

Children are generally able to act out or physically move to a position. It is more difficult for a child to look at a picture or at another person and identify and name the position. Find pictures of objects or people that are located in either an "up" or "down" position. Give the children practice in naming the position from looking at it.

Mother Goose Drama

Keep a collection of small objects that relate in some manner to Mother Goose rhymes. For example, you could have a tiny pie for "Little Jack Horner" or "Four and Twenty Blackbirds," a toy sheep for "Bo Peep" and "Little Boy Blue," or a small pail for "Jack and Jill." Each child can choose an object and recite the nursery rhyme, while role-playing the character.

Many/Few

Let the children go on a walk and collect acorns. Then use them in a variety of ways to teach the concepts of "many" and "few."

Have the children pretend that they are all squirrels. Some of the squirrels are very hungry—they should be given many acorns to eat. Some of the squirrels are not very hungry—they should be given just a few acorns to eat.

Use different sizes of containers. Which containers will hold many acorns? Which containers will hold just a few acorns?

First Day of School Activities

The transition from home to school is difficult for some children. Here are some ideas that may help on the first day of school.

1. Show a series of pictures and tell stories that relate the school with home. These pictures and stories could be about fathers and mothers, brothers and sisters at play, grandmothers and grandfathers, teachers and helpers, etc.
2. Have each child tell about one interesting thing he or she saw on the way to school.
3. Let each child tell what he/she likes best in the classroom.

Good Morning Game

Play a "Good Morning Game." Have the children sit in a group in front of you. Choose one child to stand with his/her back to the group. Choose another child to say "Good Morning!" Have the child who is standing guess who said "Good Morning."

Look at Me

Pass around a hand mirror and let each child look at himself/herself. Point out something special about each child, and then let the children talk among themselves about the things that are special.

After each child has had a chance to look and talk, let the children draw pictures of themselves. The teacher may wish to show these and let the class guess who it is.

Learn about Squirrels

Show a picture of a squirrel. Talk about what squirrels look like, how they scamper up trees, where they live, and why they gather nuts. Show the children an acorn.

The Scarecrow

Once upon a time, a grandmother who lived in the country had a large cherry tree. It was loaded with red cherries that were almost ripe. Now this grandmother's favorite grandson, Jack, was going to visit her, and she wanted to bake him a cherry pie as a surprise. But she had a big problem. The cherries weren't ripe enough to pick yet, but the blackbirds were eating them all. The blackbirds didn't care if the cherries were ripe or not, and they didn't care that the grandmother wanted to use them in a special pie.

Grandmother didn't know what to do. She wanted to have cherries for Jack's pie, but how could she stop the blackbirds from eating them all? She had to find some way to frighten the birds away. She thought and thought and thought. Finally she had an idea. Do you know what she did? (Let the children make guesses until scarecrow is suggested and then develop it on the flannel board.)

Grandmother took a stick and stuck it in the ground. She hung an old shirt on it. She tied a bundle of straw on it for a head. She tied on some old ragged overalls. She fastened old gloves for hands. When the wind blew, it flopped around like a person, and the birds didn't dare go near to eat any more cherries.

Now, Grandmother's funny scarecrow could move his head. I'll show you how and you can move your head that way, too. (With head relaxed, bob forward, to one side, backward, and to the other side. Dangle arms and shake hands as if blown by the wind. Finish with the poem below.)

The old scarecrow	His arms swing out;
Is such a funny man.	His legs swing, too.
He flops in the wind,	He nods his head
As hard as he can.	In a "how-do-you-do?"
He flops to the right,	See him flippity-flop
He flops to the left,	When the wind blows hard,
He flops back and forth,	The funny scarecrow
Till he's most out of breath.	In our back yard.

Autumn Owl

 and and =

I Am Special Because . . .

_____

_____

Colored by: _____

A NOTE TO PARENTS: This week we are talking about how special each of us is. Your child's response to the statement "I am special because . . ." is written at the top of the paper. Tell your child why **you** think he/she is special. Cut the bottom note off this paper, and hang the picture on your refrigerator.

Children love finger plays and listening to the rhymes in poetry. Begin September with one of the finger plays and gradually add the others throughout the month. Spend time on finger plays daily. We all enjoy doing things that we have mastered.

I Wiggle

I wiggle my fingers.
I wiggle my toes.
I wiggle my shoulders.
I wiggle my nose.
Now no more wiggles are left in me.
So I will sit still as still can be.
(Follow directions in verse.)

Friends

I have two friends,	*(hold up two fingers on left hand)*
And they have me;	*(hold up one finger on right hand)*
Two friends and me,	*(bend each from left to right)*
That's one, two, three.	*(hold up fingers while saying "1, 2, 3")*

Two Little Houses

Two little houses closed up tight.	*(two closed fists)*
Open the window and let in the light.	*(spread hands apart)*
Ten little people tall and straight.	*(hold up ten fingers)*
Ready for school at half past eight.	*(fingers make running motion)*

That's Me, Complete!

I have ten little fingers and ten little toes	*(hold up)*
Two little arms and one little nose.	*(raise arms)*
One little mouth and two little ears.	*(point)*
Two little eyes for smiles and tears.	*(smile)*
One little head and two little feet.	*(shake)*
One little chin, that's ME, complete!	*(hold arms up)*

The Squirrel

Whisky, frisky	
Hippity, hop.	*(hop)*
Up he goes	*(stretch arms up)*
To the tree top.	
Whirly, twirly	*(spin around)*
Round and round.	
Down he scampers	*(sit down)*
To the ground.	

One, Two, Three

One, two, three.
One, two, three.
How many children
Make one, two, three?
_____ and _____ and _____ make three.
Please come and stand in front of me.

(Use the names of children in the class in the blanks. After three children respond, call upon another three until all the children have had a turn. This poem can serve as an experience for roll call.)

Fun with Hands

Roll, roll, roll your hands,
As slow as slow can be.
Roll, roll, roll your hands,
Do it now with me.
Roll, roll, roll your hands,
As fast as fast can be.
Roll, roll, roll your hands,
Do it now with me.

(Continue this action rhyme by substituting these phrases: Clap, clap, clap your hands; Shake, shake, shake your hands; Stamp, stamp, stamp your feet.)

Look, It's Me

Look in the mirror.
Whom do you see?
It's someone special.
Look, it's me!
(Let the children take turns holding a hand mirror.)

Little Bo Peep

Little Bo Peep has lost her sheep,
And can't tell where to find them.
Leave them alone and they'll come home,
Wagging their tails behind them.

Little Jack Horner

Little Jack Horner,
Sat in a corner,
Eating a Christmas pie.
He put in his thumb,
And pulled out a plum,
And said, "What a good boy am I."

Humpty Dumpty

Humpty Dumpty sat on a wall,
Humpty Dumpty had a great fall.
All the king's horses, and all the king's men,
Couldn't put Humpty Dumpty together again.

Hickory, Dickory, Dock

Hickory, dickory, dock.
The mouse ran up the clock.
The clock struck one,
The mouse ran down.
Hickory, dickory, dock.

Jack Be Nimble

Jack be nimble,
Jack be quick,
Jack jump over the candlestick.

Sing-a-Song of Sixpence

Sing a song of sixpence, pocket full of rye,
Four and twenty blackbirds baked in a pie.
When the pie was opened, the birds began to sing,
Wasn't that a dainty dish to set before the king?

Mary, Mary, Quite Contrary

Mary, Mary, quite contrary,
How does your garden grow?
With silver bells and cockle shells,
And pretty maids all in a row.

Jack and Jill

Jack and Jill went up the hill,
To fetch a pail of water.
Jack fell down and broke his crown,
And Jill came tumbling after.

Busy Squirrel

The little gray squirrel makes a scampering sound,
As she gathers the nuts that fall to the ground.
She buries the nuts in a secret dark place,
And covers them over with hardly a trace.
Little gray squirrels always seem to know,
That the robins are gone and it's time for snow.

Five Friends

Five good friends went out to play.
It was a bright and sunny day.
One good friend said, "I can't stay."
Then there were four friends left to play.
Four good friends went out to play.
It was a bright and sunny day.
One good friend said, "I can't stay."
Then there were three friends left to play.
Three good friends went out to play.
It was a bright and sunny day.
One good friend said, "I can't stay."
Then there were two friends left to play.
Two good friends went out to play.
It was a bright and sunny day.
One good friend said, "I can't stay."
Then there was one friend left to play.
One good friend went out to play.
It was a bright and sunny day.
One good friend said, "I can't stay."
Then there were no friends left to play.
(Choose five children to pantomime this rhyme.)

Squirrel

Whirlee, twirlee,   *(Twirl index fingers around each other.)*
Look at the squirrel,
Sitting in the tree.
Stuffing nuts in her cheeks,   *(Puff up cheeks.)*
One, two, three.

Silly Face

Silly face, silly face, what do you see?
I see a sleepy face looking at me!
Sleepy face, sleepy face, what do you see?
I see a mad face looking at me!
Mad face, mad face, what do you see?
I see a surprised face looking at me!
Surprised face, surprised face, what do you see?
I see a sad face looking at me!
Sad face, sad face, what do you see?
I see a happy face looking at me!
Happy face, happy face, what do you see?
I see another happy face looking at me!
(Turn this rhyme into a flannel board activity. Make or find pictures of silly, sleepy, mad, surprised, sad, and happy faces. Have the children in your class make these facial expressions.)

Who Feels Happy Today?

Who feels happy at school today?
All who do, snap your fingers this way.
Who feels happy at school today?
All who do, clap your hands this way.
Who feels happy at school today?
All who do, wink your eye this way.
Who feels happy at school today?
All who do, fold your hands this way.
(Ask "What makes you feel happy? Can we think of other things to do with our bodies when we are happy? Show us a motion that you like to do.")

What I Can Do

I can spin just like a top.
Look at me! Look at me!
I have feet and I can hop.
Look at me! Look at me!
I have hands and I can clap.
Look at me! Look at me!
I can lay them in my lap.
Look at me! Look at me!
(Have the children act out this rhyme. Ask "What else can your feet do? What else can your hands do?")

Wiggles

A wiggle, wiggle here,
A wiggle, wiggle there.
Wiggle your hands,
Up in the air.
Wiggle your shoulders,
Wiggle your hips,
Wiggle your knees,
And move your lips.
Wiggle, wiggle, wiggle,
And wiggle and bend.
Wiggle, wiggle, wiggle,
And this is the end!

Two Little Squirrels

Two little squirrels,
Were scampering through the wood.
Two little squirrels,
Were looking for food.
Bushy Tail found two nuts,
Bright Eyes found two more.
How many nuts were there,
For their winter store?

Busy Little Bushytail

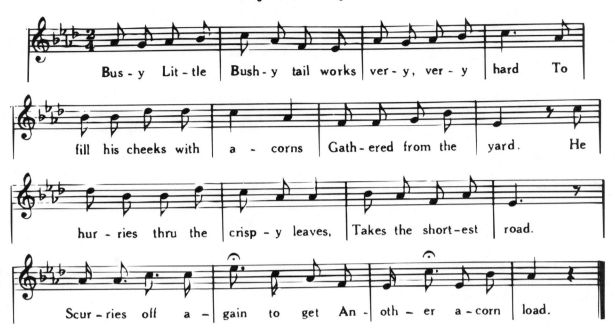

Bus - y Lit - tle Bush - y tail works ver - y, ver - y hard To
fill his cheeks with a - corns Gath - ered from the yard. He
hur - ries thru the crisp - y leaves, Takes the short - est road.
Scur - ries off a - gain to get An - oth - er a - corn load.

Continued Activities

Lollipop Game (*continued from Learning Games, pages 33–35*)

This activity encourages children to talk in a group and works on the skill of matching.

The teacher uses construction paper and tongue depressors to make the lollipops. Draw or paste pictures, shapes or colors on the lollipops. Make sure that you make two identical sets of lollipops. (Use sets of pictures of things that you have been talking about during the month of September: squirrels, apples, trees, school houses, objects found in the classroom.)

Version 1: The teacher passes out one set of lollipops to the children, so that each child has at least one lollipop. The teacher keeps the other set and asks, "Who has the apple?" (or whatever picture is on the lollipop). The child with the matching lollipop will respond.

Version 2: Pass out all the lollipops to the children and let them walk around and discover who has their matching lollipops.

Mr. Yuk or Mr. Yum (*continued from Learning Games, pages 33–35*)

Bring in many small containers, filled with things for the children to smell; for example, lemonade, soap, vinegar, syrup, jam, coffee, baby powder, hand lotion, cinnamon, etc. Explain to the children that they must decide if the smell belongs to Mr. Yuk (things that don't smell good) or if the smell belongs to Mr. Yum (things that do smell good).

Stress that if the child doesn't know what the smell is, and even if he/she thinks it smells good, he/she should never taste it. Perfume smells good, but we do not drink it.

Going on a Picnic (*continued from Learning Activities, pages 22–24*)

The teacher will need a picnic size basket and cards with pictures of foods and beverages.

Tell the children that they are going to go on a pretend picnic. Pass out the picture cards. Then ask "What shall we bring on our picnic?" Each child looks at the picture he/she has and tells about the food or beverage depicted on it. Then he/she places it in the picnic basket.

Alternate Activity: Show the children all the pictures and discuss what the foods are. Let the children choose as a group from all the cards what they would like to bring on their pretend picnic.

A Special Person

(Sing these verses to the tune of "The Farmer in the Dell.")

I am a special person.
I am a special person.
I am a special person.
And I will tell you why.
I have two hands to feel with.
I have two eyes to see with.
I have two ears to hear with.
And that is why.

I am a special person.
I am a special person.
I am a special person.
And I will tell you why.
I have a nose to smell with.
I have a mouth to taste with.
I am a special person.
And that is why.

The Fuzzy Caterpillar

Late in summer and early in autumn, if you look around you, you will find caterpillars in sunny places. They shine in their furry coats and go squirming along as though they were in a hurry. They seem to be looking for something and they really are. Before winter comes, they must find safe places on twigs or leaves where they can spin coverings around themselves and sleep all winter. These sleeping caterpillars are called cocoons. When spring comes, they stretch and they find out that they have changed into moths or butterflies. They spread their damp wings in the sunlight and fly out into the fresh air.

Tell me what the caterpillar said in this song. What did someone ask him?

Suggestion: "Sing the first part of the song to me. I will be the fuzzy caterpillar and answer you." (A good singer may be the caterpillar and sing back to the class or to another child who sings well.)

Friends

With a gay lilt

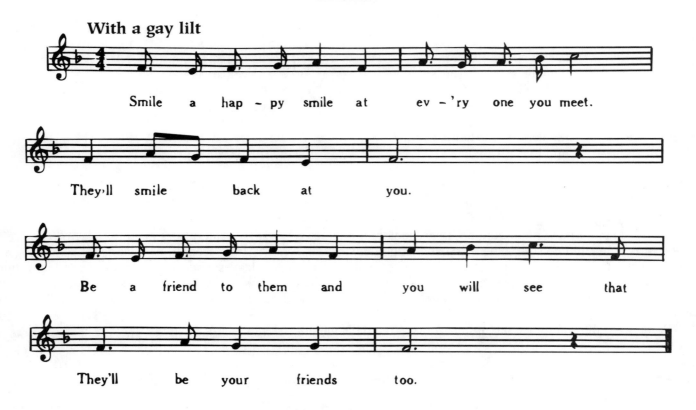

Smile a hap – py smile at ev – 'ry one you meet.

They'll smile back at you.

Be a friend to them and you will see that

They'll be your friends too.

Taking Turns

Tak – ing turns is ver – y wise.

Push – ers nev – er use their eyes,

Wast – ing time for you and me

And them – selves, as you can see.

My Photograph

Take a photograph of each child in your room. Mount each picture on a piece of cardboard and print the child's name on the other side. Attach a string to the top, so it can be hung on a wall or bulletin board.

These cards are wonderful for teaching name recognition. Each morning the children can look for their names and turn the cards over to see if they are correct by discovering if their photographs are on the backs.

After the children have learned to identify their names (or if they have learned where their cards are placed on the wall), the teacher can rearrange the display of cards so that the children are continually challenged.

What Do Your Mommy and Daddy Do at Work?

Collect old clothes and props in which the children can dress up; for example, hats, coats, briefcases, shoes, play tools, purses, office supplies, etc. Encourage a play session of dressing up like Mommy and Daddy at work.

When you are busy collecting things, keep in mind the upcoming November unit on *Community Helpers.*

Popcorn Balls

Children love to "help" in the kitchen. Celebrate the new school year by having a "friendship party."

Here is a fun recipe your class can make for the party:

> ¼ pound butter
> 12½ oz. package small marshmallows
> Salt
> 1 package small gumdrops
> About 5 cups of popped corn

Melt the marshmallows in heated butter. Let cool and stir in the popped corn and gumdrops. Put a few drops of cooking oil on each child's hands. Give each child a heaping tablespoon of the mixture. Decorate with sliced gumdrops and slices of licorice.

The Five Senses

Prepare five large sheets of paper on which are written the following statements: "I have two eyes for seeing"; "I have two ears to hear with"; "I have one nose to smell with"; "I have one mouth to taste with"; "I have two hands to feel with."

The children can paste pictures depicting each sense under each statement. For example, under "I have two ears to hear with," the children can paste pictures of things which make a sound that they can hear.

This activity could last a week. Choose one sense each day for Monday through Friday.

Applesauce

After a discussion about September and the apple picking season, provide the experience of making applesauce. Present this activity the day before you plan to make the applesauce, so that each child can bring an apple from home. This will make the child feel more involved and will be less expensive for you or your school.

Here is the recipe:

> 10 apples
> 1 cup water
> 2 cups sugar

Peel, core, and quarter the apples. Add water and sugar. Cook until soft. To save on the cleanup, serve in small paper drinking cups with disposable spoons.

Fabric Lotto

This will give children the experience of observing and matching printed pieces of fabric.

You will need fabric scraps, pinking shears, poster board, and glue. Cut several pieces of poster board, 9" x 9". Cut fabric squares to measure 2" x 2", using a variety of fabrics. Cut two squares of each fabric used, and use a pinking shears so that the fabric will not ravel. Glue one of each of the two alike squares to the poster board. Put nine different squares on each board. Each board should be different. The second square of each fabric will remain as a swatch for the teacher or leader.

To play the game, give a board to each child. The teacher or leader holds up one 2" x 2" swatch at a time. If a child has fabric on his or her board exactly like the one being held up, he/she takes the swatch and places it on top of the matching fabric. The game is played until everyone has matched all the fabric on his or her board.

You can make this game more simple or more complex by varying the fabrics used. For example, construct boards with only solid colors of fabrics, with only plaid fabrics, or with only striped fabrics.

Hard-Boiled Humpty Dumpty

Teach the children the rhyme "Humpty Dumpty." Hard-boil an egg for each child, and let it cool. Then let each child draw Humpty Dumpty's face on his/her egg.

The children can either take the eggs home to eat, or they can eat them for snack time at school. The children will really be able to see that when Humpty Dumpty cracks, no one will be able to put him back together again.

Caterpillar Hunt

Explain to the children how a caterpillar turns into a beautiful butterfly. Find a book or pictures to illustrate it. Then take the children on a caterpillar hunt. If you are lucky, you will find a real caterpillar on your walk, maybe even more than one.

Find a large glass jar (such as a mayonnaise jar). Place a twig, some grass, and the caterpillar in the jar. Hopefully, the caterpillar will begin to spin a cocoon and by spring, you may have a butterfly flying around your room.

Mother Goose Wheel

Cut out three poster board circles as shown. The first and third circles should be the same size; the middle one should be an inch larger in diameter. Divide the large wheel into six equal sections. Draw a circle in each section, and in each circle paste a nursery rhyme picture. On the first wheel cut out a circular window that matches the pictures on the middle wheel. On the back to the third wheel, make an easel stand as shown.

To play the game, the child should spin the middle wheel. The child then recites the nursery rhyme that appears in the window, and names the words that rhyme.

Middle wheel

Front wheel

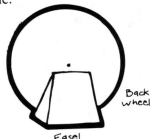

Easel

Back wheel

Instant Pictures

Bring an instant camera to the classroom. Four and five-year-olds usually can understand how to take a picture. Let them take pictures of each other. If you have a class of three-year-olds, it would be best for the teacher to take the pictures. Once you have the pictures, there are many fun activities for which you can use them.

1. Pass out the pictures to the children, making sure that no one has his/her own picture. The children then have to walk around the room and each must find the person in the picture that he/she is holding.
2. The children can practice saying the names of other children when looking at the pictures.
3. Make a bulletin board or wall display for your classroom with the children's pictures.

Matching Faces

This game will give the children the experience of matching identical faces, or sorting people into specific sex or age categories.

Cut out pictures of faces from magazines, making sure that you have two identical pictures of each face. Glue each face on a separate piece of construction paper. These "face cards" will last much longer if you cover them with clear contact paper.

To play the game, place all the cards face down. Turn over two cards at a time. If the faces match, the player can keep those cards. If they do not match, the cards are turned back over.

The children can also sort the cards into different categories, for example, by sex, by age, etc. Children can have fun putting different cards together to make families, too.

How Does It Feel?

Read very slowly to give the children a chance to respond to this list of nice things to touch. Read only a few items at a time. This quiet tactile activity will give the children an opportunity to share ideas. (You could also make a "feel" book: paste in pieces of fabric, foil, a zipper, sandpaper, and other things for children to feel and discuss.)

1. The softness of a bunny's fur. (Which animals have soft fur? I will pass around a piece of fur for you to feel.)
2. The floppy feel of tired arms. (Dangle your arms and let your head flop.)
3. The warm, wet sand between your toes. (Imagine that you are at the beach. Can you feel sand between your toes?)
4. The slippery feel of finger paint. (Tell me how finger paint feels. Do you like to feel it? Why?)

The Growing Tree

Draw a large tree, and use it to measure and mark the height of the children in the class. Children really enjoy seeing how big they are and how much they are growing.

Redo this activity in the middle of the year and at the end of the year. You can also use this information to chart who has grown the most, how many children are the same size, etc.

Refrigerator Pickles

Ask each of the children in your room to bring a cucumber. Have extras on hand for those children who are unable to bring one. Here is a great-tasting and easy recipe for pickles:

9 cups of thinly sliced cucumbers	1 tablespoon celery seed
1 sliced onion	2 cups sugar
1 cup sliced or diced green pepper	1 cup vinegar
2 tablespoons salt	

Mix together cucumbers, onion, and green pepper. Mix salt and celery seed; pour over the cucumbers. Add sugar and vinegar.

Dinosaurs

A long, long time ago, there weren't any people living here on the planet Earth. But even though there weren't any people, lots of animals lived here then. These animals were very different from the animals that live here now. We are going to learn about one very interesting group of these animals, the ones called "dinosaurs."

Dinosaurs lived in nearly every part of the world, and there were many different kinds. Some of the dinosaurs were very big. Some were even twice as big as an elephant! Other dinosaurs were more like the size of animals that live today.

Some dinosaurs spent most of their time in the water. Others lived on the land, and there were even some dinosaurs who could fly like birds. What did dinosaurs eat? Well, lots of them ate plants and the leaves of trees. But some of the dinosaurs ate other animals, sometimes even other dinosaurs!

You might wonder how we know about dinosaurs if they lived on Earth before people did. There are scientists who study dinosaurs. These scientists have a special name: "paleontologists." Paleontologists look for dinosaur bones buried in the ground. They study the bones they find, and try to find out how all the bones fit together. It's like doing a puzzle. When they have figured out how the bones fit together, the paleontologists connect all the bones with pieces of wire to make what they call the "skeleton" of the dinosaur. After studying the skeleton, the scientists can make drawings of what they think the dinosaur looked like when it was alive.

There are no real dinosaurs alive today, even though you may have seen make-believe dinosaurs on television. All the dinosaurs died a long time ago. Scientists don't know why all the dinosaurs died. Some people think that the weather changed and that not enough food grew for the dinosaurs to eat.

But even if you can't see a live dinosaur, your teacher can show you pictures of dinosaur skeletons and drawings of what scientists think the dinosaurs looked like. Maybe there is even a museum in your city that has a dinosaur skeleton you can visit.

Note to Teachers: Have on hand plenty of pictures of dinosaur skeletons and drawings of dinosaurs. Small plastic dinosaurs are also good, and they are quite inexpensive. Your local library should have a variety of books and other resources. Toy stores and bookstores are good places to check, too. If you are lucky enough to have a science museum nearby, as we do here in St. Paul, you should be able to find a lot of resources for the dinosaur unit.

Many of the concepts here will be difficult for small children to comprehend fully, but they will enjoy learning about dinosaurs anyway. You may be surprised how dinosaurs are integrated into the children's play.

Halloween Party

A Halloween party during the school day is a very important experience for a preschooler. Some preschoolers may not have the experience of trick-or-treating on Halloween, or may not be able to attend a community party.

A Halloween party at school will also provide the opportunity for preschool children to see for themselves that all those witches, ghosts, and goblins are really just other children. As exciting as Halloween can be, it can also be a scary experience for young children. Be sure to stress that it is all pretend and that it is only other children like themselves dressed up in costumes.

You may have a few skeptics in your classroom who will still choose to believe that everything about Halloween is very real, especially if you have three-year-olds. I have found it helpful to tell true "witch and ghost believers" the story of why we carve jack-o'-lantern faces out of pumpkins—all witches, ghosts, goblins, or anything else that might be scary, are frightened away by jack-o'-lanterns. Nothing scary can come to your home or your school if you have a jack-o'-lantern. It is amazing how reassuring that story can be. It is the same principle as using an aerosol can to spray away monsters that young children sometimes believe are hiding in their closets.

On the day of your Halloween party, be sure to have a few extra costumes on hand. Funny hats, big shirts, sheets, and make-up will work well. This way no child will have hurt feelings if he/she forgets a costume.

Another fun Halloween activity is to let the children make their own tape recording of scary sounds. Squeaky doors moving, chains rattling, kids screaming, footsteps, etc. are all sounds that can be easily made by the children in your classroom.

Autumn Is a Colorful Time

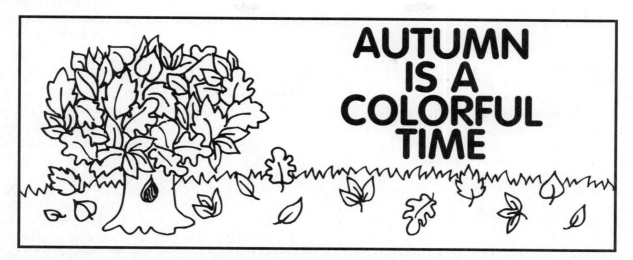

Take the children on a nature walk to collect colorful leaves. Press the leaves with a cool iron between pieces of waxed paper.

The background of the bulletin board is done in blue and green construction paper, to represent the sky and grass. Use brown construction paper for the trunk of the tree. You will need to put up white construction paper as a background for the leaves on the tree.

Now fill in the white background on the tree with all the waxed leaves. The more waxed leaves you use on the tree, the more spectacular the tree will look.

Happy Halloween

The background of this bulletin board should be black paper. The teacher makes a large yellow moon with a black silhouette of an owl flying through the night.

Day 1 Project: The children should draw and cut out pumpkins from orange construction paper. Eyes, noses, and mouths should be cut out of black construction paper and pasted on the pumpkins. Add green construction paper stems.

The pumpkins should be placed along the bottom of the bulletin board, with a small sign saying, "The Pumpkin Patch."

Day 2 Project: Use white tissue paper. Crumple a ball of tissue for stuffing the ghost's head. Place a sheet of tissue paper over the ball of crumpled tissue and tie a string around the neck of the ghost (you could also use a rubber band). Now the children can paste eyes on the ghosts, or they can use a felt tip pen to draw the eyes on.

Place the ghosts on the bulletin board so they look as if they are flying around the moon.

An Apple a Day . . .

You will need paper plates, red tissue paper, and white glue. Add a small amount of water to the white glue so that it can easily be applied with a paintbrush to the back of the paper plate. Once the paper plate is covered with glue, the child may place small pieces of the red tissue paper on it.

When the tissue paper has dried, you will probably have to trim along the edge of the paper plate. Use green construction paper to make a stem. It is also fun to use green pipe cleaners as small worms, either on the apple or coming out of the top of the apple. Children usually think the addition of a worm is very funny.

Place these "apples" on a bulletin board or use them for a wall display.

Hooray for Halloween

Use a black background for this bulletin board. In the center of the bulletin board or wall display, the teacher should put up an old run-down house made out of tagboard. Place near the house a brown, leafless tree. Let the children create monsters, bats, pumpkins, ghosts, etc.—anything that the children think should be in a Halloween scene. This is a bulletin board that can be added to and worked on for many days.

They Used to Live Here

Make a background for this bulletin board, using light blue paper at the top and green paper at the bottom. Make a volcano from gray paper. Add gray cotton balls to show smoke coming out of the volcano. (Put cotton balls in a paper bag containing gray powdered tempera paint. Shake well and you will have gray cotton balls.)

Give the children 12" x 18" pieces of white paper and ask them to draw pictures of dinosaurs. Have them color their pictures and cut them out. Place them on the bulletin board. Add trees and other landscape details.

Halloween Trick-or-Treat

Make a Halloween scene background for this bulletin board, with a haunted house, a broken fence, clouds, and a large full moon. Find pictures in magazines of children. Full-page ads for clothing will work the best. Have the students cut out the pictures and pin or tape them to the background.

Now have the children cut out ghost costumes from white fabric or construction paper. The children will probably need your assistance in drawing the proper size costumes before cutting them out. Make the costumes short enough so that the feet of the children in the pictures can be seen. Have the children pin the ghost costumes over the pictures.

This bulletin board may help children who are fearful of Halloween. They can see that the scary ghosts are just children dressed up in costumes.

Wanda the Witch

In the deep dark forest near the town of Timbergrove lives a grouchy old witch named Wanda. Now Wanda is no ordinary witch. For you see, instead of riding a broomstick, Wanda rides a flying machine.

Every Halloween night, or so folks say, Wanda the Witch emerges from the deep dark forest. She flies over the countryside in her most unusual flying machine.

Legend has it that Wanda the Witch did not always have this flying machine. Many Halloween nights ago all the young witches of the deep dark forest outside Timbergrove decided to play a trick on Wanda the Witch.

The young witches did not like Wanda because she was fat, ugly, and grouchy. Besides that, she had a big wart on the tip of her nose which made her look very mean. When the young witches teased her about her ugly nose, she would shoo them away with her broomstick.

On one particular Halloween night the young witches played a trick on old Witch Wanda. While she was preparing for her nightly cruise that Halloween, they stole her faithful broomstick and hid it where she would never find it.

"My broom! Where's my broom?" Wanda the Witch screamed when she discovered her faithful companion was not in its usual place.

Wanda the Witch was furious. If she couldn't find her broomstick, she wouldn't be able to fly around the neighborhood and scare the children of Timbergrove.

When the other witches flew out of the deep dark forest that night, Wanda the Witch was still looking for her broomstick.

"Drats!" said Wanda the Witch and she stomped her foot. "I'll not be left behind."

Quickly she began to assemble odds and ends into a huge pile. In a flash she constructed the most unusual machine anyone has ever seen. When it was finished, she leaned back on her heels, twitched her nose, waved her hand, and Presto!, the machine began to make a roaring sound. Wanda the Witch put on her big pointed hat, grabbed her black cat under her arm, jumped onto the seat of that most unusual flying machine, and away she flew.

Needless to say, Wanda the Witch was the talk of the town of Timbergrove. She made quite a sight as she flew over the treetops that Halloween night.

Every Halloween night since, the children of Timbergrove meet in the town square as soon as it is dark and wait for Wanda the Witch to fly over in her most unusual flying machine.

Story Activities

1. Have each of the children draw a picture of what they think Wanda the Witch's unusual flying machine looked like.
2. As a class project, bring in boxes, scrap material such as old cans, buttons, foil, string, yarn, etc., and have the children construct Wanda the Witch's flying machine.
3. Let the children pantomime the story as you read it.

Mystery Mansion

(The children can pretend to be Tim, a lost boy on a spooky Halloween night.)

Tim had to stay late after school and he was **walking** home. He wasn't paying attention to anything in particular. He **kicked** a rock, **ran** up to it, and **kicked** it in a different direction several times. It was becoming dark and stormy; large black clouds filled the sky, hiding the round yellowish moon. Tim noticed evening was coming and thought he better get home. The boy **turned around** to the **left** and then to the **right.** This wasn't his block; where was his house? He **scratched** his head. Tim **ran** to the end of the block, but nothing looked familiar. He decided to try to retrace his steps. He was **walking backwards.** No! That wasn't right. It was dark now, so he **walked** quickly down the block. Suddenly there was his house, but it appeared that no one was home since there were no lights on.

Skipping up the walk, Tim **unlocked** the door, and **slowly tiptoed** inside. But there were still no lights—the switches didn't work. This was spooky! The boy began to **shake.** What should he do? First Tim needed some light, and he remembered a flashlight in the kitchen. Slowly he **felt his way, arms outstretched,** feeling for furniture. He **fell** and **slowly got up, rubbing his knees** and be **bent over to rub his sore toes.** In the kitchen, he **stretched** on tiptoes to reach the top shelf. Tim **climbed** on the counter to reach higher yet. There it was! He **jumped down.**

The boy decided to investigate the house further. He heard a noise upstairs. Slowly he **climbed** the stairs and **peeked** around the corner, **dropping** the flashlight. It rolled under a bed. Tim **got down on his hands and knees** and **crawled** under the bed. He heard heavy footsteps coming up the stairs. Thud! Thud! Tim **froze.** He was so scared he didn't know what to do. Tim **huddled in a ball** to make himself as small as possible. Thud! Thud! The footsteps walked into the room. Thud! Thud! They turned and went into the next room. Tim **crawled** out from under the bed and **bent down** to grab the flashlight. He quietly **tiptoed down** the stairs and **raced** to the door. It was locked! He **skipped** to the back door. It was locked! He was trapped!

Tim went to a window and **lifted up** the heavy glass. He **squeezed** through the opening and **jumped** to the ground. He landed in some thick bushes, so to get out he had to **slide sideways,** and **squat down,** walking like a duck. Reaching the sidewalk, Tim **ran** to the end of the block where a street light was located. He **sat** down in the grass to catch his breath. "Tim! Tim!" Someone was calling his name. It was his sister. Tim had been on the wrong block and his sister came to find him. He wouldn't forget this spooky Halloween.

After reading the story to the children, have a discussion of Halloween safety:
1. Go trick-or-treating with an adult, never alone.
2. Consider attending a community party.
3. Take only wrapped treats and let an adult inspect the treats before any are eaten.
4. Go to the homes of friends only, never to strangers.
5. Do not run.
6. Stay on the sidewalk if possible.
7. Carry some kind of light.
8. Wear a safe costume, one that cannot be tripped on and that is easily seen in the dark.
9. Keep your mask off until you get to the door.

Tale of a Black Cat

(As you read this story, draw the lines on the chalkboard.)

Once there was a little boy named Tommy. There's a T that stands for Tommy.

Tommy's house was not a very good one. So he built a new wall on this side of it. And then he built a new wall on that side of it. You can see that now Tommy had two nice rooms in his house, though the rooms weren't very big.

Next he put in windows to look out of—one in this room and one in that room.

Then he made a tall chimney on this side of his house. And then he made a tall chimney on the other side of his house. After that he planted some grass beside his door, like this.

Not very far away from Tommy's house there lived a little girl named Sally. There's an S that stands for Sally.

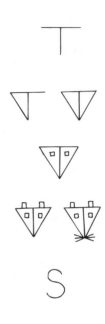

When Tommy had finished his house, he decided to go and tell Sally about it, so he came out of his door and walked along this way, over to where she lived. Sally was glad to see Tommy. Tommy told her all about how he had built two new walls in his house, and put in windows, and made two tall chimneys, and planted grass in front of his door. "And now, Sally," said Tommy, "I want you to come over and see how well I've fixed things."

"I'll put on my jacket and go right back with you," said Sally. But when she was ready to start, she said, "Let's go down in the basement first and get some apples to eat on the way."

So they went down into the basement like this.

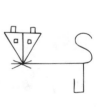

They got some apples, and then they came back up, like this.

Now they started for Tommy's house, but it was hard to walk on the bumpy road. They had gone only a few steps when they fell down, like this.

However, they got back up quickly, like this.

Tommy and Sally walked along until they were nearly to Tommy's house, when they fell down again, like this.

And they were no sooner on their feet, like this, than they fell down once more, like this.

But they were nearly to Tommy's house now. Tommy and Sally got up and were going into the yard straight toward the door, like this, when Sally pointed toward the doorstep and shouted, "O-o-o-oh! Look at the big Black Cat!"

Soap Flakes Finger Paint

Ingredients: Soap flakes, water, tempera or food coloring.

Beat soap flakes in a small amount of water until it is the consistency of whipped cream. Add color. Mix well.

This type of finger paint may be used on a smooth table top or on finger paint paper. Use fall colors, such as red, orange, yellow, and brown.

Fall Plaque

Use the plastic lid from a coffee can. Trace around the lid on colored construction paper. Cut out and glue the construction paper on top of the lid.

Collect weeds, seeds, seed pods, dried grasses, etc. Glue these to the inside of the lid.

Glue a paper clip on the back to hang it. You can also poke two holes through the lid and tie a cord through it.

Autumn Tree

Materials: 12" x 18" piece of blue or green construction paper for mounting the tree; 2" x 9" piece of brown construction paper for the trunk; 9" x 9" piece of white construction paper and red, yellow, orange, and brown tissue paper for the leaves; liquid laundry starch.

Using starch, "paste" pieces of tissue paper on the 9" x 9" white construction paper, overlapping the edges. Let dry overnight.

Draw a circle on the back of the piece of white paper and cut it out. Paste the trunk and the tissue paper collage onto the 12" x 18" construction paper.

Sprayed Leaves

Collect leaves on a nature walk. Pin the leaves on construction paper and spray with spray paint, or use a toothbrush dipped in paint over a screen.

My Paper Owl

Cut owls out of brown construction paper. Paste on small circles of white paper for eyes. Cut two holes through the lower part of the owl and push a small twig through the openings. You have seated the owl on the branch of a tree.

The children will have fun going on a walk to find the twigs.

Pumpkin Puppets

Have the children draw and cut out pumpkins from orange construction paper. The eyes, noses, and mouths should also be cut out. Paste yellow strips across the back of the cut out spaces for the eyes, nose and mouth. Paste a small green square on the top of each pumpkin for a stem. Paste the finished pumpkins on paper bags to make interesting hand puppets. Arms may be attached with brads.

Help the children make up a story to dramatize, using the completed puppets.

Sponge Painted Ghosts

Using a white crayon or white chalk, draw the shape of a ghost on black construction paper. Let the children use small sponges to dab on white paint to fill in the insides of the ghosts.

Balloon Jack-O'-Lanterns

You will need an orange balloon for every child in your room. Blow up the balloons. Using felt tip pens or magic markers, let the children draw jack-o'-lantern faces on the balloons.

Hang the jack-o'-lantern balloons from the ceiling. They will make great decorations for your Halloween party.

Fall Trees

Let the children paint with orange, yellow, red, and brown paint. After the paint is dry, those children who are able to use scissors can cut out leaves. The teacher may need to cut out the leaves for the younger children.

Cut a tree trunk out of brown construction paper and tape it to a wall or bulletin board. Use the children's leaves to decorate the tree.

Leaf Mobiles

You will need a cereal box, thread, scissors, and tape. Cut a 1" strip the length of the box. Tape it into a circle. Punch 6 holes in the strip.

Have the children collect colorful fall leaves on a nature walk. After the leaves have been collected, press with a cool iron between pieces of waxed paper. Punch a hole in the waxed paper leaves and tie them with strings of different lengths to the circular strip.

Each child could make his/her own, or you can use this as a group project.

Paper Plate Pumpkins

Make jack-o'-lantern faces on paper plates. Paint the plates orange and let them dry. After the plates are dry, they can be decorated with scraps of construction paper or fabric.

It is fun to have a jack-o'-lantern decorating contest. Let the children vote for the scariest pumpkin face, the funniest pumpkin face, the goofiest pumpkin face, the friendliest pumpkin face, etc. I always like everyone in the preschool to be a winner, so be sure to have enough categories for everyone in your room.

Nurse's Cap

Provide the experience of making nurse's caps. Be sure to include the boys. There are many male nurses these days, but that may be something that you will need to explain to the children.

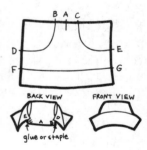

Begin with a 12" x 18" piece of white construction paper for each hat. Mark point A at the halfway point on the 18" side, and then mark two more points 2" on each side of this point. These will be B and C. Mark a point 5" down from each corner, D and E, and with a magic marker, draw a curved line from B to D and from C to E. Mark a line 3" from the bottom edge, F to G. The child can then cut along the curved lines. Then he/she folds the paper up, creasing on the marked line, FG, and glues points B to D and C to E, overlapping to fit his/her head. This may be stapled by the teacher, if preferred.

After the children have completed the caps, let them use them when role-playing in the hospital play area.

Jack-O'-Lantern Stick People

Color jack-o'-lantern faces on 9" x 12" manila paper. Draw "stick" bodies, legs, and arms. Press hard; don't leave any white spaces in the colored areas. Paint over the entire picture with black paint. Paint in rows from one edge of the paper to the other, using plenty of paint. Do not repaint.

Eye Masks

Outline the forms of eye masks with a pencil on stiff paper. Cut them out and cut holes for eyes. Paste or glue a stick, such as a sucker or ice cream stick, to one end for the holder. Then decorate the stiff paper and holder with paint. You could also paint only the holder, and decorate the stiff paper by pasting colored construction paper on it.

Clay Dinosaurs

Have the children make dinosaurs out of clay. Let them create any type of dinosaur or "monster" that they would like.

Display all the dinosaurs on a table top landscaped with rocks, grass, twigs, etc. This will be a very impressive display showing what the earth looked like during the time of dinosaurs.

Paper Plate Owl

For this activity, you will need paper plates (the kind with ridged edges), circles of orange construction paper for eyes, V-shaped pieces of orange construction paper for bills and claws, a magic marker, brown tempera paint, and glue.

Using the magic marker, draw cutting lines on each paper plate (refer to illustration at left). Have the children cut their plates on the lines, then paint the pieces of the paper plate with brown tempera paint and let dry. Staple the owls' wings to the bodies for the children. Then have the children glue the eyes, beaks, and claws onto their owls.

Halloween Spiders

Make creepy spiders for a Halloween art project. Use two flat white paper plates—a smaller plate for the head and a larger one for the body. Overlap the plates slightly and staple them together. Have the children paint their spiders black on both sides.

Punch four holes on each side of the body. Punch two more holes at the "neck" of the spider. Insert a pipe cleaner in each pair of punched holes, and bend it to look like legs. Thread black yarn through the holes in the neck so the spider can be hung up. Glue small white pom-poms or plastic moveable eyes on the head.

(Joyce M. Cini, Garden City, NY)

Plastic Spoon Witch Puppet

You will need plastic spoons, moveable eyes, felt, pipe cleaners, yarn, and construction paper for this project. Have the children glue the various materials to the spoons to create their witches. Pipe cleaners can be used for hands, and a pipe cleaner brooms can be made, too. Use yarn for the witches' hair.

Nighttime Paint

Prepare some light gray tempera paint. Give the children each a sheet of paper and tell them to color a picture of an orange pumpkin sitting in some green grass. Tell them to color the pumpkin a very strong orange color so that it will show through the "nighttime" paint they will be adding to the picture.

After the pictures are colored, have each child paint the gray tempera paint over his/her entire sheet of paper, making the pumpkin picture a very scary "nighttime" picture.

Trick-or-Treat Bag

Have the children decorate small square-bottomed paper bags to carry their Halloween candy in. Fold the bags over at the top to reinforce, and attach handles.

If you are more ambitious, you could have the children make "black cat" trick-or-treat bags. Shape the tops of the bags to look like cat ears. Have the children add cat features and attach black tails to the lower sides of the bags.

Halloween Night

Color the Halloween pictures on the bottom of this page. Cut them out and paste them by the haunted house.

Dinosaur Match

Draw a line to match the picture
of the dinosaur to its skeleton.

Owls Play at Night

The teacher explains to the children that owls do not sleep at night like children do. Owls sleep during the day when it is light outside, and play and fly at night when it is dark outside. Today the children are going to take turns pretending that they are owls playing and flying at night.

Have the class stand in a circle. Choose two children to be the "owls." Blindfold the two children, and walk them into the middle of the circle. Tell them to pretend they are owls flying at night. They must try very hard not to bump into each other.

The children standing in the circle are to help keep the blindfolded children in the circle. When the two "owls" have bumped, another two are chosen.

Encourage the owls not to fly too fast. The idea is to end up bumping into each other, not to crash!

Loop-De-Loop

Place a clothesline on the floor in a varied loop pattern. The child is instructed to walk from loop to loop without touching the rope. If successful, the child can attempt to hop from loop to loop.

Tell the children that it is time for the birds to start thinking about flying south for a warm winter. The loop to loop pattern is the path that the birds must fly. Place a picture of autumn at the beginning of the path to represent the cold north, and place a picture of the sun or a warm climate to represent the south at the end of the pattern.

Who Is in the Haunted House?

Place many 1' x 1' squares of paper all over the floor. Under one of the squares, place a picture of a haunted house.

On the teacher's signal, the children should follow the commands:

1. Walk to a square and stand on it.
2. Walk to a square and kneel on it.
3. Move to another square by sliding on your stomach.
4. Move to another square by sliding on your bottom.
5. Move to another square by crawling on all fours.
6. Move to another square by hopping.
7. Move to another square by walking backwards.

When you have given six or seven directions, ask the children to pick up the squares and discover who is in the haunted house.

Rearrange the squares and play again.

Towel Fun

To continue the autumn theme, tell the children they are squirrels playing outside on an autumn day.

Each child should have his/her own bath size towel. The child places his/her hands, feet, and knees at various positions on the towel according to directions. Once spread out on the gym floor, the child can follow these directions:

1. Hands in front and feet in back—go forward.
2. Go in reverse.

4. Push hands on the towel.

6. Ice skate with feet on towel.

8. Sit in cross-legged position and twist around on towel.

3. Just knees on the towel.

5. Feet on towel—walk with hands.

7. Knees on half towel—throw arms up to slide forward.

The Bean Bag Game

The children form a single circle. All the children face the center with their hands behind their backs. One child is "it" and stands outside the circle. This child walks around the circle and drops the bean bag into one of the children's hands. The child who was given the bean bag chases "it" and tries to tag him or her before "it" can reach the empty place in the circle. If the child tags "it," he/she gets the bean bag and is the new "it."

Busy Feet

Two children sit on chairs, small enough so that their feet are on the floor. The chairs should be placed close enough so that the children can play the game successfully.

Have the children take off their shoes. One child pushes a ball with his/her feet toward the other child. That child, in turn, stops the ball and pushes it back. By being barefoot, the children can curl their feet around the ball. They may use one or both feet. As they are successful, the children may move the chairs farther apart.

Flying Witch

Tell the children to pretend that they are witches flying through a moonlit sky. The teacher demonstrates to the class by spreading his/her arms wide and "flying" around the room. The teacher then places two bean bags about 10' apart on a straight line. It is important that the bean bags be spaced far enough apart so that the child can leap over each one without taking steps in between. The teacher then runs with his/her arms wide apart and takes off on one foot in a springing leap over one bean bag, lands on the opposite foot and then proceeds to spring over the next bean bag.

As the child successfully accomplishes this, place three bean bags in succession, so that the child alternates his/her legs in the leaps. Keep adding bean bags until the child achieves success in alternating legs in all of the leaps.

Flashlight, Flashlight, Where Are You?

Turn the lights off in the gym or classroom. The child focuses his/her eyes straight ahead. The teacher shines a flashlight to the right side of the child. The teacher can flash it a certain number of times or move in a particular pattern (circle, square, etc.). The child then can draw the pattern that was flashed or can call out the number of times the light was flashed. The teacher then shines the light to the left side of the child and repeats the procedure.

For variation, the child can repeat the pattern with his/her own flashlight. This activity is good for visual memory and projection as well as peripheral awareness. The idea is to develop rapid movement in the child.

Children always think games and activities in the dark are fun, especially during the month of October.

Scary Movements

Have the children pretend that they are out on a walk on a dark, scary Halloween night. The teacher can say movement words that the children can pantomime. Some good words to use are: wiggle, shiver, tremble, shake, creep, crawl, sneak, pounce, jump, squirm, slither, tingle, and hide.

Pantomime Autumn

Have the children in your class pantomime the following actions. Discuss why they are a part of the autumn season.

1. Squirrels gathering nuts.
2. Leaves floating to the ground.
3. People raking fallen leaves and putting them in bags.
4. Birds flying south.
5. Animals getting ready to hibernate.

The Walking Board

This activity is for developing muscle coordination and should be used throughout the year. Make the walking board from a piece of two-by-four about 8' long; a bracket is built to hold the board (see the diagram at the left).

The 4" surface is used by beginners. Later, the board is turned on edge and the 2" surface is used. Here are some suggested exercises:

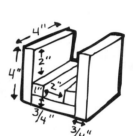

1. Walk slowly to the end of the board (moving slowly forces the child to balance).
2. Walk forward, arms held sideways.
3. Walk backward, arms held sideways.
4. Walk to the middle, turn, and walk sideways.
5. Walk forward, keeping the left foot in front of the right foot all the way.
6. Walk forward with an eraser balanced on the head.
7. Tiptoe across.
8. Hop across.
9. Walk to the middle. Pick up an eraser and walk forward.
10. Walk forward with eyes closed.
11. Walk sideways with eyes closed.

Cattails

Collect milkweeds and cattails. Take the children outside on a windy day, and let them chase the seeds from the milkweeds and cattails as they fly in the wind. This is a nice way for children to learn that not all seeds are planted in the ground by people.

The Balance Board

Make a balance board from a 16" x 16" square platform of wood. Attach the platform with a wing nut and bolt to a small post, 3" high and 5" on the sides. Refer to diagram at left.

Put a covering of ribbed rubber matting on the platform. This will help the children grip with their feet when balancing.

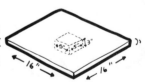

Dinosaur Tag

Have the children pretend that they are dinosaurs. Choose one child to be "it," the largest dinosaur. This child chases the other dinosaurs until one is tagged. The tagged dinosaur then becomes "it."

Dinosaur Bone Hunt

Cut out several kinds of "dinosaur bones" from heavy cardboard. Hide the "bones" outside or in the classroom.

Tell the children that they are going to pretend to be paleontologists, the scientists who study dinosaurs. Paleontologists find bones from dinosaurs in the ground, and these bones are the things that have taught us about dinosaurs. Have the children hunt to find the bones.

Real bones would be fun to use in this activity, too, if you are willing to go through the work of cleaning them.

Directions: Children color and cut out owl parts. Help them attach wings with brads at x's. Having a finished sample to show will be a great help to the children.

Pumpkin Puzzle

Name_____

 and and  =

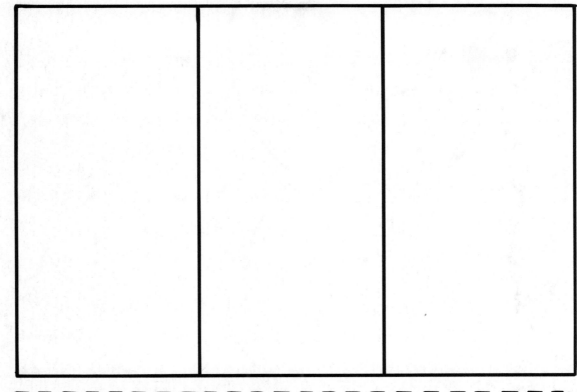

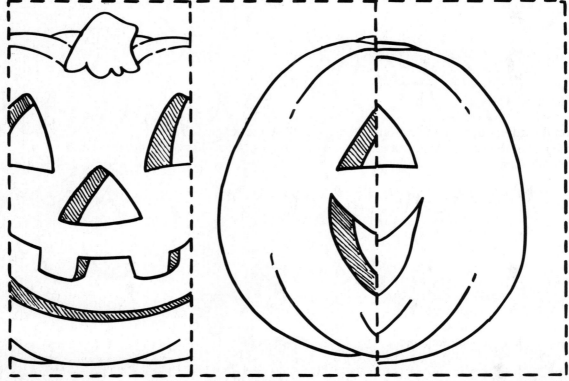

What's Up

This lesson emphasizes the positional concepts of up/down and high/low.

You will need a flannel board and flannel board cut-outs of a tree, of birds that fly like owls, ducks, and geese, and of ground animals like squirrels, mice, raccoons, etc.

The ground animals can climb up and down the tree. The birds can fly up and down in the sky. You can discuss which animals are high and low. Let the children take turns placing the animals on the flannel board and telling you where they are.

Autumn Jobs

Show the children a study print (or a picture you have drawn) of a family outside getting ready for fall. Discuss how families share jobs to be done in the fall. Some members rake leaves, some members bag the leaves, some cover flowers.

Encourage the children to discuss the pictures. Label the actions. Pantomime the actions.

Big/Little

You will need a bag of big and little leaves. Let the children sort the leaves by size.

1. Use a big box for the big leaves and a little box for the little leaves; or
2. Tape two sheets of paper on the wall. Draw a big leaf on one sheet and a little leaf on the other sheet. Let the children tape the leaves on the appropriate sheets.

Is She Happy? Is She Sad?

Prepare pictures of ghosts, pumpkins, or witches' faces depicting a variety of expressions.

Use these pictures as an oral language lesson. "Does she look happy? Why? Can you think what might have happened?" Or, "She seems angry, doesn't she? Can you imagine why?"

Another time, use two pictures together. Children can make up explanations of the interrelationships.

It's on My Back

The teacher will need cut-out shapes of a ghost, pumpkin, witch, owl, and scarecrow, and pins.

The teacher calls two children to play. They must face away from her and close their eyes while she pins a picture on the back of each child.

These two children are then led to the center of the group. They face each other. They may open their eyes, and when the teacher says "Go," they try to jockey about to see each other's back. The first child to succeed calls, "I see!" They stop and the child tells what he/she saw in a sentence, such as "I saw a black cat!" If the child is right, he/she turns and the second child may say what is on the other's back. New cut-out shapes are chosen to repeat the game.

During the rest of the school year, you can use colors, shapes, seasonal symbols or everyday objects to play this game.

A Real Pumpkin

Bring a large, real pumpkin to school for the children to assist in carving. The teacher can carve the face and the children can have the fun of scooping the insides out. This is a great activity for teaching the concepts of in/out and inside/outside. They are actually taking something that is "in" and putting it "out." Encourage that vocabulary.

Turn this into a science lesson. Discuss the reason a face is carved in a jack-o'-lantern—to supply air for the candle to burn.

Use a jar and a votive candle to demonstrate how fire needs air to burn. Leave the cover off the jar and watch the candle burn. Put on the cover. Watch the flame go out.

Special Note: SAVE THE SEEDS! You will need them for another lesson.

Make Stories Live

Reading to children and telling stories are probably the best things that a teacher or parent can do to increase language development. The more language to which children are exposed, the more language they are going to use and understand.

When you are telling stories, be sure that you are familiar with the story and that you are making it fun. The children will also learn through your expressions and attitudes. Show pictures often and discuss the details of the pictures.

Tell stories, don't just read them. Use flannel board characters, puppets, and everyday objects when telling stories, but keep in mind that the gadgets you use should enhance your stories, not overwhelm them. Let the children reenact parts of the stories or retell the stories themselves.

Storytime at the preschool level can be a very special time. Make it as meaningful and delightful as you possibly can.

Operation

Find pictures of people in magazines. Cut out one person for each child in your class. Remove a part of each person—an arm, a leg, the stomach, etc. When you give the magazine people to the children, explain that the children are doctors and that the people have come to them for operations to get repaired. Ask each of the children if he/she can name the part of the person that is missing. After each child has named the missing part, show the children the body parts that have been cut away. Have each child find his/her magazine person's part. When the child has matched the correct part to his/her person, he/she can perform the operation by pasting the person and the missing part together on a sheet of paper.

My Band-Aid Story

Give each of the children in your class a band-aid. Tell them to put the band-aids anywhere they want to on their bodies—head, hands, knees, feet, etc. It doesn't matter where they want to put their band-aids.

After the children have put on their band-aids, ask each child to make up a story about how he/she got hurt. This can really be a fun activity. Some children will retell real experiences and other children will make up exciting "pretend" stories.

Balloon Voices

Blow up a balloon. Let the air escape by manipulating the opening of the balloon. The air can be made to sound like a voice. Encourage each child to tell a story of what the balloon is saying to him/her. The teacher can use a tape recorder and record the responses of the children. Children always think it's fun to hear themselves on tape.

Let's Make Halloween Sounds

Ask the children to make the sounds that a witch, ghost, cat, squeaky door, and bat make. Make a tape recording of the children's scary sounds and use it as a background tape during your Halloween party.

Autumn Activities

The following activities will probably take your class two days to complete. On the first day, walk to a neighborhood field or park. Look for and collect seeds, leaves, and other signs of fall.

You can use these materials in the classroom in a variety of ways. Sort seeds according to type: seeds that fly, seeds that "hitchhike," seeds that are planted by animals or birds, seeds that pop and are scattered, seeds that float in the water. The children could also make collages, prints, or sponge paintings, using the collected material.

Tall/Short Dinosaurs

Prepare pictures or cut-outs of various-sized dinosaurs to use on the flannel board. Have the children compare the heights of the dinosaurs. Encourage them to use the words "tall" and "short" when describing the dinosaurs.

Pumpkin Faces

Prepare three sets of pumpkin faces, three identical pumpkins in each set. Follow the examples at the left.

Show the children three pumpkin faces at a time—two that are the same and one that is different. Ask the children to show you which are the same and which one is different. Once the children are able to point to the correct pumpkin faces, encourage them to use the words "same" and "different" when they respond to your questions.

You could also use the pumpkin faces for matching activities. Show the children one pumpkin face and ask them to find another one that is either the same or different from the one that you are holding.

Loud/Soft Sounds

Children enjoy listening to CD's or tape recordings of various sounds. Play the sounds both loudly and softly, and have the children identify which are loud and which are soft.

The children may enjoy making their own tape recording of loud and soft sounds.

Halloween Safety

Have a discussion with your class about Halloween safety. Find out how much information the children have about being safe on Halloween. Below are some guidelines for your discussion.

1. Go trick-or-treating with an adult. Never go alone.
2. Consider attending a community party.
3. Take only wrapped treats, and let an adult inspect the treats before any are eaten.
4. Go to the homes of friends only, never to the homes of strangers.
5. Do not run, and stay on the sidewalk if possible.
6. Carry some kind of light.
7. Wear a safe costume, one that can't be tripped on and that is easily seen in the dark.
8. Keep your mask off until you get to the door.

Rough/Smooth Touch

Have a box filled with various materials that are rough or smooth: sandpaper, cotton, silk, nylon, crumpled foil, wood, etc. Ask the children to shut their eyes and then feel the materials. They should describe the textures using the vocabulary words "rough" and "smooth."

Halloween Match

Draw lines, matching the shapes.

Ghost Puzzle

Directions:
Children cut out ghost parts, arrange on a large piece of black construction paper, and glue down.

and   =

PASTE

TSD1896-4 *The Preschool Calendar*

Four Little Owls

This little owl has great, round eyes.
This little owl is of very small size.
This little owl can turn her head.
This little owl likes mice, she said.
This little owl flies all around,
And her wings make hardly a single sound.
(Pretend a desk or table is the tree. One child is the owl; another, the sun. The owl sleeps. The sun goes down. The owl awakens and flies away to look for mice to feed her babies. The sun comes up and the owl goes back to her "tree.")

Three Little Pumpkins

Three little pumpkins,
Sitting on a fence.
A witch came riding by,
"Ha, ha, ha, ha, ha," she said,
"I'll take you all and make a pumpkin pie."
(Make three pumpkin cut-outs and one witch cut-out, use them with this poem, on the flannel board.)

Autumn

Autumn winds begin to blow;	*(blow)*
Colored leaves fall fast and slow.	*(make fast and slow falling motions with hands)*
Twirling, whirling all around.	*(turn self around and around)*
Till at last, they touch the ground.	*(fall to ground)*

Three Little Witches

One little, two little, three little witches,	*(hold up fingers one by one)*
Ride through the sky on a broom.	*(move hand quickly "through the sky")*
One little, two little, three little witches,	*(hold up fingers again)*
Wink their eyes at the moon.	*(wink one eye while making circle with arms)*

The Witch

A funny old woman with a pointed cap.	*(hands peaked above head)*
On my door went rap, rap, rap.	*(make rapping motion with fist)*
I was going to the door to see who was there.	*(swing arms as if you were walking)*
When off on her broomstick she rode through the air.	*(sail hand high through air)*

Autumn Leaves

Leaves are floating softly down;	*(make "floating down" movements with hands)*
Some are red and some are brown.	
The wind goes swish through the air;	*(make "swish" motion with one hand)*
When you look back, there are no leaves there.	*(hold hands out in front, palms up)*

Here Is the Witch's Tall Black Hat

Here is the witch's tall black hat.	*(hold arms together over head)*
Here are the whiskers on her cat.	*(index fingers and thumbs are put together and pulled back and forth under nose)*
Here is an owl sitting in a tree.	*(circle eyes with fingers)*
Here is a goblin! Hee, hee, hee!	*(hold hand on stomach area)*

Little Ghost

I saw a little ghost,	*(hold hands over eyes)*
And he saw me, too!	*(point to self)*
When I said "Hi"!	*(wave hand)*
He said, "Boo"!	*(both hands out front on "Boo")*

Jack-O'-Lanterns

Five little jack-o'-lanterns sitting on a gate.
The first one said, "It's getting late."
The second one said, "I hear a noise."
The third one said, "It's only some boys."
The fourth one said, "Let's run, let's run."
The fifth one said, "It's Halloween fun."
Then "oooooo" went the wind, and out went the light,
And away ran the jack-o'-lanterns, on Halloween night.
(Use as a flannel board poem. Make 5 pumpkins.)

Sore Toe

This little dog has a sore toe.	*(put up piece for dog with sore toe)*
This little dog said, "Oh, no!"	*(put up a second dog)*
This little dog said, "That's bad."	*(put up a third dog)*
This little dog cried, "How sad."	*(put up a fourth dog)*
This little dog, helpful and good,	*(put up a fifth dog)*
Ran for the nurse as fast as he could!	*(put up "nurse" dog)*

(Make flannel board pieces: 1 dog with a sore toe, 4 dogs that are the same, and 1 "nurse" dog.)

Halloween

Leaves are falling! Leaves are falling!	*(twirl on tiptoe)*
Pumpkins calling! Pumpkins calling!	*(cup hands to mouth)*
Halloween! Halloween!	*(jump high in the air, kick feet together, clap hands over head)*
Witches riding! Witches riding!	*(pretend to gallop on broomstick*
Goblins hiding! Goblins hiding!	*(crouch down, hide head under arm)*
Halloween! Halloween!	*(jump high in the air, kick feet together, clap hands over head)*

(Beat the rhythm on a drum, while the children chant the words and dramatize the poem.)

Raking Leaves

I rake the leaves	*(make raking motion)*
When they fall down,	*(raise arms and let fingers fall gradually)*
In a great big pile.	*(measure)*
And when there are	
Enough of them,	
I jump on them a while.	*(jump three times)*

Little Ghosts

The first little ghost floated by the store.
The second little ghost stood outside the door.
The third little ghost tried her best to hide.
The fourth little ghost stood by my side.
The fifth little ghost near the window sill,
Gave everybody a great big thrill.
The five little ghosts were all my friends,
And that is the way that this story ends.
(Make puppet ghosts by rolling up a ball of newspaper, laying a large square of white sheeting over it, and tying at the neck. Draw eyes and mouth with a black felt-tip pen.)

Four Big Jack-O'-Lanterns

Four big jack-o'-lanterns made a funny sight,
Sitting on a gatepost Halloween night.
Number one said, "I see a witch's hat."
Number two said, "I see a big, black cat."
Number three said, "I see a scary ghost."
Number four said, "By that other post."
Four big jack-o'-lanterns weren't a bit afraid.
They marched right along in the Halloween parade.
(Let the children take turns dramatizing this poem.)

Ten Huge Dinosaurs

Ten huge dinosaurs were standing in a line.
One tripped on a cobblestone, and then there were nine.
Nine huge dinosaurs were trying hard to skate.
One cracked right through the ice, and then there were eight.
Eight huge dinosaurs were counting past eleven.
One counted up too far, and then there were seven.
Seven huge dinosaurs learned some magic tricks.
One did a disappearing act, and then there were six.
Six huge dinosaurs were learning how to drive.
One forgot to put in gas, and then there were five.
Five huge dinosaurs joined the drum corps.
One forgot the drumsticks, and then there were four.
Four huge dinosaurs were wading in the sea.
One waded too far out, and then there were three.
Three huge dinosaurs looked for Mister Soo.
One gave up the search, and then there were two.
Two huge dinosaurs went to the Amazon.
One sailed in up to his head, and then there was one.
One lonesome dinosaur knew her friends had gone.
She found a big museum, and then there were none.
*(Make "ten huge dinosaurs." Use on the flannel board
or as stick puppets.)*

The Owl

There's a wide-eyed owl,	
With a pointed nose,	*(make point with index fingers)*
With two pointed ears,	*(show with hands)*
And claws for his toes.	*(show with hands)*
He lives high in a tree.	*(point)*
When he looks at you,	
He flaps his wings,	*(flap hands)*
And he says, "Whoo, Whoo."	

Eight Giggling Ghosts

Eight giggling ghosts,
Like to give you a fright,
When they come out to play,
On a Halloween night.
One ghost laughs,
And one ghost giggles;
One ghost ha-ha's,
And one hoots and wiggles.
One ghost cackles,
And one ghost roars;
One ghost guffaws,
And one rolls on the floor.
Eight giggling ghosts,
Aren't much of a fright,
When they come out to play,
On a Halloween night.
*(Make "eight giggling ghosts." Use on the
flannel board or as stick puppets.)*

Inside the Sheet

My brother is inside the sheet,
That gave an awful shout.
I know, because those are his feet,
That I see sticking out.
And that's his head that waggles there,
And his eyes peeking through—
So I can laugh, and I don't care.
"Ha!" I can say, "It's you!"
*(Use as a flannel board rhyme. Make a boy
and a ghost costume to cover him.)*

Halloween Ghost

There once was a ghost,	*(extend hand and wiggle fingers)*
Who lived in a cave.	*(form hollow with palm for "cave")*
She scared all the people	*(point to children)*
And the animals away.	
She said "Boo" to a fox,	*(point)*
She said "Boo" to a bee,	*(point)*
She said "Boo" to a bear,	*(point)*
She said "Boo" to me!	*(point at self)*
Well, she scared that fox,	*(nod head "yes")*
And she scared that bee.	*(nod head "yes")*
She seared that bear,	*(nod head "yes")*
But she didn't scare me!	*(shake head "no")*

Halloween Goblins

On Halloween, we hear much about goblins. Children dress like goblins and try to scare people. The stories we read about goblins tell us that they play tricks and do mischief on Halloween night, but no one ever catches one. What happens to the goblins in this song after they have done their tricks?

MYSTERIOUSLY

Gob - lins, on the night of Hal - low - een,

Hide a - way so they can not be seen, Play such tricks as

softly

they can do, Dis - ap - pear and fright - en you.

Suggestion: Point to someone on the last word of the song, making it scary.

Move to Music

Play music on the piano appropriate for running, marching, hopping, etc. Change the tempo often so the children are able to move fast and slow.

Tell the children that they are fall leaves in a forest on a windy day. When the music is fast, the wind is blowing them very hard. When the music is slow, the wind is blowing them very gently.

Listen to the Sounds

The teacher needs to use a piano or other musical instrument.

Divide the children into three groups—the "witch" group, the "ghost" group, and the "black cat" group.

Explain to the children that the high notes are the black cats screeching, the middle notes are the witches cackling, and the low notes are the ghosts saying "Boo, boo, boo!"

The teacher should make each of the sounds several times while playing the musical instrument. This will enable the children to associate which sound belongs to which group.

The children should now be ready to play the game. In random order, play the three sounds one at a time. The appropriate group should respond to the sounds that they were assigned.

Special Note: These types of activities, including activities where the emphasis is on loud and soft sounds, can offer you the opportunity to spot children who may have hearing difficulties.

Percussion Instruments

Children enjoy playing "orchestra" to the rhythm of a musical selection. Tapping, clapping together, striking, shaking, or beating instruments, when done lightly and in rhythm, produces a pleasant effect as an accompaniment to music. The performance gives great satisfaction to the children.

The teacher can make many interesting percussion instruments out of everyday objects. Below are some suggestions:

Jack and Jill Shakers: tubes from rolls of paper towels with ends sealed and beads inside. The shakers may be covered with decorative paper.

Rattle Caps: bottle caps strung on a wire ring or a coat hanger.

Clatter Cups: two paper cups sealed together with tape and about three marbles inside.

Brrrrt Block: a board with ridges sawed across it. Play by scraping with a big nail or thin stick.

Clickety Clothespins: 8 or 10 upside down clothespins nailed or screwed to a thin board from the underside. Play with a thin stick or tongue depressor.

Timmy Tambourine: two paper plates sewed or tied together with bells tied on.

Dribble Drum: 1 pound coffee can, ⅓ full of water, inner tube stretched over top, tied on tightly or sealed with heavy rubber binders.

Halloween Is Coming

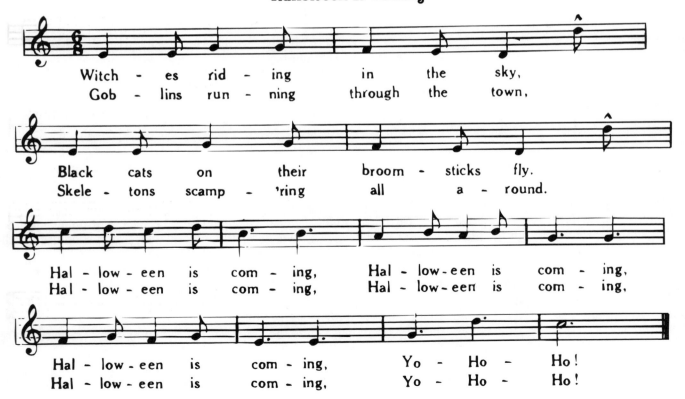

Witch - es rid - ing   in   the   sky,
Gob - lins run - ning   through   the   town,

Black   cats   on   their   broom - sticks   fly.
Skele - tons scamp - 'ring   all   a - round.

Hal - low - een   is   com - ing,   Hal - low - een   is   com - ing,
Hal - low - een   is   com - ing,   Hal - low - een   is   com - ing,

Hal - low - een   is   com - ing,   Yo - Ho - Ho!
Hal - low - een   is   com - ing,   Yo - Ho - Ho!

Goblin in the Dark

Sing this to the tune of "The Farmer in the Dell." Have the children form a circle. One child is chosen to be the goblin. The children sing:

The goblin in the dark,	The goblin takes a witch,
The goblin in the dark,	The goblin takes a witch,
Hi-ho on Halloween,	Hi-ho on Halloween,
The goblin in the dark.	The goblin takes a witch.

At the end of this stanza, the child who is the goblin chooses another child to be the witch. The song continues with "the witch takes an owl," "the owl takes a cat," "the cat takes a ghost," and "the ghost goes 'Boo!'" The song ends with this stanza:

They all scream and screech,
They all scream and screech,
Hi-ho on Halloween,
They all scream and screech.

In Prehistoric Times

In Pre-his-tor— ic Times, they say, Huge mon-sters walk'd upon the ground. Great mam-moths and big di-no-saurs, Lived
here and all a-round. Long—necked dra-gons
in the seas. And pter-o-dac-tyls, fly-ing in the sky. In
pre-his-tor-ic times, a cir-cus was al-ways pass-ing by.

Color Cards

The autumn season brings about many color changes in a large portion of the United States. This is a good time of the year to talk about all the colors.

As a class project, have the children make posterboard color cards. Cut a piece of red posterboard, 12" x 18". Look for red pictures in magazines. Cut and paste the red pictures onto the red posterboard. Cover the posterboard with clear contact paper. Repeat with other colors.

Keep these posterboard color cards up all year. They make great room decorations.

Feed the Owl

You will need a large owl made out of heavy tagboard. Cut a mouth opening wide enough so flash cards of everyday objects, seasonal symbols, colors, shapes, or specific vocabulary you may be currently working on in your classroom may be inserted into the owl's mouth.

Ask one child to stand behind the owl. A second child stands in front of the owl, chooses a card, and states what is on the card. If he/she is right, the owl "eats" the card. If not, the child (or teacher) behind the owl pushes it back and thus the owl "spits it out."

Toast Pumpkin Seeds

You will need the pumpkin seeds that the children scooped out of the pumpkin (see Language Activities, page 53).

> 2 cups pumpkin seeds, rinsed clean
> 1½ tablespoons melted butter
> 1½ teaspoons salt

Add melted butter and salt to seeds. Spread on cookie sheet rubbed with salad oil. Bake in 250° oven until crisp and brown, about 2 hours.

Haunted House

The teacher should bring a large box, big enough for children to get inside.

Crooked doors and windows can be cut out of the box, and the box can be painted by the children. This makes a very exciting "play haunted house."

If you are unable to find a large box, decorating a sheet to look like a haunted house works well, too. The sheet can be draped over a table for the children to play under.

Triangle Witch

Each child will need: 3 medium sized black triangles for the arms and hat; 1 large black triangle for the dress; 1 small yellow triangle for the broom; 1 circle for the head.

Have the children paste the shapes on construction paper to make the witch.

Hair, facial features, the brim of the hat, and broom handle can be added with color crayons.

Halloween Party

A Halloween party is a very special event in a child's preschool experience. Let the children dress up in their costumes and parade around the school. "Pin the Tail on the Cat," or "Pin the Hat on the Witch" are fun games.

A party is not much fun without something good to eat. Let the children help you create "Rice Krispie Pumpkins." Here is an easy recipe:

> ¼ cup butter
> 1 10-oz. package regular marshmallows or 4 cups miniature marshmallows
> 5 cups Rice Krispies

Melt the marshmallows and the butter. Add the Rice Krispies. Put a drop of cooking oil on each child's hands. The cooking oil will help keep the marshmallows from sticking.

Each child should form a circle from the marshmallow and Rice Krispie mixture. They can then be frosted with orange frosting and decorated with raisins.

Vegetable Store

This is the time of year that many parents are harvesting their home gardens. Ask each of the children to bring in something that was grown at home, or to bring in a fresh vegetable that was purchased at the store. Wash the vegetables and cut them into serving-size pieces. Arrange them in bowls and set up a produce stand or a vegetable store. Give each of the children a small bag and let them go shopping in the store.

Once the shopping is done, let the children taste all the vegetables. Make a large chart. On the chart have a column for each vegetable. Graph the number of children who liked each vegetable. Which vegetable was liked the most? Which vegetable was liked the least?

Hospital Dramatic Play

Set up a "hospital" in which the children may play. Include the following "departments":
- A reception desk with a telephone, a place for people to sign in, and a loudspeaker to call for the doctors.
- A kitchen, including a table where cooks can fix trays of food for the patients.
- A ward—use kindergarten mats that are placed in rows on the floor.
- An operating room, including a low table for the patient, with a small table nearby to hold bandages, splints, plastic hypodermic syringes without needles (from disposable hospital kits), and stethoscope.
- An examination room—this would be an area near the admissions desk where patients may be weighed and measured.

Be sure to discuss with the children all the jobs that are found at a hospital. There are many people that work at a hospital besides doctors and nurses.

Face Bingo

You will need chipboard, a marking pen, and scissors.

Cut a 9" square piece of chipboard. Divide the square into nine equal square boxes with the marking pen. Draw a face in each square, showing eyes, nose, and mouth. Each of the faces should be different (see illustration).

Cut nine 3" squares out of another piece of chipboard. Draw a face on each 3" square, to match the different faces on the large board.

This will give the children the experience of matching identical faces.

Match the Size

On a rectangle of chipboard, draw geometric shapes graduated in size. Mark only the outline of the shape, but complete the rest of the figure, as illustrated at the left. Cut identical graduated shapes of chipboard or tagboard to fit the outlined shapes.

Orange Milk Sherbet

1 envelope unflavored gelatin	1 cup orange juice
3 cups milk	¼ cup lemon juice
2 cups half-and-half	¾ teaspoon salt
1½ cups sugar	yellow and red food coloring

In a saucepan, sprinkle gelatin over 1 cup of the milk. Cook over low heat, stirring constantly, until gelatin dissolves. Set aside. In a large bowl, combine the rest of the milk with remaining ingredients. Gradually stir in gelatin mixture. Pour into cake pans, cover with foil, and freeze.

Autumn Color Change Game

Talk about how the leaves change color in the autumn. Into what colors do the green leaves turn? Then play this autumn color change game.

Mount autumn colors on 3" x 6" pieces of tagboard. Divide the colors evenly among the members of the class. Have the children sit on the floor in a circle, holding their color cards in front of them. Choose one child to be "it." This child should stand in the center of the circle. Call out two colors words, for example, "red and yellow." The children holding red and yellow cards should then try to change places, while the child who is "it" tries to beat one of the children changing places to his/her new home. If "it" succeeds, the child left out becomes "it," surrendering his/her color tag to the former "it."

Variation: When the colors are called, the children holding color cards may skip around the outside of the circle. "It" skips after them, trying to tag one of the other children. The first child tagged becomes the new "it."

Hibernating Animal Puzzles

Discuss the word "hibernation" with your class. Explain that chipmunks, squirrels, bears, and skunks are some of the animals that sleep or rest all winter long when it is cold in the north.

Find pictures of these animals, and glue them on tagboard. After the glue is dry, cut the pictures up into puzzle pieces. The children can work on the puzzles alone or in groups. Store the puzzles in envelopes.

Read "Ideas of Interest"

There are so many misconceptions about the dinosaurs. It's important to give the children accurate information. Read the information about dinosaurs on page 36 to your class, and discuss it with them. Have pictures available to show to the children.

Alive/Not Alive

By the time you reach this activity, the children should understand that there are no dinosaurs alive today. Dinosaurs used to be alive, but they are all gone now. We do have some animals that look a little bit like the dinosaurs, though, like the Komodo Dragon, chameleons, horned toads, iguanas, etc.

Find pictures of dinosaurs and of the animals mentioned above. Have the children identify them as alive or not alive.

Pumpkin Pudding

3 cups mashed pumpkin
3 cups milk
3 eggs
1 cup sugar
dash of nutmeg, ginger, cinnamon, salt, and cloves
graham cracker crumbs

Beat the eggs, then add the sugar and beat together. Beat the pumpkin into the eggs and sugar. Use a hand beater and let the children take turns beating. Stir in the milk, then the spices. Cook in the top of a double boiler until thick. Pour in paper cups and sprinkle with graham cracker crumbs.

Caramel Apples

Dip small apples into melted caramel, and if desired, into chopped peanuts. Place on a buttered cookie sheet. Push a craft stick in the top of the apple. These will make a wonderful treat for a Halloween party.

The holiday of Thanksgiving is one that is celebrated in many classrooms throughout the United States. The story of Thanksgiving is taught and often re-enacted by the children. For the importance of teaching about this historic event, *The Preschool Papers* has included a special section on the origin of Thanksgiving. This article was written by Bill Rosenfelt, editor in chief at T.S. Denison. Mr. Rosenfelt is the author of six different state history books. A special one to us in Minnesota is *Minnesota: Its People and Culture*. Not only is Mr. Rosenfelt an historian and editor in chief at T.S. Denison, but he was also a classroom teacher for many years.

A Teacher Note
on the Origin of Thanksgiving

The first white settlers in the American colonies and settlements were accustomed to giving thanks to their God for the blessings of their time. Since food was scarce in early times, these people depended on the rich soil of the new land to produce corn and other foods to carry them through the harsh winters. Many of their first food-growing efforts were a result of knowledge shared with them by their neighbors, called Indians. These Native Americans were also accustomed to giving thanks to their "Great Spirit" for providing them with food.

Many tribes or clans provided for their food needs by simple farming. Corn, squash, and other root vegetables were already in cultivation when the white settlers arrived, and there is much historical evidence to indicate that these people shared both their farming knowledge and their supplies of food with the settlers.

These Native Americans observed a harvest festival in the fall which featured food they had grown, as well as animals and wild fowl (deer and wild turkey) that their hunts provided. They held feasts, gave thanks to their "Great Spirit," and enjoyed a day or more of gala festivities with hosts of friends and relatives. Some historians believe that the first Thanksgiving celebration observed by the white colonists was one to which they had been invited by their Native American neighbors.

From this early observance, the celebration of our traditional Thanksgiving was born, a day each year that we set aside for special observance, a day for special gatherings of family and friends, and for traditional foods such as roast turkey, squash, corn, and pumpkin pie. It is truly an American tradition, and it started with the very first Americans, the people called Indians by those first white settlers.

Editorial Comment. You might plan to tell this story of the first Thanksgiving to your children, then follow the activity by having the children bring pictures from magazines or newspapers that show current aspects of the Thanksgiving observance. Then allow each child to tell what Thanksgiving means to them. It not only encourages creative self-expression, but it also stimulates feelings for their cultural heritage.

Families

I felt that November would be a good month to include a "Families" unit.

For small children, family members are generally everyone and everything that they love: parents, the puppy, grandparents, brothers and sisters, special friends, the next door neighbor, a favorite doll. Children seem to be the best believers in the extended family concept.

When talking about the family unit, be sensitive to the many kinds of family structures that exist today. Not all families are made up of mom, dad, kids, and a pet. Family structures can include stepparents, stepsiblings, divorced parents, single parents, special friends, adoptive parents, extended families, one-child families, etc. Give value and meaning to all family units—each is special and has unique needs. Children should be proud of their families, no matter what kinds of relationships are involved.

Here are two important objectives in teaching a preschool unit on "Families."
1. Help the children identify the people who are important to them. Be sure to treat the child's feelings for these people as important. The child will feel more secure knowing that there are many people who care about him/her.
2. Help them learn to identify some of the relationships within a family. (For example, Grandma is Mommy's mom, Aunt Liz is Daddy's sister, etc.) These are very difficult relationships for young children to understand, but they delight in hearing about them. My own five-year-old loves to hear stories about when I was little, and she is fascinated by the fact that her two big uncles are my "baby" brothers.

Community Helpers

When teaching the "Community Helpers" unit, stress the fact that a community is only as good as the people who live in it. To ensure a well-balanced and organized community, all of us need to cooperate, to be considerate, and to follow rules. Plan a discussion of how children can be helpful and make their community a better place. In my classrooms I often had a large poster on the wall entitled "Friend of the Week." On Friday afternoons, we would put up on the poster a picture of the child who had been the most considerate, tried the hardest, or who was the best at being a good friend. The children loved it!

Be aware of stereotypes when talking about various occupations. Let the children know that men can be teachers and nurses, and women can be doctors and police officers.

Our Community Helpers Make the Wheels Go Around

Make a large white circle. Draw in the rim and the spokes of a wheel. Print the name of a helper on each spoke. Cut out a fire fighter's hat, a bus, an envelope, a blackboard with letters and numbers printed in chalk, a garbage can, a grocery bag, a doctor's bag, and a police officer's blue hat. Pin these on the outside of the circle opposite to the correct spoke. Print the caption under the wheel.

You can add as many pictures or objects as you would like to the bulletin board. The more things you put by each of the community helper's names, the more attractive the bulletin board will look.

When you put up this bulletin board, do it with your class. Ask the children who they think each of the pictures or objects belongs to. Find out how much they know about community helpers. Tell them that these are the people about whom they are going to be learning this month.

Can You Find My Turkey?

Each of the children will be making a hand print for this bulletin board.

Using a paint brush, put brown paint on the thumb and palm of the child's hand. The other fingers should each be painted a different color. After the entire hand has been painted, press the child's hand on a 7½" x 10½" piece of white or beige construction paper. When the hand prints are dry, the children may draw on legs, eyes, and the red wattle which hangs under the turkey's chin.

Mount each turkey hand print on a piece of 9" x 12" construction paper. Display on the wall or bulletin board.

Look Both Ways

The "Transportation unit" will provide you with an excellent opportunity to discuss street safety. Most preschoolers are not as yet crossing the street by themselves, but it is not too soon for them to learn about looking both ways before they cross a street.

On the bulletin board, put up two long strips of black paper for the street. Let the children design and create their own cars for the street. Put up the caption "Look Both Ways Before You Cross."

Thanksgiving Turkey

The outline shapes of the turkey and the pumpkin are drawn on paper the size of the bulletin board with the sky and grass background painted around them. Mark each section of the turkey and pumpkin with the color to be used.

Crumple scraps of tissue paper (about six inches square) into tight balls. Put a dot of paste on the background, and press the ball on it. Outline each section with the balls. Then work to the center, placing the tissue paper balls close together, and filling in each section to make a solid color.

Families Play Together

Talk with your class about the kind of play situations that their families enjoy. Tell the children to each draw a picture showing some game or activity in which their family participates. Drawing a picture of people in action may be too complicated for the children, so tell them that they can draw a picture of an object, a game, or a place. They don't have to draw a whole scene.

Have each child tell you what his/her picture is about. Write what the child says on the bottom of the picture. Mount the drawings on colored construction paper and display on a bulletin board or wall.

Horn of Plenty

The horn of plenty will be a large display in your classroom. Divide your class into equal groups. Each group will be responsible for a section of the horn of plenty. One group will make the horn, and each of the other groups will be responsible for one piece of fruit.

Have the children make the horn of plenty by tearing pieces of brown paper and then gluing them onto a piece of construction paper that is in the shape of a horn. This will give the horn a textured look. The fruit is made by pasting small crumpled pieces of tissue paper onto heavy construction paper. Display on a bulletin board or wall.

The following story is a popular Ojibwe story as told to Sherrill Flora by Sally Hunter, who is an Ojibwe from the White Earth Reservation in Minnesota. She has worked with a team of Indian teachers, Rick Gresczyk and Collins Oakgrove, telling stories and teaching Indian culture in the Minneapolis Public Schools.

Storytelling is an important aspect of Indian culture. Indian people have used stories as an educational device to teach morals, to teach about animals and nature, and to teach about human folly. Traditionally, such stories were told in the winter when the snow covered the ground and the animals were asleep and could not hear the stories. After all, it is impolite to talk about someone when they can hear you.

In the story you are about to read, and in many Ojibwe stories, you will hear about Wenaboozhoo. It is important for your children to understand that Wenaboozhoo has special powers.

How the Rabbit Got Long Ears

A long time ago, the rabbit Waabooz was very plain looking. He was sort of medium brown with short ears. He didn't like the way he looked. Waabooz thought he was too plain looking. "No one ever notices me," he thought. "I'm so plain." Waabooz wanted to be noticed, but instead of doing something good, he decided to do something awful. Waabooz decided to tell a lie!

Waabooz called all the animals in the forest together. He called the bear. He called the squirrel. He called the moose. He called everyone and they all came. "What is it? Why did you call us?" said the animals. Waabooz said, "I know something you don't know. I know something you don't know." The animals said, "What is it, Waabooz?" Finally, when Waabooz got everyone's attention, he said, "The sun, the moon, and the stars are going away. They will never shine again. I know it is true. The sun, the moon, and the stars are going away. They will never shine again. I know it is true."

And what do you think would happen if the sun, the moon, and the stars went away? There would be no sunshine and light for the plants to grow and the animals could not find food.

Well, the animals became so frightened that they began to run and gather food and eat and eat and eat! Running and eating, running, and eating. The deer were munching the leaves. The bears were munching the berries. And Waabooz sat in the bushes laughing and laughing and thinking, "They noticed me!"

About that time, who do you suppose came walking along? Wenaboozhoo, and he saw all the animals running and eating. They were frantic! Wenaboozhoo asked the bear, "Why are you running and eating? What's wrong?" The bear said, "I can't talk to you now. I'm too busy." So Wenaboozhoo asked the deer. The deer said, "I can't talk to you now. I'm too busy." So Wenaboozhoo asked the squirrel. The squirrel said, "I can't talk to you now. I'm too busy."

Finally, a little chipmunk came up to Wenaboozhoo. The chipmunk said, "It was Waabooz. He told us the sun, the moon, and the stars were going away forever. We are trying to get food before it is too dark and too cold." Wenaboozhoo said, "Where is Waabooz?" Waabooz was in the bushes. He wasn't running or frightened. He was laughing and laughing.

Wenaboozhoo reached down and pulled Waabooz up by his ears. When he did this, Waabooz' ears stretched. Waabooz now had long ears. Wenaboozhoo shook him and asked, "Did you tell the animals that the sun, the moon, and the stars were going away? Did you scare them by telling a lie?"

"Yes," said Waabooz. "It was I. I just wanted to be noticed." Wenaboozhoo reached down and gave Waabooz a split lip.

So whenever you see a rabbit, you will notice that he has a split lip, because Waabooz told a lie, and he has long ears, because Wenaboozhoo lifted Waabooz by his ears.

Wenaboozhoo called the animals together and had Waabooz tell them the truth. The sun, the moon, and the stars will always be with us.

Taking a Trip

On Sunday, Bradley Bear told his mother that he wanted to go to Disneyland. "I want to ride on Space Mountain," said Bradley. "How will you get there?" asked his mother. "I'm going to take the train," he decided. "Have a good time," called his mother.

(put up label for Sunday)
(put up bear)

(put up train)

On Monday, he told his father he was going to the beach. "I want to look for seashells and fly my kite," said Bradley. "How will you get there?" asked his father. "I'll sail on a boat," he explained. "Don't forget your bathing suit," laughed his father.

(take off train and Sunday, put up Monday)

(put up boat)

On Tuesday, he told his mother that he thought he would visit his grandmother because she was always glad to see him. "How will you get there?" asked his mother. "I'll zoom in an airplane in the sky," he shouted. "Tell her I said hello," smiled his mother.

(take off boat and Monday, put up Tuesday)

(put up airplane)

On Wednesday, Bradley planned a trip to the zoo. "I like to watch the elephants," he said. His mother asked how he would get to the zoo. "I'll wait at the bus stop for the bus," he said. "Be home for lunch," joked his mother.

(take off airplane and Tuesday; put up Wednesday)

(put up bus)

On Thursday, Bradley wanted to go camping in the mountains. "I like to sleep in a tent with my sleeping bag," he said. "How will you get there?" asked his father. "I'll go in a car and drive to the mountains," said Bradley. "Drive carefully," laughed his father.

(take off bus and Wednesday, put up Thursday)

(put up car)

On Friday, he wished for a trip to the moon. "How will you get to the moon?" questioned his mother. "I'll float high in the sky in a hot air balloon," he said. "Sounds like fun," his mother told him.

(take off car and Thursday, put up Friday)

(put up balloon)

On Saturday, he said, "Today I'm going next door to play with my friend." "How will you get there?" asked his father. "I'm going on my roller skates," said Bradley. "Have a good time," said his father. "I will," shouted Bradley, "because I'm really going!"

(take off balloon and Friday; put up Saturday)

(take off bear; put up bear on skates)

How the Robin's Breast Became Red

Long ago in the cold Northland there was a great big blazing fire. All day and all night an Indian hunter and his son took care of it. They kept it burning brightly. There was no other fire in the whole world, and squirrels and rabbits and chipmunks would come near the fire to warm their toes before they hurried away to their winter homes. All the Indian people came to the fire to get hot coals which they used to cook their food.

Then one day the Indian hunter whose job it was to tend the fire became very sick. His son had to take care of the fire by himself. For days and days, and nights and nights, the little boy bravely kept the fire burning. He would run off into the woods to collect sticks, and hurry back to toss them on the fire. But at last the little Indian boy became very tired. He couldn't keep his eyes open any more. His head nodded, and he fell fast asleep on the ground.

In the deep woods of the Northland there lived an old white bear. He always watched the fire, his bright eyes peeking out from behind the pine trees. The bear hated all warm things, and he had wanted to put the fire out for a long time, but he was afraid of the hunter's sharp-pointed arrows. When he saw that the Indian hunter and his little son couldn't take care of the fire, the bear laughed to himself and began to step softly, nearer and nearer and nearer to the fire.

"Here's my chance!" the bear said. "We won't have any more fire in the Northland!"

The bear jumped with his big wet feet on the logs, and he tramped back and forth on the hot coals, until he couldn't see a spark. Then the bear went back to his cave in the woods again. He was sure that he had put the fire out for good.

But up in a pine tree sat the little gray robin who lived in the Northland. She felt very sorry when she saw what the white bear had done. She fluttered down to the ground, and over to the place where the fire had been. And what do you suppose she found?

There was one tiny spark of flame still burning, and one little red coal! So the gray robin began hopping and flapping her little gray wings, fanning the tiny sparks to make the fire burn again. Soon the red coals began to crackle and the flames began to burn higher and higher, until they scorched the poor robin's breast, but she never minded at all. She was happy that the fire was beginning to burn again.

When the fire was burning cheerily once more, the Indian boy woke up and the robin flew back to the pine tree. But the old white bear just growled and growled. He was mad when he saw that the fire was safe. And the robin, who had always been just a gray color all over, looked down where the flames had burned her breast, and saw that it had turned a beautiful golden red. After that, every gray robin had a pretty red breast too, for the robin who saved the fire was the grandmother of all robins.

The people of the Northland love the robin very much, and this is the story they tell of how she came to have her red breast.

Story Activities:
1. Have each child draw a picture of a robin with a red breast.
2. Let the children take turns acting out the story as you read it. The children can be the Indian hunter, the Indian boy, the bear, and the robin.
3. Show the children pictures of robins.

Grocery Store Collage

As a class project, have the children take turns pasting labels from items bought in a grocery store on a large sheet of paper. If you prefer to have the children do this as an individual project, they could each make their own grocery store collages on smaller sheets of paper.

Ask parents to help by sending labels to school. You can also use the grocery store advertisement section of the newspaper for pictures of things found in the grocery store.

Trash Mobile

Discuss with the children that it is the responsibility of the garbage collector to pick up everyone's trash in the neighborhood. Today they are going to be the neighborhood garbage collectors.

Let the children take a walk and collect trash, the things that people have forgotten to throw in a trash receptacle. (The children should wear gloves.) Discuss how the litter got there and why people should use trash receptacles. If broken glass or sharp metal pieces are found, a lesson on safety should be included.

Make a mobile from all the things collected on the walk. You can make one large class trash mobile, or each child could make his/her own. Attach the trash to dowel sticks with wire or string and suspend it from the ceiling. The mobile will serve as a reminder that trash belongs in the trash can.

Corn on the Cob

Each child should be given a sheet of stiff paper or tagboard with the outline of corn on the cob. The children can fill the inside of the corn by pasting or gluing real kernels of corn (unpopped popcorn).

Tell the children that it was the Indian people who taught the Pilgrims how to grow corn. The Pilgrims on Thanksgiving were thankful that they had learned about corn from the Indian people.

Painting Shells

Small inexpensive shells can be purchased through most hobby or craft stores.

The children take turns at the paint table. Each may paint the inside and outside of the shell. A hole can then be drilled in the top and a piece of black string can be used for stringing.

These can be Indian necklaces when they are completed.

Paper Sack Turkey

Use a square-bottomed paper sack. Fold the sack flat for coloring. Use brown crayon on the sides to color body feathers. The open end of the sack will be colored to represent bright tail feathers. The sack is stuffed with newspaper and a pipe cleaner closes the end so that the tail feathers spread out. Cut a double head from red paper and attach to the square end of the sack along the sides. Mr. Turkey might like a nest. A cardboard box filled with torn paper will do nicely.

Teachers Provide Fun or Finger Paint With Pudding

Begin this wonderfully messy activity with a discussion about teachers. Emphasize that it is part of a teacher's job to plan activities for children to do while they are at school. Today you have planned something really fun for them—finger painting with pudding.

Use instant pudding. I have found it very easy to make the pudding in a large jar with a tightly sealed cap. Instead of using an electric mixer, it works just as well to shake the jar. The children love taking turns shaking the pudding, finger painting with the pudding, and of course, eating their artistic creations.

Shoe Box Train

This project will take two days. Ask each child to bring a shoe box from home. On Day One, each child should paint his/her shoe box a different color. Make sure that one child paints his/her shoe box black (for the engine) and that another child paints his/her shoe box red (for the caboose).

On Day Two, have the children paste on wheels and windows cut from construction paper. Then connect all the shoe boxes. Children are always very impressed with how big and how long their classroom train is. It is a lot of fun to leave it on display for the parents to see.

Balsa Plane

Balsa wood pieces can be glued together with many types of glue or cement to make airplanes. Cut balsa blocks with knives or small hand saws, and balsa sheets can be cut with scissors or knives. Balsa wood is excellent for making toys which are small or light in weight. You can buy it in blocks and sheets at most toy or hobby shops.

Rocket

You will need a toilet paper roll for each child in your classroom. Following the example on the left, glue the paper shapes to the roll to make the rocket.

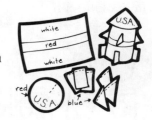

Sail-a-Boat

Cut the shape from the top of an egg carton. Pipe cleaners may be used to hold paper towel sails. The children may want to decorate the paper towel sails before they glue them to the pipe cleaners.

Carton Turkey

Paint and paste a head and a tail to a salt carton or oatmeal carton to make a turkey.

(It is a good idea to always ask the parents of the children to save things such as salt cartons, egg cartons, paper towel and toilet paper rolls, etc. They can always be used for something creative.)

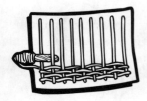

Weaving Rugs

Prepare cardboard looms (one for each child) and string with yarn. Be sure to use an uneven number of strings. Provide yarn and wooden ice cream sticks for shuttles.

The children should begin at the bottom left and put the shuttle over one string, under the next, etc. across the bottom. Then they start back, going under the first string, alternating thus and pushing down the yarn tightly until the card is filled. The child can take it home on the card or it can be taken off. Many of these woven squares could be sewed together to make a large rug.

Canoes

You will need cereal boxes or cardboard, tape, and craft or ice cream bar sticks. Follow the example on the left. Fold the paper lengthwise. Cut the top and corners, not the bottom. Tape the ends together. Pieces of craft sticks will hold the sides apart.

Let's Build a Family

Tell the children that today they are going to make a pretend family. Have them cut pictures out of old magazines or catalogs for the various members of their pretend families, and glue or paste the pictures onto large sheets of construction paper.

When the project is completed, ask the children to tell the class about their pretend families. Encourage the children to use correct terminology to describe the relationships of the family members.

Turkey Planter

Have the children each color a small Styrofoam cup brown. Draw a turkey head on a folded piece of paper, and cut out the head (refer to illustration at left). Glue a toothpick in between the two turkey heads.

Fill the Styrofoam cup with dirt and have the child plant a cutting of a geranium in it. If the geranium cutting has nice leaves, it can serve as turkey tail feathers by itself. Otherwise, stick colored toothpicks in the cup for a nice turkey tail. Stick the toothpick from the turkey's head in the front of the cup.

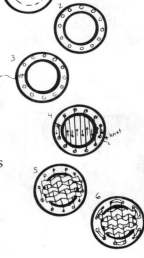

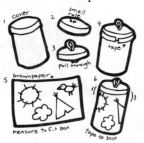

Tom-Toms

Prepare a box for each child in your class. Remove the top of the box, and punch a small hole in the middle. Pull a loop of twine, tied with a large loose knot, through the hole. Then replace the top and tape it on (this way the box can be carried on the child's wrist).

Have the children color brown wrapping paper with bright-colored Indian designs. Have books that show examples of traditional Indian art, or draw some examples on the blackboard with colored chalk. Cover the sides of the boxes with the decorated brown paper.

Weaving

You will need a plastic lid from a 3-pound coffee can and a 6' length of cord or heavy string for each child in your class, as well as a scissors and a single hole punch. Collect any or all of the following materials to use for texture in the weave:

Smooth	*Rough*	*Hard*	*Soft*
plastic straws	bark	sticks	tissue
cellophane	weeds	wire	fur
plastic bags	sandpaper	reeds	velvet
silk	wool	seeds	feathers
foil	burlap	plastic beads	cotton
Styrofoam	steel wool		chamois
leather	rope		

This is how you begin weaving:
1. Cut out the center of the coffee can lid with the scissors, leaving a ¾" wide edge.
2. Using the punch, make holes around the edge of the lid.
3. Tie one end of the 6' length of cord or heavy string through one of the holes in the lid.
4. Thread the cord through the holes as illustrated, then tie a knot.
5. Cut the textured material into strips and weave them through the strings.
6. Weave one of the textured materials in and out of the holes around the lid.

Thankful Collage

You will need a large piece of newsprint for the background of the collage, scissors, glue, and lots of magazines with pictures of food, homes, clothing, etc. Have the children cut out pictures of things for which they are thankful, and mount the pictures on the newsprint. Have the children discuss why they are thankful for the things that they chose.

Teepee Tracing

Directions:
Have children trace designs and then color..

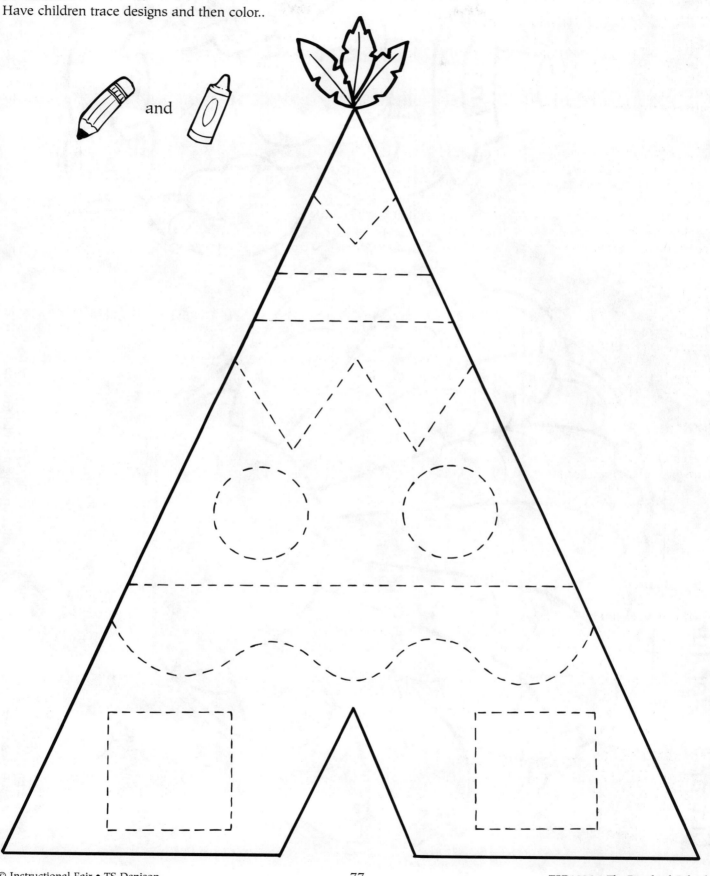

and

Cut and Color Turkey

Directions:
Have children color and cut out the turkey and its tail. Attach turkey to tail with brads at x's. It's a good idea to have one already made so the children have a model to follow.

Trash Toss

The child should use his/her dominant hand, and crush scrap or "trash" paper with arm stretched out to one side. He/she then attempts to do the same with the other hand as that arm is stretched out to the side. The child may try both arms stretched out and crushing paper with each hand.

After all the trash is crushed, the children can toss it into the recycling container like a bean bag toss game.

Discuss with the children the importance of making sure all the trash lands in the container. What would our community look like if our garbage collectors left trash on our streets?

Ladder on the Floor

You can use a real ladder, or with tape, mark a "ladder" on the floor. Tell the children that they are fire fighters practicing how to use a ladder so they can rescue people from tall burning buildings.

1. Child walks forward with both feet on each side of the ladder.
2. Child walks forward on the right side of the ladder.
3. Child walks forward on the left side of the ladder.
4. Child steps forward between the rungs of the ladder, alternating his/her feet.
5. Child steps backwards between the rungs of the ladder, alternating his/her feet.

Auto Dodge

The children should pretend that they are cars driving through their community in heavy traffic.

This activity should be done in a very large circle. The children should get on their hands and knees, and on a command from the teacher, they race around inside the circle. They may not bump into another child or leave the circle area. As the children move about, they weave in and out, moving in all directions. On a second command, they come to a halt (freeze).

Turkey Hide

Tell the children to pretend that they are turkeys and Thanksgiving Day is almost here! They will need to find somewhere very safe to hide if they do not want to become Thanksgiving dinner.

One child is chosen to be "it." He/she leaves the group and hides. The rest of the children count out loud to 20 (or as high as they are able). Then they separate, searching for "it." The first child to find him/her keeps quiet and hides along with "it." The second does the same, and so on, until all the children are hiding in the same spot, packed together.

The first player to find "it" becomes "it" for the next game.

Forms of Hopscotch

When playing hopscotch during the "Community Helpers" unit, tell the children that they are bus drivers. They must be sure to hop and stop on every square so they don't forget every stop on their route. Below are some interesting forms of "Hopscotch."

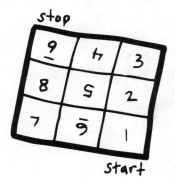

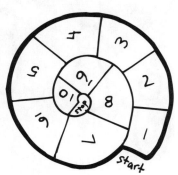

Choo-Choo Dodge

You will need a ball for this activity. The class forms a large circle. Four children are selected to go in the middle. They line up, one behind the other, hands on the hips of the person in front of them. The last of the four children is the "caboose." The other children must pass the ball around the circle and keep it moving quickly. The inside people try to avoid having the caboose hit. The engine or front child is very important. He or she always tries to face the ball being thrown. When the caboose is hit, four new children enter the circle.

Bean Bag Rope

You will need to suspend a bean bag on a rope from the ceiling. The children take turns standing on the mat about a leg's length from the bean bag. The bean bag is lowered to the pupil's waist. The child attempts to kick the bean bag with either foot. Repeat with the opposite foot. If successful, raise the bean bag two or three inches. One foot always remains in contact with the ground. The child is permitted to rise on his/her toes, but may not leave the ground. A mat must be used for safety.

A Bouncing Ball Game

All of the players form a circle. Choose a boy and a girl to stand in the center. These two players bounce balls in time to music played on a CD or tape player. When the ball is missed, another player takes that child's place in the center. The other members of the circle who are able to so do may count the number of times the balls are bounced. Whether the children are able to bounce the ball or not, give each one a turn.

Turkey Race

Choose teams. Two children, one from each team, run "turkey fashion" (stooped, with hands on hips) from one line to another. They must also gobble as they race. If one gets out of position to gain speed, he or she is taken away by the "farmer" (one of the other children).

The team having the most "turkeys" left at the end of the race is the winning team.

Push the Turkey Obstacle Course

You will need plastic bowling pins, or cones, and a playground ball. Arrange the pins or clubs to form an obstacle course. They can be set up without any definite shape or pattern. Leave a lot of room between the pins to insure success. The children should try to push the ball through the obstacle course using their feet. Explain to the children that the ball is the turkey and they are trying to get the turkey home for their Thanksgiving dinner.

If using feet is difficult for the children, let them use their hands.

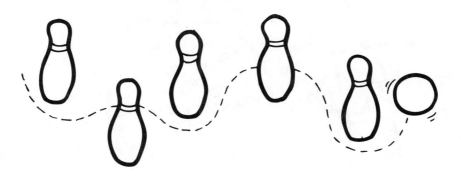

Babies

Many preschool children have an infant sibling or have been hearing talk about another baby on the way. Talk about babies with the preschoolers. How do babies move? They wiggle, turn over, lay on their backs and stomachs with their heads up, kick their feet, bat with their hands, crawl, pull themselves up to standing position, walk, and finally run. Have the preschoolers imitate the movements of a baby.

Make Yourself Tall

People come in all different sizes in a family. Children are small, adults are tall. Tell your class that today they are going to pretend that they are many different sizes, just like the people in their families. Have the children stretch, crouch, spread arms and legs wide, etc., following these directions:

1. Make yourself tall.
2. Make yourself taller.
3. Make yourself wide.
4. Make yourself wider.
5. Make yourself small.
6. Make yourself smaller.
7. Make yourself big.
8. Make yourself bigger.
9. Make yourself short.
10. Make yourself shorter.
11. Make yourself long.
12. Make yourself longer.

Spinning Tops

You will need gym mats and a soft lawn or carpeted area. Have the children choose partners. Tell them to stand facing each other with their toes almost touching, holding hands tightly. Have them lean back until their arms are straight, keeping their feet in place.

Tell the children to start moving their feet, taking tiny sidesteps to make a circle. As they step faster and faster, they will feel just like spinning tops.

Do What I Do

"Do What I Do" is similar to "Follow the Leader." Divide the class into four groups: a senior citizen's group, an adult's group, a children's group, and a pet's group.

Have each group take a turn demonstrating the different ways people in their group might move. For example, have the senior citizen's group get in a line, while the other children remain seated as the audience. The children would then move in ways that senior citizens move.

Over the River

Many children celebrate Thanksgiving at their grandparents' homes, and they may also have heard the song "Over the River and Through the Woods, to Grandmother's House We Go." Tell them that they must jump over the river to get to Grandmother's house for Thanksgiving dinner.

Make the "river" by laying out two parallel lengths of string on the floor, placing masking tape on the floor, or using chalk on the playground. Tell the children to jump over the river. If their feet touch the lines, they will get all wet. As the children get better at jumping, move your "river" boundaries wider and wider apart.

Circle Turkey Tag

Have the children join hands and make a big circle; then have them drop their hands and take one giant step backward. (This will make a generous space between players.) Demonstrate which way the children should turn so that they will all be facing clockwise around the circle.

Tell the children that they are turkeys in the forest. They certainly don't want to be caught and turned into Thanksgiving dinner. When you say "Go," everyone should start running, keeping in their big circle. Each child should try to tag the person ahead. If a child is tagged, that means that he or she is going to be Thanksgiving dinner and must go into the center of the circle. Continue until there is only one turkey left before Thanksgiving.

 TSD1896-4 *The Preschool Calendar*

Match the Twins

Name_____

Train

Attach cotton balls for puffs of smoke.

I Sent a Letter

Have the children dictate letters to you that they can send in the mail to their parents. The children can also include drawings that they have done in their letters. Encourage the children to think up a lot to say. Let the children fold their letters and put the stamps on. Older preschoolers may wish to print their own names and try addressing the envelopes.

Children also love to receive mail. Ask the parents to send their child a letter at school. How much fun to get mail at school, especially if it is from Mom or Dad!

Police Officer, Find My Child

You will need a police officer's hat as a prop. One child is chosen to play the role of the police officer. He/she is sent from the room. Meanwhile, the class decides who is going to be "lost," and who is going to play the role of the parent. The parent then stands up and the police officer is called in. Dramatic play ensues:

Parent: "Oh, police officer, please find my child."
Police Officer: "Is it a girl or a boy?"
Parent: "It is a boy."
Police Officer: "What color was his/her shirt? What color was his/her eyes? What color was his/her hair?"

The parent tries to describe the child who is lost without looking at him/her, which would give the game away. The police officer tries to "find" the child by the simple description.

What Would You Do If . . .

Discuss with your children what you would do if:
1. you see a fire down the street.
2. you see another child playing with matches.
3. you discover that your own house is on fire.
4. you smell smoke in your house.

Discuss the usefulness of fire:
1. to heat the home.
2. for cooking.
3. to get rid of waste.
4. in factories.
5. in industries.
6. in camping.

Hats

You will need a wide variety of real hats or paper hats, which represent various community helpers. Let the children take turns trying on a hat and telling you who would wear the hat, and something about the particular job that the hat represents.

For What Things Are You Thankful?

Discuss with your children what the word "thankful" means. Encourage the children to talk about things for which they are thankful.

As a class project, make a large poster of the children's drawings or pictures that they have cut out of magazines depicting things for which they are thankful.

Grandmother's House

Tell the children that they should pretend that they are going to Grandmother's house for Thanksgiving.

Get ready. Get in the car. What do you see out the window? A cow? A barn? A woods? Stop for gas. Do you see Grandmother's house? Stop the car. Get out. There are Grandmother and Grandfather. What good smells are coming from the kitchen?

Where Do You Hurt?

Let the children take turns playing "Doctor." The doctor's patients should come to him/her complaining that some part of the body hurts. Encourage the children to name as many parts of the body as they can.

Providing a doctor's kit can make this experience more fun. The doctor should try to correct the complaint.

Toy Vehicles

Display many kinds of toy vehicles. Discuss each, allowing children to contribute their thoughts. After discussion, let the children play with the toys.

Transportation Pictures

Display pictures of the following means of transportation: truck, bus, car, train, plane, ship, rocket. Ask the following questions and let the children decide which vehicle answers the question.

1. Which one is used for going to the moon?
2. Which one travels on tracks?
3. Which one carries vegetables from farm to city?
4. Which one goes through the air?
5. Which one do we park in our garage?
6. Which one stops in many cities and carries many people?
7. Which one travels on the ocean?

Take a Mayflower Journey

Display pictures of the Mayflower. Then draw the outline of the sail of the Mayflower on a large sheet of newsprint. The children can cut out the sail and mount it on the blackboard or on a pole they can hold upright during the "voyage." They can also paint long strips of cardboard or newsprint brown. These will be used for the sides of the ship. Place chairs in the area that is to be the ship, and tape the brown strips of paper to them, enclosing the area.

To take the "Mayflower Journey," all the children will go aboard the "ship" and pretend they are sailing to a new land. They will talk about the high waves and the sea gulls flying. They will cook and eat and play and be sick. Then someone sights land through a long tube that is the spyglass. They decide to send a small boatload of people ashore to see if it is safe. The people go ashore, walk about, and then return to the ship. The others go ashore in the longboat a few at a time.

In Order

A familiar story is selected, and illustrations of major events in the story sequence are mounted on uniform pieces of cardboard. (A discarded or mutilated story book will often have a second usefulness for this purpose.) If desired, numerals may be placed on the reverse side as a means of checking the order.

One child is called on to select "what happened first," and so on. The attention is centered on achieving proper sequence and placing cards in proper left-to-right order. Later, as other stories are added, children may use this as a table activity for individual manipulation.

Where is the Turkey Hiding?

Prepare a small cut-out turkey, or if you have one, use a small toy turkey. Tell the children that the turkey is very nervous because he knows that he may become Thanksgiving dinner. He is going to run away and hide. The children are the Pilgrims and it is their job to find the turkey.

Put the turkey in various locations in your classroom, in plain view for the children to see. Encourage the children to describe where the turkey is hiding, by using such statements as, "**under** the table," "**next** to the chair," "**on** the desk," "**in** the box," etc.

Tell Me about Your Family

Start the discussion by telling the children some things about your own family. Children love hearing that their teacher really does have another place to go besides school. Some small children actually believe that their teachers sleep at school!

Then give each of the children a turn to talk about their own families. Children who need encouragement should be prompted with questions such as "Do you have any brothers or sisters? Are they older than you? Do you have any pets?" etc. End your discussion by having each of the children draw a picture of his/her family.

My Family's Hobbies

Children are always interested in learning about other children's parents. Send a note home to the parents of the children in your class, asking if they would be interested in coming to school to talk about a special interest or hobby they may have (i.e. playing the guitar, sewing, rebuilding cars, bicycle racing, etc.). You would be surprised how many people are willing to come to school and share their special skills.

Family Helpers

Talk about the concept of helping. What is helping? What makes a good helper? Why should families help each other and help around the house? What kinds of things do you do at home that are helpful? What are some of the helpful things that other members in the family do? What would it be like at your house if no one was helpful?

The Remembering Game

This game will help develop visual memory. Have the children sit in a large circle. Place six objects in the center of the circle (for example, a book, a block, the paste jar, a crayon, a pencil, and a ruler). Have one child close his/her eyes. Tell another pupil to remove one of the objects. Then have the child open his/her eyes and tell which object has been taken away.

Indian Names

The Indian people give their children names that have special meanings. Give your children some examples of Indian names translated into English (Running Bear, Morning Star, etc.). Have each child think up a name like this that he/she would like to use at school for a whole week. Try to encourage the children to choose names that will have special meaning for each of them.

Indian Picture Words

Explain to the children that the Indians used a different kind of writing than we use. Some of the Indians used small pictures in their writing.

Draw some examples of picture writing on a large sheet of paper on the easel or on the blackboard, and explain what each symbol represents. Have the children copy the examples on their own pieces of paper.

The children may enjoy using these designs on other Indian-related art projects, like headdresses, blankets, and tom-toms.

Comparing Thanksgivings

Show the children pictures of the first Thanksgiving feast and of Thanksgiving dinner gatherings of today. Discuss the differences and draw simple line figures illustrating the differences. Among the things that can be compared are how the food is prepared, what kind of clothing the people are wearing, what kind of food is being served, who is invited to the dinner, etc.

Pilgrim Hat

Color the hat pieces. Cut them out
and paste them on the Pilgrim hat.

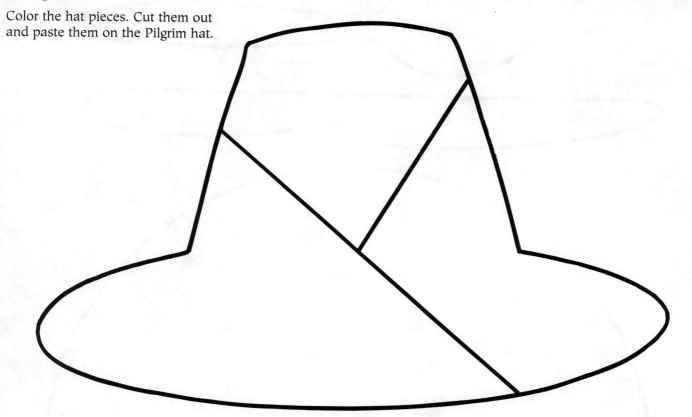

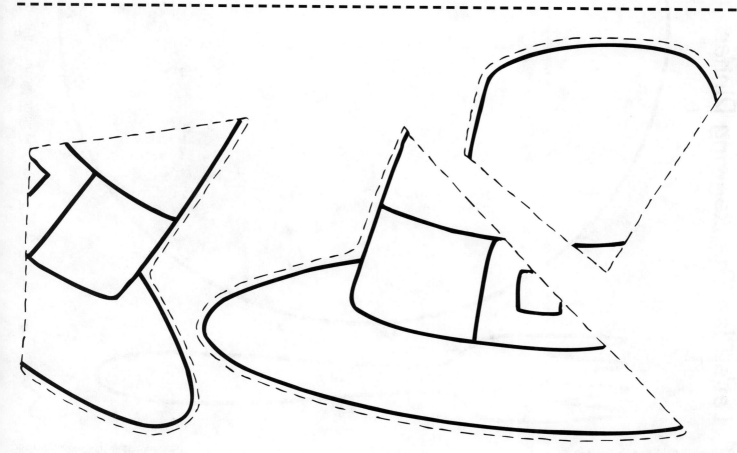

Let's Plan Thanksgiving Dinner

Name _____

Cut and paste pictures of food you would like to eat on Thanksgiving.

Five Strong Police Officers

Five strong police officers, standing by a store.	(hold up hand, fingers extended)
One became a traffic cop, and then there were four.	(bend down thumb)
Four strong police officers, watching over me.	
One took home a lost child, and then there were three.	(bend down another finger)
Three strong police officers, dressed all in blue.	
One stopped a speeding car, and then there were two.	(bend down another finger)
Two strong police officers—how fast they can run!	
One caught a bad person, and then there was one.	(bend down another finger)
One strong police officer saw some smoke one day.	
She called the firefighter, who put out the fire right away.	

Once There Was a Pilgrim

Once there was a Pilgrim	(extend one finger up)
Who tried every way	(nod head)
To catch a turkey	(raise left hand sideways, fingers spread, put right fist next to it, for "turkey")
For Thanksgiving Day.	
She said "caught you" to the turkey,	(make catching motion, make "turkey-nod" head motion)
She said "caught you" to the hen	(make a catching motion)
She said "caught you" to the pumpkin,	(make a catching motion)
She said "caught you" to me!	(point at self)
Well, she caught that turkey	(nod head "yes," hold arms close to body)
And she caught that hen.	
She even got the pumpkin	(hold hands close to body)
But she didn't catch me!	(shake head "no")

Mr. Turkey

Mr. Turkey's tail is big and wide.	(spread hands)
He swings it when he walks.	(swing hands)
His neck is long, his chin is red,	(point)
He gobbles when he talks.	(open and close hand like a mouth)

Our Community Helpers

Some people bring us produce,
And drinks all fresh and cold.
Some people work in shops and stores
Where many things are sold.
Some people bring us letters
And they take more mail away.
Some people stop the traffic
To help us on our way.
Some people move our furniture,
And put it in a van.
Some people take the garbage,
And empty every can.
(Ask children to tell what other people do
to help us. "What does a weather person
do? A sailor that goes to sea?" Let them
choose the helpers they would like to be
when they grow up.)

Different People

This person drives a taxi.
This person leads a band.
This person guides the traffic
By holding up a hand.
This person brings the letters.
This person rakes and hoes.
This person is a funny clown
Who dances on tiptoes.
(Invite the children to choose which
person they would like to be and to
pantomime the action, asking the class
to identify the worker. Ask them to use
no words, only hands, feet, and bodies.
Ask, "Did we leave out anyone? Who?
Shall we add your person to the poem?")

Thanksgiving

Mr. Turkey went for a walk
On a bright, sunshiny day.
And on the way he met Mr. Duck,
Gobble, Gobble . . . Quack, Quack.
And they both went on their way.
(The children can take turns playing the
parts of the turkey and the duck. This is
also a fun poem for the flannel board.)

The Family Car

Sometimes I ride in the family car.
The engine jerks so we cannot go far.
Pop, pop, pop, pop, pop, pop, pop!
Pop, pop, pop! Juggle, jiggle, JAT!　　　*(children repeat)*
What is the matter?　　　*(children repeat)*
Why, the tire is flat! Sssssssssssss!　　　*(children make sound)*

Choo-Choo Train

This is a choo-choo train,　　　*(bend arms at elbows)*
Puffing down the track.　　　*(rotate forearms in rhythm)*
Now it's going forward,　　　*(push arms forward, continue rotating motion)*
Now it's going back.　　　*(pull arms back, continue rotating motion)*
Now the bell is ringing.　　　*(pull bell cord with closed fist)*
Now the whistle blows.　　　*(hold fist near mouth and blow, "Toot, Toot")*
What a lot of noise it makes,　　　*(cover ears with hands)*
Everywhere it goes.　　　*(stretch out arms)*

The Airplane

The airplane has big wide wings.　　　*(stretch out arms)*
Its propeller spins around and sings.　　　*(make one arm go around)*
Vvvvvvvv!　　　*(make the sound)*
The airplane goes up in the sky.　　　*(lift arms up and then down)*
Then down it goes, just see it fly!
Vvvvvvvv!　　　*(make the sound)*
Up, up, and up; down, down, and down;　　　*(make continuous up and down movements)*
Over every housetop in our town.
Vvvvvvvv!　　　*(make the sound)*

The Turkey

A turkey I saw on Thanksgiving,
His tail was spread so wide.　　　*(make fist for turkey and spread fingers of other hand for tail)*
Shhh . . . don't tell that you've seen him,　　　*(make "shhh" sound with forefinger to lips)*
For he's running away to hide.

My Bicycle

One wheel, two wheels on the ground;　　　*(revolve hand in forward circle to form wheel)*
My feet make the pedals go round and round;　　　*(move feet in pedaling motion)*
Handle bars help me steer so straight,　　　*(pretend to be steering a bicycle)*
Down the sidewalk, through the gate.

I Am Thankful

I am thankful for pets.
I am thankful for school.
I am thankful when I
Can swim in a pool.
I am thankful for home,
And the food that I eat.
I am thankful for all
The new friends that I meet.
I am thankful for health,
And for my family.
I'm especially thankful
That I am just ME!
(Ask: "Could anybody in this class have written this poem? Does it say what you might have said about being thankful? Tell us something for which you are thankful and I will write it on the board. Why are you glad that you are YOU? Did you pronounce the first sound in the word 'thankful'? Say the word with me: 'thankful.' Show me something in this room for which you are thankful.")

Five Little Pilgrims

Five little Pilgrims on Thanksgiving Day.	*(hold up one hand, fingers extended)*
The first one said, "I'll have cake if I may."	*(point to thumb)*
The second one said, "I'll have turkey roasted."	*(point to 2nd finger)*
The third one said, "I'll have chestnuts toasted."	*(point to 3rd finger)*
The fourth one said, "I'll have pumpkin pie."	*(point to 4th finger)*
The fifth one said, "Oh, cranberries I spy."	*(point to 5th finger)*
But before they ate any turkey or dressing,	
All of the Pilgrims said a Thanksgiving blessing.	*(hold hands in prayer)*

Thanksgiving Turkey

Hobble goes the turkey,	*(put hands on hips, squat down,*
See him strut along.	*and walk "turkey "fashion)*
"Gobble" says the turkey.	*(rise up slightly, stretch neck)*
He'll not be here long!	*(run and hide)*

Love

Kiss, kiss, kiss.	*(make kissing sound)*
One, two, three.	*(count)*
I love you.	*(put hand on heart)*
Do you love me?	

Turkey

Turkey, turkey,	*(put left hand with fingers spread behind right fist)*
Big and fat.	*(show space between left and right hands)*
Change into Thanksgiving dinner,	
Just like that!	*(clap hands)*

(Make a reversible turkey stick puppet. Put the turkey on one side and Thanksgiving dinner on the other side.)

See My Family

See my family! See them all!	*(hold up one hand)*
Some are short, and some are tall.	*(hold up thumb, hold up 3rd finger)*
Let's shake hands, "How do you do?"	*(clasp hands and shake)*
See them bow, "How are you?"	*(bend fingers)*
Father, Mother, Sister, Brother,	*(hold up 3rd finger, 2nd finger, 4th finger, thumb)*
And me; all polite to one another.	*(hold up 5th finger)*

The Family

Here's Mommy and Daddy and the baby,	*(point to thumb, 2nd finger, 5th finger)*
That makes three.	
Here's sister and brother,	*(point to 3rd finger and 4th finger)*
Making five in the family.	

Use as a flannel board rhyme.

My Teepee Home

Many years ago, when our country was very young, there were Indians living in tribes all over the land. They lived in the woods. They lived on the deserts and in the mountains. Many of them used tents for shelter. Some tribes called these tents wigwams or teepees. The Indians had to hunt, fish, and raise corn for food. They shot buffalo, wild turkeys, and deer. They feasted on the meat and made teepees and clothing out of the skins. To make a teepee, the Indians set up a framework of poles tied to pegs driven into the ground. Then they stretched skins over the frame, leaving a hole at the top to let the smoke out. To make the teepees attractive, the Indians painted pictures and designs on them.

I am going to sing a song a happy Indian child likes to sing. What is the Indian child proud of.?

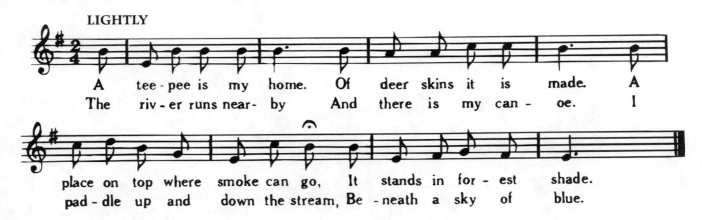

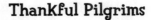

Thankful Pilgrims

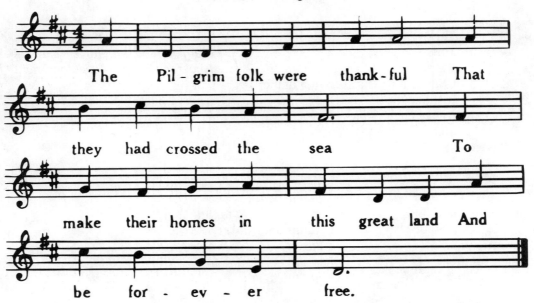

The Bus Stop

You will need to arrange chairs to represent a bus station or bus stop.

A child is chosen to be the bus driver. The bus driver stands first in line with several children behind him/her, all with hands on the shoulders of those in front, forming the "bus." The other children are waiting at the bus stop.

To play this music activity, the bus driver should begin to "drive" or lead the others around when the music is loud. When the music begins to get soft, he/she should head towards the bus stop. When the music stops, one more child "gets on the bus." When the music starts up, the bus driver may begin to drive again.

After all the children are on the bus, play the game in reverse, so that all get off the bus at the bus stop.

My Rolling Wagon

Perhaps one of your most useful toys is your toy wagon that can be used in so many ways. It seems that wherever children are playing, a wagon is not far away. It can be a car, a bus, a train, a truck, or a popcorn wagon.

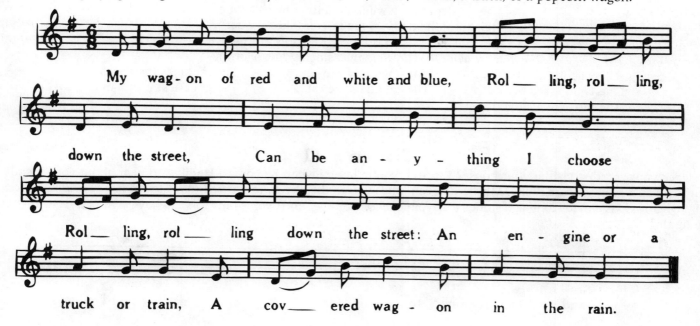

My wag-on of red and white and blue, Rol ___ ling, rol ___ ling,

down the street, Can be an - y - thing I choose

Rol ___ ling, rol ___ ling down the street: An en - gine or a

truck or train, A cov ___ ered wag - on in the rain.

The Turkey and the Pumpkin

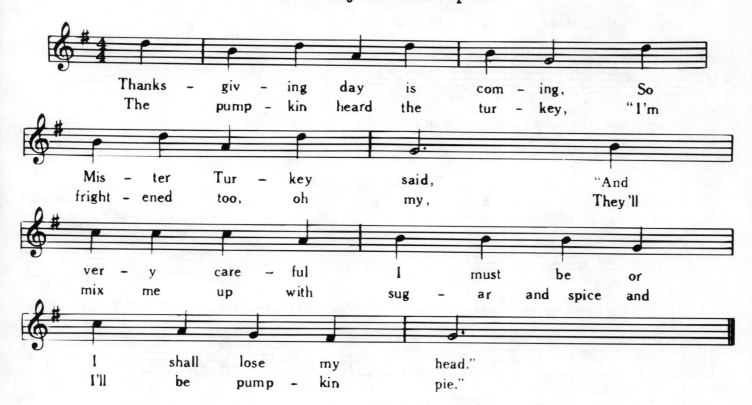

Thanks - giv - ing day is com - ing, So
The pump - kin heard the tur - key, "I'm

Mis - ter Tur - key said, "And
fright - ened too, oh my, They'll

ver - y care - ful I must be or
mix me up with sug - ar and spice and

I shall lose my head."
I'll be pump - kin pie."

The Farmer in the Dell

The farmer in the dell, the farmer in the dell,
Heigh-ho, the dairy-o, the farmer in the dell.
The farmer takes a wife, the farmer takes a wife.
Heigh-ho, the dairy-o, the farmer takes a wife.

Continue in the same manner, singing the following.

The wife takes the child.   The dog takes the cat.   The rat takes the cheese.
The child takes the nurse.   The cat takes the rat.   The cheese stands alone.
The nurse takes the dog.

Grandpa and I

Does your grandpa visit at your house? I'm sure you're happy when he comes. He likes to hear about your friends, your toys, and what you are doing. Maybe he even takes you to the circus, to the zoo, downtown, fishing, riding, or out walking. Grandpas can tell long-ago stories that you love to hear over and over again. You can have a good time with your grandpa.

Grand - pa came to our house one day. I'm
ev - er so hap - py be - cause he will stay. We can go walk - ing out
un - der the sky My wag - on, my pup - py, my Grand - pa and I.

The Coming Feast

When we think of Thanksgiving and a big dinner, what is usually the most important thing in the meal? Name a few other things we like to go with it. Listen for the good things in this song that is called "The Coming Feast."

Tur - key on the plat - ter, Pud - ding in the pan! Thanks-
giv - ing pie is steam____ing. I'll eat as much as I can.

Which Store?

Use a cardboard box at least 12" x 12" x 6". Mark a rectangle on each of the four sides of the box. These will represent store windows for four different kinds of stores. Paste pictures in these windows of items that would belong in the particular store.

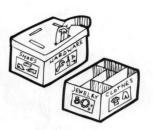

Cut four slots in the top of the box near the center edge of each side. Make cards with pictures of items that can be bought in these stores. The children put the cards in the corresponding slots.

If desired, divide the inside of the box into four sections as shown, keeping the cards separated.

Our Grocery Store

This activity should become a permanent part of the play area in your classroom.

Save empty grocery store items such as cans, cereal boxes, egg and milk cartons, etc., and create your own grocery store. This will encourage wonderful creative play. The children can role-play a shopper, a cashier, a sacker, or a butcher.

You can fill your grocery shelves with two of everything and use the items for matching. The children can also sort the items by shape and size, and place the items on the shelves according to a positional direction (top, middle, bottom, next to, etc.).

Mail Carrier Game

You will need envelopes, poster board, clear contact paper, pictures, marking pen, used stamps, and glue.

Cut poster board into pieces that will fit into the envelopes. Glue a picture, shape, or color onto the poster board. With the marking pen, write the name and address of each child playing the game on separate envelopes. Glue a used stamp on each of the children's envelopes. Place a picture card in each envelope. Do not seal envelopes so that they remain reusable.

The teacher or one of the children acts as the mail carrier and passes out the envelopes. The teacher starts the discussion by saying that everyone has received something in the mail. The children open their "mail" and describe what they have received. Anything can be put in the envelopes. You may choose letters, numbers, colors, shapes, or pictures. This makes flashcards a lot more fun!

Match Letters

Discuss with your children the fact that teachers help you to learn. Today they are going to be teachers and correct each other's work.

Prepare for each child a card with his/her name on it, and individual cards with the letters of his/her name. The children should match the small letter cards to the letters on their name cards.

Have the children work with partners. When each child has finished matching the letters in his/her name, they should exchange places and correct each other's work.

Doctor, Help Me!

Cut up pictures of people from magazines into several puzzle pieces. Cut as many puzzle pieces as you know that your children will be able to put back together.

Tell the children that they are each going to be doctors and help someone who has been hurt. They must help the hurt person by putting them back together.

Let the children put together their "hurt" persons and glue or paste the pieces on paper.

Corn Bread

Follow the recipe on the package of corn meal. Show how the Indians had to grind their corn. Honey is a very good topping for the corn bread.

Following the Rules

Discuss the significance of the colors red, yellow, and green in controlling traffic. Talk about traffic signs. Why is it important to observe what they tell us to do? Guide the conversation to include the duties of the police officer or the traffic cop.

Mark part of the room off into streets. Assign two or three children to be police officers. It will be their job to set up the miniature traffic signs at the proper places. Use signs that have the same color and shapes as those used by the highway department. (If you do not purchase the signs, make them out of heavy cardboard.)

Several children may dramatize the role of "motorists" trying to observe the traffic rules. Provide pencils and paper pads for the tickets the police officers will give to the drivers who fail to follow the regulations.

Transportation Tic-Tac-Toe

Prepare charts of cut-out pictures of transportation vehicles and arrange them on a tic-tac-toe grid. For group use, the grid may be covered with plastic on which an X or O may be marked with a soft grease crayon or felt pen without destroying the chart. For smaller individual charts, use buttons or blocks of contrasting colors to cover the pictures.

The players are selected, and marks or markers assigned. Each side or player, in turn, names one object on the chart and marks it if named correctly. The first team or player to have marks on three squares in a horizontal, vertical, or diagonal row is the winner.

You can make many variations of this game. Change the charts and make the tic-tac-toe game for colors, furniture, toys, shapes, clothes, story characters, foods, etc.

Parachute

Parachutes are a lot of fun to make and probably even more fun to play with. Use scraps of thin fabric in the shape of a square. You can also use handkerchiefs. Tie strings on each corner. Bring the strings together and tie around a weight. You can use a variety of things for the weight: rocks, paper weights, blocks, etc. It is fun for the children to experiment with the weights on the end of the parachutes. Who has the fastest parachute? Who has the slowest parachute?

Chippewa Bannock

On the day of your Thanksgiving celebration, have the children make Chippewa Bannock, or fried bread. Here is how you do it:

You will need measuring cups, measuring spoons, a bowl, a stirring spoon, and an electric frying pan.

2 cups flour	¼ teaspoon salt
1 tablespoon shortening	1 teaspoon soda in ½ cup water
1 cup sour milk	

Combine shortening, milk, salt, soda and water; mix in flour. Pat into large circle in greased electric frying pan. Bake in hot electric frying pan for 30 minutes. You may need to turn the bread.

Thanksgiving Celebration

Have the children celebrate the Pilgrim's first Thanksgiving with the Indians. Read the "Teacher Note" article on page 67 to get some extra ideas of how the children can reenact this part of history.

Photographs of Our Families

Ask the children to each bring a photograph of his/her family to school. Collect all the pictures. Hold the pictures up, one at a time, covering up the part of the photograph showing the child who is in your class. Ask the children if they can guess whose family is in the picture.

After the children have guessed, let the child whose picture it is talk about his/her family. The child can tell who each person in the photograph is and mention something special about his or her family. Mount the pictures on a bulletin board for display.

Button Buzzer

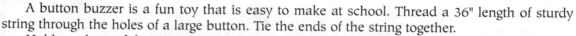

A button buzzer is a fun toy that is easy to make at school. Thread a 36" length of sturdy string through the holes of a large button. Tie the ends of the string together.

Hold one loop of the string in each hand, with the button in the center. Hold one hand still, and rotate the other to "wind up" the string. Wind it up quite tightly.

Pull firmly out with both hands until the string is stretched tight. Move your hands closer together, and the string will rewind. Keep moving your hands slowly apart, then together again. The button spins and makes a happy buzzing noise.

Tell the children to teach their families how to play with the button buzzer.

Hideaway House

Set four chairs back to back, a short distance apart, to form a square. Drape a large blanket or sheet over the chairs to make the "Hideaway House." You could also drape a blanket over a table.

Let the children take turns playing in the Hideaway House. Several children may enjoy playing in the house together, but you should honor the request of the child who wants to play alone. The preschool child, away from home and part of a large group for the first time, sometimes needs a place where he or she can be alone.

The children will also enjoy playing "House" and "Families" in the Hideaway House.

Sweet Potato

Many families have sweet potatoes for Thanksgiving dinner. Here is a fun activity you can do with a sweet potato. Have each child put a sweet potato in a glass jar filled with water. Put the jars in a sunny window. Watch the roots and stems grow.

Popcorn

Show the children popcorn while it is still on the cob. Then let them help you remove the kernels and pop the corn. Tell the children that popcorn is one of the things that the Indians shared with the Pilgrims at the first Thanksgiving dinner.

Cranberries

Thanksgiving always makes me think of cranberries. Have the children help make cranberry sauce.

2 cups sugar
1 cup water
4 cups cranberries

Cook water and sugar until it reaches the boiling point. Add cranberries. Cook until they crack (about five minutes). Refrigerate. Serve in small paper cups.

Happy Holidays! December is such an exciting month, filled with bright colors, many different holidays, and many different traditions. Christmas and Hanukkah are often the first two holidays that come to mind, but many other holiday traditions are celebrated, not only in the United States, but worldwide.

Activities are provided for four different holiday traditions: Christmas, Hanukkah, St. Nicholas Eve, and St. Lucy's Day. Activities centered around holiday traditions are always a lot of fun to do with preschoolers, because preschoolers are such wonderful "believers."

The Christmas activities concentrate on the symbol of Santa Claus and his reindeer. Santa seems to be a symbol that is acceptable to many different religions.

In the "Story of the Month" section, you will find the historical background of the Hanukkah celebrations. There is also a reproducible activity sheet of a menorah. The menorah can be completed in one day or you can have your children add one candle each day for the eight days of Hanukkah. Adding one candle a day may give the children a better understanding of how long Hanukkah actually lasts.

M.J. Moll is the author of the following article. M.J. is a psychologist at Comprehensive Childcare Services, located in Yellowknife, Northwest Territories, Canada (near the real North Pole). Comprehensive Childcare Services is unique in that it meets the particular needs of the north. Parents go on duty travel, holidays, or courses, and since they are either at Yellowknife for short periods of time, or passing through on their way further north or south, their children must be looked after.

M.J.'s article will provide you with a realistic look at life near the North Pole. Santa is not the only person who lives there!

Life Near the Real North Pole
written by M.J. Moll

Those of us who live near the North Pole are all real, and we do carry on daily survival as well as living fulfilled lives in the land of the midnight sun!

Yes, we do have daylight for at least six months of the year, from the vernal equinox (March 21) until the summer solstice (June 21). Each day lengthens by about six minutes until at summer solstice we have 24 hours of daylight. From that point on until the winter solstice, each day shortens by six minutes. The autumnal equinox (September 21) marks the point at which we have 12 hours of daylight and 12 hours of night. From this point until the 21st of December, our days shorten dramatically, and we live in what I call constant gray to dark, until in December it is dark 24 hours a day.

Starting in September, we get the most fantastic displays of northern lights. The entire sky is lit up, sometimes in technicolor, sometimes only in white light, and these bands or waves of light dance across the sky. The sight is spectacular, and awesome. These are our first signals that cold is coming. I feel, too, that as the sun retreats (starting really in September), it gets colder, more distant, and almost hostile. These are my "anthropomorphisms" regarding the sun.

In summer, we go camping. We can go places where no other human being has been, and we are alone. We canoe, build our campfires, pick berries, cook our meals, and we will not see any other human being during that entire time. So it important when we leave our town that we file a "flight plan" with the police or friends, and if we do not return at the given time, someone will come looking for us. You see, the terrain is all so very similar and you cannot orient yourself by the sun or stars, so you need to leave very precise directions as to where you are going.

Our children growing up here learn to recognize the limits of human beings and the power of nature very quickly. Because once you stray beyond town limits there is no way orient yourself, so you must go prepared, with matches, an axe flares, a survival kit, proper clothing, and a small cache dried food. You must also know the proper signals to lay out in case of emergency. Our children learn these things.

Summer terrain is Precambrian shield rock, bog, and water. Winter terrain is Precambrian shield rock, ice, and snow. We have trees which grow about as tall as our houses: mostly poplars and willows. Our flowers are fireweed, cinquefoils, sassafras, primroses, and a few dandelions. Our gardens are sparse, because the growing season is so short. Higher north, there is vegetation of the same sort, only it very much shorter. For instance, a willow bush may grow only as high as six inches at maturity, and flowers grow very close to the ground for protection against the wind.

Our insect life is limited, but what insects we have—mosquitoes, black flies, no-seeums—make themselves very evident when they bite.

We have lived here for eight years, and enjoy life here. It is the last frontier on earth for the mind and body of people. Here one can be what one dreamed of being, for what there is not, you can make or build or create.

Colors

I have not outlined an exact way to teach colors, although I have provided activities to enhance the teaching of colors. I have always preferred to think that colors are an area that should be continually discussed and should be a daily part of the preschool curriculum. Preschoolers should be in an environment which naturally lends itself to the noticing and the naming of colors throughout the day. I added color activities during the month of December because it is such a colorful month. Take time to point out all the colors that the decorations add to our environment during December. Let the children make color books or posters about their favorite colors.

Winter Wonderland

You will need to cut out Christmas tree shapes from green paper. Construction paper will work, but poster board is better.

Let the children glue decorations on their trees. Beads, seeds, sequins, popcorn, buttons, scrap material, felt, or anything that resembles a tree ornament will work.

After the trees are decorated, take glue and squeeze it onto the tree as if it were tinsel or lights. Then shake glitter over the tree.

Display the trees on a bulletin board that has white paper for snow and blue paper for the sky. Title your display "Winter Wonderland." With this title, the bulletin board can stay up through January.

Santa Is Coming to My House!

You will need to draw Santa in his sleigh and his eight reindeer, or use commercial bulletin board cut-outs that you may have on hand.

Let each child create his/her own house or apartment building. Use colored construction paper for the houses. Print the children's names on the front doors.

Use black paper as a background for the display. After all, Santa only comes to children's houses at nighttime.

On the day of your holiday party, tape a piece of candy to each of the chimneys. It is fun to see how long it takes the children to notice the "surprise."

The North Pole

Use white paper as a background for this bulletin board or wall display. Along the bottom, tape or staple strips of torn white paper for snow. Cut-outs of pine trees may be added. Glue pieces of cotton on the pine trees and they will look as if they are covered with freshly fallen snow. A red and white striped pole should be put up with a sign at the top saying "The North Pole." Santa's workshop can be added in the background.

What a Beautiful Tree!

This bulletin board is a lot of fun for children. Make a large tree by gluing cupcake papers to a background. Add a brown trunk. Have the children create presents to put under the tree.

You will also be using this bulletin board in a lesson after the Christmas holiday ("Top /Middle /Bottom," *Language Activities,* page 116). Don't take it down until after you have read this activity.

Snowy, the Snow Person

Use a light blue background paper. Staple three very large circles to the bulletin board to form a snow person. Glue pieces of coal on for the eyes. Staple a child's sweater and stocking cap on the snow person. Have the children glue cotton on the snow person. The children may also add cotton at the bottom of the bulletin board.

As a fun addition, the children can each make a small snow person for the bulletin board. Have them glue a small doily to a medium-sized doily, then add features using paper, felt, construction paper, or color crayons.

Happy Holidays

Prepare a wreath cut-out for each child, using paper plates or construction paper. Precut small squares of green tissue paper.

Have the children fill their wreaths with the tissue paper by wrapping a tissue paper square around the tip of a pencil, dipping the pencil into glue, and pressing the tissue paper onto the wreath. Add a construction paper or ribbon bow. These three-dimensional wreaths are very attractive.

St. Nicholas Eve

Dutch children watch for St. Nicholas, a tall man with a white beard, dressed in a bishop's robe and a tall pointed hat. He comes on December 3, St. Nicholas Eve. On that evening, children put their shoes before the fireplace. They stuff hay and carrots into the shoes for St. Nicholas' horse.

If the children have been good, St. Nicholas leaves candy in their shoes. If they have not been good, St. Nicholas leaves coal in their shoes.

When Dutch settlers came to the new world, they brought St. Nicholas with them. If you try to say the words "St. Nicholas" very fast, you can almost hear "Santa Claus."

Celebrate St. Nicholas Eve in your room.

St. Lucy's Day

Swedish children look forward to St. Lucy's Day which is December 13, and this day leads to Christmas. A girl wearing a crown of pine boughs and seven lighted candles awakens the family and serves them cakes and coffee. On Christmas an imaginary white-bearded dwarf brings gifts in a sleigh.

Celebrate St. Lucy's Day by serving the children coffee cake and milk.

Hanukkah

This is the Jewish holiday known as the Feast of Lights. This happy eight day celebration comes in the winter and is a time of presents and parties. Long ago, when a foreign king and his army took over Israel and the temple there, the Jews fought their enemy for three years and at last they won. Lights were always kept burning inside the temple, but finally there was only enough oil left for one more day. Then the great miracle occurred. The light burned for eight days and nights, giving the Jews enough time to prepare more oil. Ever since then, Jews around the world celebrate Hanukkah by lighting one candle each night of the eight nights until all are lit on the last day of the holiday.

Reindeer Training

(This is a Christmas story in which the children can pretend they are the reindeer, crawling on hands and knees, or they can simply pantomime the activities.)

It was a month before Christmas, and as usual, everyone at the North Pole was very busy. Even the reindeer were preparing by building up their strength for the long hard ride delivering presents on Christmas Eve.

The reindeer woke up early, **stretching, shaking their heads,** antlers, and **whole bodies.** They then **swept** their stalls and **put down** fresh hay. Prancer was hungry, so one of Santa's helpers gave them some oats and water for breakfast. They **chewed** their food slowly and carefully. Dancer decided to have some fun, so she **pushed open** the door with her head and **motioned** for the others to join her.

They all **skipped** out of the barn into the heavy snow. The deer **ran** and **hopped first on one foot, then on the other,** and finally **on both feet.** They **skipped** from the pine trees to a brook which they **leaped** across. The snow was so soft and fluffy that the deer **sat down** and **rolled** in it. They then **stood up** and **shook** the snow off. Vixen had an idea—he wanted to play hide and seek. The rest all agreed, **jumping up and down** with excitement. Blitzen was "it," so the others **scurried, crouching down** behind snowdrifts or behind trees.

Suddenly, all the reindeer **stood still.** They heard a bell jingle so they **raced** back to the barn. Santa's Helper lined the deer up for their flight exercises. While she counted, the deer **stood on the tips of their hooves** and **stretched** to the top of their antlers. They **sprang** into the air and **floated** back. The deer **jumped forward** as far as possible, then **backwards.** They **hopped on one hoof** and **then the other.** The reindeer **stood up** straight and **bending at their middle,** they **touched their hind hooves ten times.** The most important exercise was to practice **galloping in place** to build up their leg muscles. Last of all, the reindeer **stood on their hind legs** and **squatted five times.**

The supper bell rang and the reindeer **herded** into their stalls for a special delight of peanut butter and cheese which they **chewed** slowly and carefully. Tired from all their training and fun, Santa's deer **curled up** in the soft hay, closed their eyes, and went to sleep.

⋀⋀⋀ Story of the Month ⋀⋀⋀

Holidays touch the culture of home and every nation of the world. They enrich the lives of individuals and give cohesiveness to society. People of different cultures understand the purposes for particular festivities and beliefs and realize that many of them overlap.

Christmas in Mexico

Christmas begins in Mexico on December 16 and ends with the observance of Epiphany, January 6.

Many Mexican families share in the work of preparing for the Christmas season. After they have finished their work, these Mexican families load all of their treasures in cars and go to the cities to sell their wares.

In every city there are puestos or market stalls. Across the front of each stall are hung piñatas.

The celebration of La Posada begins on December 16 and continues for nine nights, the last night on Christmas Eve. The families may observe La Posada by meeting at nine different family homes on nine different nights; or they may celebrate at the same house with only the family present.

La Posada begins with a recitation of the rosary by the head of the house. Then children carry lighted candles and march around the house. The children leading the procession carry images of Mary and Joseph. At the door of each room, they will beg for admission to the "Inn," but are turned away. Finally, they reach the room where an altar is seen. This is the stable they may enter. There is a manger in the stable, but it always stays empty until Christmas Eve.

Following religious ceremonies is the breaking of the piñata. When broken, the children find that it contains goodies of every kind and small toys or whistles.

On Christmas Eve, the Babe is placed in the manger and everyone sings praises to the Infant. Singing, dancing, and fireworks are seen with another piñata and festivities conclude with attendance at Mass.

Mexican children write letters to the Christ Child, listing their wishes for gifts. They place their shoes at the foot of the bed the night of Epiphany, January 6.

My Special Friend

I have a special friend; he's as jolly as can be. You can guess who he is if you play this game with me. In the center of the paper, draw a circle:
Step 1:

Draw a smaller circle for a mouth that says, "Ho, Ho!"
Step 2:

Above the mouth place a cute red nose and mustache white.
Step 3:

To this face add the eyes that sparkle ever so bright.
Step 4:

On top of his head draw a red hat with white trim.
Step 5:

Have you guessed that it's Santa? It really is him!

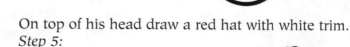

A Jolly Fellow

Make flannel board pieces to use with this story.

This story starts just like all stories—once upon a time. Once upon a time, there were two children—a boy named Charles and a girl named Susan. Late one evening in December, it was time for Charles and Susan to go to bed. Their mother called, "Charles, Susan, it's time for bed." But Charles and Susan asked just what you do sometimes. "Oh, Mother, can't we please stay up just a few more minutes?" They wanted to stay up and wait for someone very special to come.

Mother looked puzzled, but she said, "Well, just a few more minutes." So Charles and Susan went over by the fireplace where it was nice and warm, and they each rolled up in a big, comfortable chair and waited and waited for someone to come. And while they waited, they fell asleep. As they slept, "Whoosh" went the wind, and down the chimney into the fireplace dropped two big, big boots on the warm, warm floor. But Charles and Susan slept and slept and waited and waited for someone to come.

"Whoosh" went the wind, and down dropped a pair of short, short pants on the big, big boots on the warm, warm floor. And still Charles and Susan slept and slept and waited and waited for someone to come.

"Whoosh" went the wind, and down dropped a long, long jacket on the short, short pants on the big, big boots on the warm, warm floor. And still Charles and Susan slept and slept and waited and waited for someone to come.

"Whoosh" went the wind, and down came a pair of long, long sleeves on the long, long jacket on the short, short pants on the big, big boots on the warm, warm floor. And still Charles and Susan slept and slept and waited and waited for someone to come.

"Whoosh" went the wind, and down dropped a pair of fat, fat mittens on the long, long sleeves on the long, long jacket on the short, short pants on the big, big boots on the warm, warm floor. And still Charles and Susan slept and slept and waited and waited for someone to come.

"Whoosh" went the wind, and then there appeared a jolly, jolly face with a long, long beard on the long, long jacket on the short, short pants on the big, big boots on the warm, warm floor. And still Charles and Susan slept and slept and waited and waited for someone to come—but someone was there!

And who do you think it was? Yes, it was jolly Santa Claus. He hummed a merry tune and he filled up a long, long stocking for Mother. Then he filled up a long, long stocking for Father, then a small stocking for Charles, and then a small stocking for Susan.

Then with a hearty laugh, Santa turned and went over to the Christmas tree. He put many beautiful shiny packages under it. Some were very small packages, some were medium-sized packages, and some were very large packages.

Then "Whoosh" went the wind, and the jolly, jolly face with the long, long beard on the long, long jacket on the short, short pants on the big, big boots on the warm, warm floor disappeared. And still Charles and Susan slept and slept and waited and waited for someone to come.

"Whoosh" went the wind, and the fat, fat mittens on the long, long sleeves on the long, long jacket on the short, short pants on the big, big boots on the warm, warm floor disappeared. And still Charles and Susan slept and slept and waited and waited for someone to come.

"Whoosh" went the wind, and the long, long sleeves on the long, long jacket on the short, short pants on the big, big boots on the warm, warm floor disappeared. And still Charles and Susan slept and slept and waited and waited for someone to come.

"Whoosh" went the wind, and the long, long jacket on the short, short pants on the big, big boots on the warm, warm floor disappeared. And still Charles and Susan slept and slept and waited and waited for someone to come.

"Whoosh" went the wind, and the short, short pants on the big, big boots on the warm, warm floor disappeared. And still Charles and Susan slept and slept and waited and waited for someone to come.

"Whoosh" went the wind, and the big, big boots on the warm, warm floor disappeared. And still Charles and Susan slept and slept and waited and waited for someone to come.

"Whoosh" went the wind, and "Whoosh" went the wind, and "Whoosh" went the wind. And it rattled down the chimney so loud that Charles and Susan woke up. And then they heard a loud merry voice say, "Merry Christmas to all and to all a good night!"

Christmas Ornament #1

Make candy canes with white pipe cleaners and narrow strips of red crepe paper or red garbage bag twisters.

Christmas Ornament #2

Use plaster of paris in a small mold (a small lid works well). Before it is dry, put a toothpick through the top to make a hole for hanging. Children may paint the ornaments with thick tempera paint. When dry, put a Christmas seal on each side. Shellac or spray with clear lacquer or plastic. Use a gold cord or colored yarn and make a loop to hang.

Christmas Ornament #3

Paint the outside of half a walnut shell. Glue a short piece of pipe cleaner to the top to form a hook. Glue cotton to the inside of the shell. Cut small figures from old Christmas cards. Glue them to the cotton and decorate with sequins.

Christmas Ornament #4

Decorate used canning lids with odds and ends of braid, fringe, rickrack, cord, sequins, etc. Hang with a pipe cleaner.

(When the children have completed all the Christmas tree ornaments, have each wrap his/her set of four in a box. These will make wonderful Christmas presents for their parents.)

Soap Flakes Wreath

Mix soap flakes with water to make a thick mixture. Add green coloring and put on paper plates with centers removed for Christmas wreaths. Add seeds or buttons for berries.

Paper Chains

Make continuous paper chains for Christmas tree decorations or for hanging from the ceiling for party decorations. Cut red and green colored construction paper into strips, and then bend them into rings. Paste the rings shut as each strip is slipped through the preceding ring.

Colored Cards

Use typing paper and color over old Christmas cards that have embossed designs. Mount the colored picture on a slightly larger piece of colored construction paper. Paste the colored picture on a folded card. Print "Merry Christmas" on the inside of the card.

Gumdrop Tree

Use a small branch of a tree or bush for the tree. Strip the leaves off the branch. Next make the tree stand upright by sticking it in a mound of clay, or in a small paper nut cup or drinking cup that has been filled with sand. Paint the tree and stand white, and stick a gumdrop on the end of each branch.

Mexican Clay Jars

The Mexican people make a lot of pottery from clay. Here is a good recipe for clay. Have the children try to make some clay pots.

4 cups flour	1 teaspoon oil
2 cups salt	food coloring
2 cups water	

Mix all ingredients together. Knead about five minutes. Allow the children to take turns kneading. Store in plastic bag. Bake at 300° for one hour to harden objects.

Hammer and Nails

Children love to pretend that they are building. Hammers, nails, and corkboard or a soft wood can be wonderful tools for fine motor skills. This is an activity that should be closely supervised.

It is fun to create a wood-working area in your classroom. Large stumps are also fun to have just to pound on.

Star Santa

Many years ago a story was told about a star that wanted to fall down to the earth and make the children happy. He did fall—down, down, down. A fat, jolly gentleman picked him up and said, "I will have a pattern of you made for all the boys and girls." Mrs. Claus made the pattern, cutting it out of red paper. The children used their white crayons and made a face on one of the points, arms and legs on other points, and a belt across the middle. The Star Santa hung on the Christmas tree and made the children happy.

Apple Santa Claus

Use a large, whole apple for the body. Attach a marshmallow to the top with a toothpick for the head. Then press raisins into the marshmallow for the eyes, nose, mouth, and ears, and press cotton under the marshmallow for the beard.

The Night Before Christmas

Fold a 9" x 12" sheet of white paper across the center. Cut a third of the way down and fold over one side so that it looks like a bed with the sheet turned down. Each child may draw a boy or girl, cut it out, and slip it into the bed. They might also cut small pieces of white for pillows.

Tote Box

This tote box is a great project because it has so many uses. The teachers may enjoy making some of their own. This tote box is meant to be used as a container for the "No Bake Oatmeal Cookies" (Learning Games/Experiential Activities, page 127). It will make a wonderful gift that the children can take home to their parents.

Remove the lid of a round box (such as an oatmeal carton) and with the point of your scissors punch holes close to the edge of the lid at opposite sides. Cut two holes toward the top of the box at the same places. Tie a large knot at one end of the yarn. Pull the yarn through the hole in the box and then through the hole in the lid. Loop it up, then down through the other hole in the lid and finally through the hole in the box. Tie a large knot at this end also. Paste a large knot of yarn or a round button in the center of the lid to make it easier to remove.

The yarn handle enables the carrier to remove the lid without losing it. It also enables the person to open it without setting it down.

Icicle

Use scraps of metallic or gift wrapping paper. Punch a hole in the top corner and fasten a string to it. Begin rolling the side corner around a straw. Hold tight! When you get near the opposite corner, put a little paste on the corner and roll to the end.

Bird Feeders

Talk with your class about the importance of feeding the birds in the winter, and then have them make bird feeders to take home.

Help the children cut large square sections out of the sides of small milk cartons. Cut out a small bird to perch on one side, and attach a string to the top so each child can carry his/her bird feeder home.

Bells

Make ornaments from egg cartons to hang on the tree. Cut apart the sections of an egg carton. Have the children paint these with tempera paints. Before the egg carton sections dry, sprinkle them with silver or gold glitter.

Attach a tiny bell to a pipe cleaner. Insert the pipe cleaner up through the center of the egg carton section. Bend the top of the pipe cleaner to make a hanger for the ornament.

Hanging Christmas Trees

Make Christmas tree cut-outs from green construction paper, one for each child in your class. Punch a hole in the top of each tree, and attach a red pipe cleaner for a handle so the tree can be hung up.

Have the children glue red pom-poms on the top of their trees, and then glue on "Froot Loops" or some other colorful cereal for the trees' decorations. They should decorate both sides of the trees.

(Nancy Hutchinson, Albany, NY)

Felt Pin Santa

Use a powder puff for Santa's head. Cut Santa's cap, eyes, mouth, and nose out of felt, and glue these to the powder puff. Attach a safety pin to the back of the powder puff.

The children can either wear the pins themselves, or they can give them as a Christmas presents. This might make a nice gift for Grandma.

Holiday Cards

Prepare several stencil patterns ahead of time. The pictures on the right will provide you with some ideas. Have the children sponge paint on top of the stencils to decorate their cards, then let the cards dry.

The children will especially enjoy this project if the cards are really sent through the mail, and their parents will appreciate receiving the cards.

Blue and Gold

Various colors are associated with different holidays and traditions, for example, red and green are for Christmas. People who celebrate Hanukkah think of the colors blue and gold. Have your children make Hanukkah placemats using these colors. The placemats may be colored with crayons, or collage placemats may be made using Hanukkah wrapping paper.

Gifts for Mom and Dad

Cut two rings from construction paper. Using clear tape, tape a piece of string to the back of a photograph of the child. Put the ends of the string on one ring and paste the other ring on top of this. Cover the tape on the back of the photograph with a sticker or paper. Write the date in gold or red ink. These make nice Christmas or Hanukkah gifts.

Holiday Shapes

Name_____

and

PASTE

and

Menorah

Color the menorah yellow.

Where Should Santa Go?

This activity teaches the language concepts of "forward," "backward," "sideways," and "around" through gross motor activity.

The children work with partners. One child can pretend to be Santa Claus and the other child can pretend to be one of Santa's reindeer. The two children hold a jump rope.

The teacher gives commands using the words "forward," "backward," "sideways," and "around." Santa and the reindeer should move together according to the directions.

Our Bodies Make Shapes

Use groups of children to make the following shapes:

1. a Christmas wreath
2. a Christmas tree
3. a Christmas tree ornament (including hook)
4. a star
5. a long chain (they can interlock arms)

If the children participating sit on the floor, the onlookers will be better able to see and follow the outline.

Color Run

Pin a small color tag on each of the children in your room. Use a wide variety of colors. The teacher calls out, "Everyone with a red tag can run." After a short run, the teacher should blow a whistle for the red tag children to sit or "freeze." Repeat this activity until all the children have had a turn.

Variation 1: Pin two or three different colors on each child, so the children have to double check to see if they have the color that the teacher called out.

Variation 2: Use a variety of motor skills when playing this game. Yellow tag children can hop, blue tag children can crawl, green tag children can walk fast, etc.

Hop on Colors

Place construction paper squares (12" x 12") of different colors all over the floor. Make sure you have three or four of each color, or enough squares on the floor for all the children in your class. The children can move from square to square by hopping. Call out, "John, hop to a blue square," "Sue, hop to a yellow square," etc.

Variation: Place white squares on the floor. Place different colors under each of the white squares. Let the children hop from square to square. When you signal them to stop hopping, each child should stop on the square on which he/she landed, pick it up, and name the color that is under the white square.

Hoola Hoops and Bean Bags

Place five hoola hoops in a straight line. The child stands behind the starting line (as shown) and attempts to throw the bean bag into the hoola hoop nearest to him/her. With each success, the child attempts to get the bean bag in the next hoola hoop, then the third hoola hoop, the fourth hoola hoop, and finally the fifth hoola hoop. This is also a good activity for teaching the concepts of near and far.

Barrel Ball

Each child is given his/her own 8½" playground ball with a shape or number on it. A barrel is placed in the middle of the circle inside a tire or something that will keep the barrel from moving or failing. The children stand on the outside of the circle. On the teacher's signal, the children throw their balls into the barrel. If successful, the child sits down at the end of the room. If unsuccessful, the child must get his or her assigned ball (with shape or number on it) without going into the circle. He/she must go all the way around the circle to get the ball. If the ball stays in the middle, the child may go into the circle to get it. If the child finds the distance from the circle to the barrel is too far, he/she may move a step closer until he or she can successfully reach the barrel.

Musical Hat

Depending on the size of the class, divide the children into groups, eight or ten in a group. Only one group plays at a time. The first group of children stands in a straight line facing the rest of the class. Give a hat to the child first in line. When the music starts (piano or tape or CD player), he or she must place the hat on the head of the next boy or girl. Each child places the hat quickly on the head of the child next to him/her. When the hat gets to the last person, it is started back in the opposite direction. The child holding the hat when the music is stopped is out of the game. Continue until only one child remains.

When all the groups have had a turn, the winners in each group compete against each other. The last child standing wins the game. To make this game seasonal, use a Santa Claus hat.

Pantomiming

Introduce words that suggest action or motion. The children may give suggestions. They take turns pantomiming these words. Below are some suggested action words:

Ball—throwing, bouncing, tossing	Boats—rowing, tossing on the waves, sinking
Bicycle—riding, pumping	Ropes—roping cattle, jumping
Skates—sliding motion	Cars—starting, shifting, driving, stopping
Needle—threading, sewing	Bird—flying, soaring
Fish—swimming, breathing	

Several children can give their interpretations of the various words. Acting out real experiences is one way to start movement sessions. Begin with something simple, such as "Show how you brushed your teeth this morning;" "Show how you would get the toothpaste out of an almost empty tube;" "Pour milk into your glass and then drink it."

Let's Exercise

Present physical exercises in the classroom. Provide enough floor space for the free movement of arms and legs. After a few practice times, the children should know their places without directions from the teacher. Start with the following simple exercises:
- From a sitting position, sit up as tall as possible, relax. Repeat a number of times.
- Place hands on the floor and crawl forward with legs held in a stiff manner.
- Walk on all fours slowly, like a turtle.
- Lie on the floor with hands above the head. Raise right leg, raise left leg. Lower right leg, lower left leg.
- Lie on the floor. Rise up to a sitting position, lean over, and touch the right toe with the left hand. Return to a reclining position. Repeat with the right hand.

Happy New Year Balloons

Give each child a blown-up balloon with his/her name on it. (Permanent markers can be used to write on balloons and the markings won't come off.) The children hold their balloons until they hear you say "Happy New Year!" Upon hearing that, the children toss their balloons in the air and sit down. After all the balloons have settled and the children are sitting, each child can then get up and try to find the balloon that has his/her name on it.

Gross Motor/Movement Activities

Kick the Bag

Have the child stand on a starting line and kick a bean bag located 2' or 3' in front of him or her. The child should be able to kick the bean bag forward without losing his/her balance. Then reverse the kicking foot and repeat the activity.

This activity is also great fun to do outdoors in the snow. Kicking in the snow and with boots on is a challenge!

Slippery Ice

Skating is one winter activity that most preschoolers aren't able to do. But you can have your children go skating inside! Tell the children to take off their shoes and move in a skating motion to this chant:

Isn't it nice on slippery ice,
To slide and slide and slide?

Indoor Sleds

Tie a rope or heavy string to one end of a large piece of cardboard. (Follow the example on the left.) Then have the children take turns pulling each other around the room on this "indoor sled." The sled will work well on carpeting.

Be sure to team up children of equal weight. A very small child trying to pull a heavy child won't work very well.

Ringle Jingle

Children enjoy using bells as rhythm instruments and as an extra prop for movement activities. Buy 6" wooden dowels. Drill holes in one end of the dowels, and tie bells through the holes.

The children will have fun using these with movement and rhythm recordings. They can dance with them and keep the beat of the song with the bells.

Speedy Santa Race

This is a relay race. Place a Christmas tree at one end of the room. Have the children line up in two lines at the other end of the room. Give each child a "present" (a box, a block—anything that will represent a present).

Tell the children that when they hear the signal, the first child in each line should run to the Christmas tree and put his/her present under it. The child should then run back to the end of his/her line and sit down. The first team finished is the winner.

Obstacle Course

This obstacle course provides experience for a wide variety of gross motor movements and skills.

1. Walk across a balance beam.
2. Climb up on a chair and jump off.
3. Jump through a hoola hoop, feet together.
4. Crawl under a table.
5. Swing on a rope and jump off.
6. Jump over a box onto a mat.
7. Crawl through a barrel.

Let the children add other equipment to the course or exchange something for another piece. Positional concepts and relationships can be strengthened by use of positional words as the child performs the activity (under the table; over the box).

Jolly Old St. Nick

Directions:
Have children
color and cut out
Santa parts.
Attach with brads
at x's. Prepare a
sample before
hand to show to
the children.

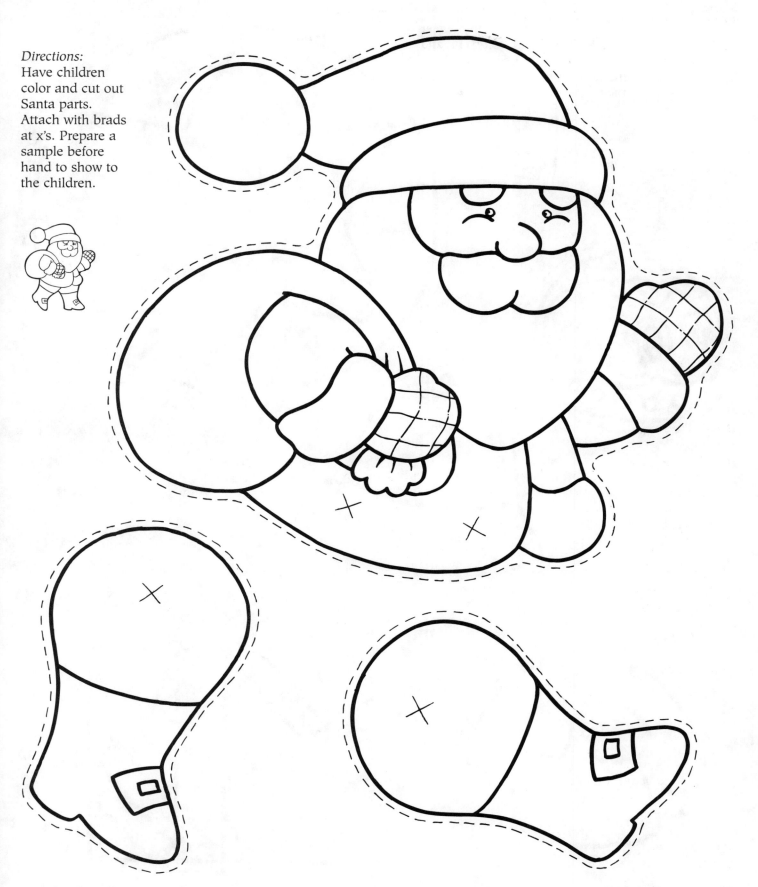

Cut and Paste Tree Decorations

Directions:
Give each of the children a tree shape cut from green construction paper. Have the children color, cut, and paste the ornaments and star to the tree. Paste the tree on a sheet of construction paper. Color, cut, and paste the present under the tree.

What Is Missing?

You will need a collection of five or six objects; these may be selected by the children from available toys and materials in the room, or may be flannel board felt cut-outs, etc.

The selected objects are placed in full view for study. Then one child is told to hide his/her eyes (or leave the room). Another removes one object. The child who is "it" is to guess what is gone. If he/she succeeds, another child is chosen to be "it" and the winner may decide what to remove.

Variation: Keep the same objects but change their arrangement or order. Then "it" must replace the objects in original order.

A Letter to Santa

Let each child dictate a letter to Santa Claus, either orally or on tape. Ask the children's parents or a high school class to write answers to the letters. Have the responses to the children's letters returned to school. How exciting to get a letter back from Santa Claus!

In Santa's Bag

Draw a Santa and put it on a bulletin board or on the wall. Give him a real sack to hold. Let each child cut a picture from a catalog of a toy that he/she would like to receive. The children can paste the pictures of the toys on cards to make them more durable. They can put the pictures "in" Santa's bag. After the pictures have been placed "in" the bag, one child can be chosen to play Santa and take the pictures "out" of the bag. It is fun to see who can remember which toy was theirs.

Tell a Story

You will need a grab-bag or draw-box containing small plastic items, such as animals, cars, doll house furniture, dolls, etc. You could also use mounted pictures.

A child draws out any item blindly; he/she must then tell a story about it. At first this may be simply naming it or telling what color it is: "This is a bear," or "I got a red ball." Later more creative statements may be encouraged; or two children may each draw an item and try to make up a joint story about both.

Variation: You can tell the children that Santa had a few toys left over this year. Let the children make up stories about who should have received the toys; why they were left in Santa's bag; what do they think Santa is going to do with them?

Gift Box

You will need to prepare gift boxes for all the children in your class. Once you have done this, the boxes can be used over and over again for a variety of activities.

Glue gift wrap paper separately on the lids and bottoms of boxes. Tack a bow on each lid. Place a small object in each box.

Have the children sit in a circle and give each one of them a gift box. The child opens the gift and tells about what he/she received.

Variation 1: The child can shake the box and guess what is in it.

Variation 2: The child can peek in the box so that no one else sees what is inside, then give clues to the other children and have them guess what is in the box.

What Does Santa See?

Have a discussion with the children about the night before Christmas. What do you do to get ready for Santa? Do you leave him a snack? Do you leave the reindeer a snack? How does Santa get into your house? Not everyone has a chimney. Are you sleeping when Santa comes? Is everyone at your house asleep when Santa comes'? How do you think Santa sees what he is doing when the lights are out in your house? What are some of the things that Santa sees when he is at your house?

Boxes Under the Tree

Wrap a wide variety of shapes and sizes of boxes. Have the children identify the shape and size by using such words as "big," "little," "tiny," "large," "small," "tall," "short," "wide," "long," "square," "triangle," "circle," "round," "rectangle," etc. After identifying the sizes and shapes, have the children think of different objects that would fit in the boxes. What would they like to find in the boxes?

Dear Santa

Have the children take turns orally finishing this letter:

Dear Santa,

I have been very good this year! I would like you to bring me a _____. Some of the very good things I have done this year are _____. Thank you, Santa!

Top/Middle/Bottom

This activity uses the bulletin board or wall display "What a Beautiful Tree!" described on page 100. Have the children help you take down the tree.

Ask the children, one at a time, to follow your directions: take down a cupcake paper from the top of the tree; from the middle of the tree; from the bottom of the tree.

The children will enjoy the activity of helping you remove the bulletin board, and will have a lot of practice in following directions using the words "top," "middle," and "bottom."

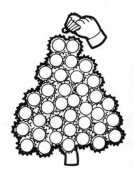

Listen to This

Children are always fascinated with the voices they hear on a tape recorder, especially if the voice they hear belongs to them or someone that they know.

Have available a tape of the teacher telling many stories or finger plays, so that individual children can "go off in a corner" to re-run their favorites. It is best if the recorder can be equipped with a headphone set.

Let the children make tape recordings of themselves telling stories.

Things That Fly

Prepare flannel board pieces for this activity by gluing small pieces of sandpaper on the back of pictures of things that fly—balloons, birds, bugs, airplanes, kites, rockets, ducks—as well as pictures of animals and transportation vehicles that don't fly. Prepare a picture of Santa and his reindeer also.

Place the picture of Santa on the flannel board. Ask the children what Santa is doing. They will tell you that he is flying. Then put up the other pictures, one at a time, and ask the children if that picture is of something that can fly.

The Peek Box

Wrap up a large box so that it looks like a gift. The top of the box should have a flap that can be easily opened and shut (refer to illustration at left). Fill a bucket with lots of objects.

Talk with the children about the presents that they will be getting at home (either Christmas or Hanukkah presents). Ask them, "Should children peek at their presents before the day that they are to have them? Of course not. But wouldn't it be fun to pretend to peek ahead of time?"

Put four or five objects in the peek box. Show the box to one child at a time. Open the flap quickly, let the child look for a few seconds, and then shut the flap. Ask the child to tell you all the things that he/she saw in the box.

After the activity, remind the children not to peek at their presents at home.

Hanukkah

Hanukkah and Christmas are the two major holidays celebrated during the month of December. If you have children in your classroom who do not know about Hanukkah, tell them about it. Bring in a menorah or ask a parent to come in and tell about Hanukkah traditions.

Call Santa on the Phone

You will need two play telephones for this activity.

Let each of the children take turns calling Santa (the teacher) on the phone. Guide the children into a conversation.

Story Game

You will need a collection of various objects, such as toys, numeral cut-outs, food, clothes, tools, etc. These should be on display in random order in the chalk tray, in a pocket chart, or on a bulletin board.

Tell a simple story, pausing to let the children choose and name the correct picture or object for blanks in the story. For example: Bobby was about to become 6 years old. He hoped his parents would give him a new **bike**. His parents were going to give him a party, and he wanted a chocolate **cake**. Bobby invited eight **children** to his party. All of the children who came liked the **ice cream**, **candy**, **games**, and **balloons**.

The children will have fun retelling the story or making up new stories.

Left or Right

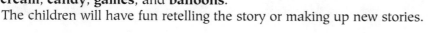

The concepts of left and right are very difficult for young children. But if you introduce the concepts, the children may begin to understand even if they aren't sure which side is left and which side is right. Here are some suggestions for teaching left and right:

- Put "bracelets" on the right wrist or ankle of each child, as shown in the illustration. This provides a concrete and tactual lesson.
- Using perfume on the girls and after-shave on the boys is another fun technique. Put the scent on the children's right wrists. They can check which are their right sides by smelling their wrists.

Cotton Santa

Color Santa's hat red. Glue on cotton
balls for the fur on Santa's hat and for
his mustache and beard.

Toy Match

Name_____

Color the toys that are the same.
Do not color the different toy.

  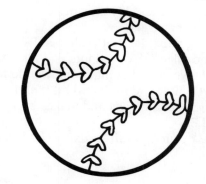

In Santa's Workshop

In Santa's workshop far away,
Ten little elves work night and day.   *(hold up ten fingers)*
This little elf makes candy canes;   *(point to little finger on one hand)*
This little elf builds streamlined trains;   *(point to ring finger)*
This little elf paints dolls for girls;   *(point to middle finger)*
This little elf puts in their curls;   *(point to pointer finger)*
This little elf dips chocolate drops;   *(point to thumb)*
This little elf makes lollipops;   *(point to little finger on other hand)*
This little elf packs each jack-in-the-box;   *(point to ring finger)*
This little elf sews dolly socks;   *(point to middle finger)*
This little elf wraps books for girls and boys;   *(point to pointer finger)*
This little elf checks off the toys;   *(point to thumb)*
As Santa packs them in his sleigh,
Ready for you on Christmas day.
(Ten children may be chosen to be the elves and to each say a line. Stick puppets or paper sack elves may be made and held up by the children as the poem is said by the group. The poem can also be used with the flannel board.)

Santa's Reindeer

One, two, three, four, five little reindeer.   *(point to one finger at a time)*
Stood by the North Pole gate.
"Hurry, Santa," called the reindeer.
"Or we will all be late."
One, two, three, four, five little reindeer.   *(point to fingers again)*
Santa said, "Please wait!
Wait for three more little reindeer,
Then we will have eight."   *(hold up three fingers on other hand)*
(Ask the children to name the reindeer: Vixen, Comet, Cupid, Dancer, Dasher, Donner, Blitzen, and Prancer. Ask "How many reindeer are there? What shall we do about Rudolph?")

Santa Is Back

Two merry blue eyes,   *(point to eyes)*
A cute little nose,   *(point to nose)*
A long, snowy beard,   *(stroke beard)*
Two cheeks like a rose.
A round, chubby form,   *(rub stomach)*
A big, bulging sack,   *(bend shoulders, hold "sack")*
Hurrah for old Santa,   *(clap hands)*
We're glad that he's back.

Con Las Manos/With the Hands

Con las manos
Aplaudo, aplaudo, aplaudo,   *(clap hands 3 times)*
Y ahora las pongo
En mi regazo.   *(fold hands in lap)*
With my hands
I clap, clap, clap,   *(repeat actions)*
And now I lay them
In my lap.
(Children will think it is a lot of fun to learn a rhyme in another language.)

The Piñata

My goodness! My goodness!
A big paper jar!   *(make large circle with hands)*
A big paper jar that is shaped like a star.   *(draw star shape in air)*
And filled full of walnuts and filled full of sweets, *(cup hands)*
Of toys and of oranges and wonderful treats.
Let's hit it and hit it and hit it until   *(pretend to hit piñata)*
The piñata breaks and makes everything spill!   *(clap)*
OLE!   *(children cry "Ole" and scramble to pick up goodies)*
(Ask your Spanish-speaking children to describe a piñata and tell about their experiences at breaking one.)

Finger Plays/Poetry

Toys

Toys, toys, toys,
For many girls and boys.
Some can talk,
Some can walk,
And some make lots of noise.
Toys, toys, toys,
For many girls and boys.
Puzzles, boots,
A horn that toots,
That every child enjoys.
Toys, toys, toys,
For many boys and girls.
A silver bike,
Shoes for a hike,
A dancing doll with curls.
Toys, toys, toys,
For many boys and girls.
A music box,
Some skiing socks,
Or a wind-up toy that whirls.

A Mouse's Christmas

Down in the cellar
One dark Christmas Eve,
A little mouse wondered
What she would receive.
She wrote, "Dear old Santa,
You know how to please,
So won't you please bring me
A small slice of cheese?"
Down in the cellar
That bright Christmas Day,
The mice knew that Santa
Had come in his sleigh.
Each little mouse
Knew how to say "Please,"
For Santa had left
More than one slice of cheese.
*(Ask: "Do you like the mouse that
wrote to Santa? Why did Santa
listen to her? Do you like the way
the rhyme ended? Why? Have
you ever written a letter to Santa?
Tell about it.")*

Gingerbread Man

Stir a bowl of gingerbread   *(stir as in a bowl)*
Smooth and spicy brown.
Roll it with a rolling pin   *(roll dough with rolling pin)*
Up and up and down.
With a cookie cutter,   *(with cookie cutter, cut cookies)*
Make some little men.
Put them in the oven   *(put pan in oven)*
Until half past ten.

I Can Be . . .

I can be:
   As tall as a Christmas tree.   *(stretch tall)*
   As round as Santa.   *(circle arms in front)*
   As tiny as an elf.   *(bend body to become smaller)*
I can:
   Bend like a candy cane.   *(bend head and neck)*
   Look like a star.   *(stretch arms and legs in all directions)*
   Prance like a reindeer.   *(prance around the room)*

Ways of Saying "Happy Christmas"

God Jul—Swedish and Norwegian
Feliz Natal—Portuguese
Froehliche Weihnachten—German
Buone Feste Natalizie—Italian
Joyeux Noel—French
Feliz Navidad—Spanish
Bozego Narodzenia—Polish
Glaedelig Jul—Danish

Five Little Bells

Five little bells, hanging in a row,
The first one said, "Ring me slow."
The second one said, "Ring me fast."
The third one said, "Ring me last."
The fourth one said, "Ring me like a chime."
The fifth one said, "Ring me at holiday time."

Santa Claus

Here is the chimney,   *(make fist, enclose thumb)*
Here is the top.   *(place palm on top of fist)*
Open the lid,   *(remove top hand)*
And out Santa will pop.   *(pop up thumb)*

Hanukkah Candles

Eight little candles
Are standing in a row.
See their pretty colors.
See their bright flames glow.
Violet, orange,
Green, red, and blue,
Yellow and pink,
And a purple one, too.
See our menorah
All shiny and bright,
Holding so many
Bright candles tonight.

The Christmas Cookie

First we mix and mix it,   *(make stirring motions)*
And stir it all around.
Then we roll and roll it,   *(make rolling motions)*
And cut it into shapes.
Bake it and bake it,   *(slide "cookie sheet" in "oven")*
That's how we make it.   *(point at self, look proud)*
Looky, looky,
It's a Christmas cookie!   *(show "cookie")*

Frost

Little Jackie Jack Frost pinched my nose,
Little Jackie Jack Frost pinched my toes.
But I ran in the house and shut the door,
And he couldn't pinch my nose any more.

Winter Cold

Hat and mittens keep us warm,   *(put hands on head, rub hands together)*
We are ready for the storm.
Zip your coat up to your chin,   *(raise hand to chin with pulling motion)*
Don't let the cold winter in.   *(shake head "no")*

Hanukkah Lights

I want to be the one who lights
The candles which will brightly glow.
I'll light them all because we know,
There is one candle for each night.
Each night of Hanukkah they'll shine,
1, 2, 3, 4, 5, 6, 7, 8, in a line.
(Glue three tongue depressors or craft sticks together to form a triangle. Repeat to make another triangle. Sprinkle glitter on them, then put the triangles together to form a Star of David.)

Five Little Spiders

Five little spiders on Christmas Eve,
Wanted to see the pretty Christmas tree.
One said, "I'm afraid to go into the room."
Two said, "We're afraid of the mop and the broom."
Three said, "I hope someone won't step on us."
Four said, "I hope that we won't cause a fuss."
Five said, "We just love pretty Christmas trees."
All said, "We hope that nobody sees."
So they crept through a hole in the wall that night,
And next morning, there was a wonderful sight.
For on Christmas Day all over the tree,
Were the shiniest webs that you ever did see.
(Have the children volunteer to be spiders and memorize the lines in quotation marks. Ask someone to tell the story about the little spiders after you have read the poem once. Draw crisscrossed lines on the board to represent a web which children can copy. Make spiders from black pipe cleaners.)

(Use pattern to make flannel board pieces.)

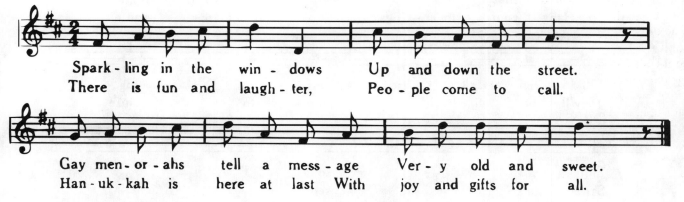

Music Activities

Christmas Shoes and Stockings

Santa Claus leaves gifts in stockings. St. Nicholas leaves gifts in Dutch children's wooden shoes. What do the children leave for Santa in this song?

Lit - tle folk in Hol - land Far, ___ far a way,
We hang up our stock - ings Ear - ly Christ - mas Eve.

Find their gifts in wood - en shoes Hap - py Christ - mas day.
San - ta Claus comes in the night, Pres - ents there to leave.

An Invitation

Part of the fun at Christmas time is inviting friends to come to your house. What does the happy child invite you to do in this song?

Next to the fire __ place, Close to the wall, There stands our

Christ - mas tree, Love - ly and tall. O, what a spark - le,

Col - or and light! Do come to see it All light - ed at night.

Happy Hanukkah

Why do you think this song is called "Happy Hanukkah"?

Spark - ling in the win - dows Up and down the street.
There is fun and laugh - ter, Peo - ple come to call.

Gay men - or - ahs tell a mess - age Ver - y old and sweet.
Han - uk - kah is here at last With joy and gifts for all.

Market Day in Mexico

I am off to mar - ket
I shall see the dan - cers

Go - ing to the vil - lage
I shall sell my bas - kets

On a sun - ny day,
To the peo - ple there.

On my bur - ro gray.
In the vil - lage square.

S-A-N-T-A

(Sing these verses to the tune of "B-I-N-G-O")
(Joyce M. Cini, Garden City, New York)

I know a man with a long white beard and Santa is his name, O!
S-A-N-T-A, S-A-N-T-A, S-A-N-T-A, and Santa is his name, O!   *(repeat this refrain after each verse)*
He fills his pack with lots of toys and Santa is his name, O!
On Christmas Eve he loads his sleigh and Santa is his name, O!
Eight reindeer pull the heavy sleigh and Santa is his name, O!
He visits all the girls and boys and Santa is his name, O!
He leaves us lots of games and toys and Santa is his name, O!

Santa's Coming Soon

f Christ - mas bells are ring - ing, ring - ing.
Hang your stock - ings in a row, and

p Child - ren all are sing - ing, sing - ing,
They'll be filled from top to toe, 'cause

f San - ta's com - ing soon.
San - ta's com - ing soon.

                   TSD1896-4 *The Preschool Calendar*

I'm a Little Snow Person

(Sing this action song to the tune "I'm a Little Teapot.")

I'm a little snow person,	*(stand with arms in a circle above stomach)*
Short and fat.	
Here are my buttons,	*(point to buttons)*
Here is my hat.	*(pat top of head)*
When the sun comes out,	*(make circle with hands above head)*
I cannot play.	*(shake head "no")*
Slowly I just	*(bend slowly down to floor)*
Melt away.	

My Red Sled

After the very first snowfall, the sleds come out. What a jolly day! Some sleds are painted red and look bright and gay against the snow. They are like wagons because they can be used in so many ways. Sometimes sleds are Christmas presents. What made the child happy in this song?

I saw a sled of beau-ti-ful red, Ver-y fine!

When old San-ta came a-long, It was mine!

Busy Christmas Time

What is going on in this song about Christmas?

Pack-a-ges come. Pack-a-ges go. Hol-ly and rib-bon and sweet mis-tle-toe!

Cook-ies bak-ing, pud-dings oh, ho! Christ-mas is here. I know, I know.

Car-ols we sing, where-ev-er we go. Christ-mas is here. I know, I know.

Suggestion: This song can be used as a walking song. Pretend that you are looking in store windows as you go down the street. When you get back to your places, will you be ready to name a beautiful present you saw?

Color Town

Tape two lengths of colored paper together. Fold as shown to represent buildings. Stand this on a table to represent the color being taught. Ask the children to find things around the room the same color as the "town." Change the color of the "town" daily or every few days. Keep this activity on display for the month or longer.

Holiday Shape Game

This is a wonderful activity for noticing likenesses and differences, and for matching. Cut poster board to measure 12" x 21". Place holiday symbols on the poster board. With a marking pen, trace around each symbol. Cover the poster board with clear contact paper. Cut a felt symbol to match each outline on the poster board. The children will enjoy matching the felt pieces to the correct outlines on the poster board.

Keep the poster board and felt pieces stored in a box for future use.

We Baked Gingerbread Men

Here is a good recipe for gingerbread men cookies. It is fun to mix all these ingredients with your class. If your children are very young or are easily distracted, you may want to premeasure all the ingredients.

Sift into a large bowl:
- 2 cups sifted flour
- 1 teaspoon soda
- ½ teaspoon salt
- 1½ teaspoons ginger
- ½ teaspoon cinnamon
- ½ teaspoon cloves

Add:
- ½ cup brown sugar
- 1 egg, beaten
- ½ cup shortening
- ⅓ cup buttermilk

Roll on lightly floured surface. Cut with a small gingerbread man cookie cutter. Bake on a greased cookie sheet for 12 to 15 minutes at 375°. Decorate with currants.

Color Wheel

Cut a cardboard circle with a 10" diameter. Divide the circle into eight equal wedges. Paint each wedge a different color. Cover the painted circle with clear contact paper. For every color wedge, paint a clothespin in a matching color. The children will enjoy attaching the clothespins to the correct parts of the wheel.

Jingle Bell

One child closes his/her eyes and stands in the center of a circle. The children in the circle pass a small bell around while the teacher counts to ten. All the children keep their hands closed and pretend to shake the bell. "It" must guess who has the bell.

Toy Matching Game

Make a background card from 12" x 12" poster board. Draw a 1" border all around it. Divide the board into sixteen 2½" squares. Mount duplicate pictures of toys on 2½" cards. Cover with clear contact paper.

Game 1: Place one set of cards face down on the board. Divide the second set equally among the players and turn face up in front of them. The players take turns turning over a card from the board. If it matches one of his/her cards, the child keeps it. If not, he or she returns it to the board, face down. The player who matches his/her set of cards first is the winner.

Game 2: Put pairs of pictures face down on the board. (For this you will need to use two boards, or only half of each set of cards.) The player turns over two cards. If they match, he/she keeps them. If not, he/she returns them to the board, face down. The winner has the most cards at the end of the game.

Piñata Game

A piñata is a clay jar filled with sweets and decorated. It is hung by a cord from the branch of a tree. The children in the neighborhood gather around the piñata, and take turns trying to break it. Each child, one at a time, is blindfolded and given a long stick. He/she gets to strike only once at the piñata. When the piñata is hit squarely, it shatters and a flood of candies pour out. The child who breaks the piñata is the hero of the day, and all the children share the candies.

Provide a piñata experience for the children. Instead of using a jar in the center of the piñata, fill a balloon with candy, blow up the balloon, and tie a knot at the end. Cover the balloon with strip papier-mâche. Below is a description of how to make the papier-mâche.

    paper towels   water
    newspapers   paint
    flour   shellac

Crush or roll newspapers to basic shape desired and tie with string. Wind with torn strips of newspaper dipped into flour and water paste about the consistency of heavy cream. Shape as strips are added. Strips of paper toweling may be added to a last layer to make a white surface for painting. When dry, paint and shellac.

Tacos

Tacos are a lot of fun to make and to eat. Give your children the experience of making tacos and learning about a food that is eaten in Mexico.

Buy the packaged taco shells and use a packaged taco sauce mix for the meat mixture. After you have all the ingredients prepared, set out everything (lettuce, tomatoes, taco shells, grated cheese, meat mixture) in individual bowls. Show the children how you put each of these things into the taco shell to make a taco. Let each of the children make his/her own.

Does It Fit?

Attach yellow cut-outs of the four basic shapes (circle, rectangle, triangle, square) by strings to a box. In the box have red cardboard cut-outs of these shapes, plus a number of different shapes, such as hearts and kite shapes.

The child is to match shapes by holding red ones to yellow ones to see if they are the same. The teacher may check when the child is finished to see if he/she has done the puzzle correctly.

No Bake Oatmeal Cookies

Have the children make these cookies as Christmas gifts for their parents.

    2 cups sugar   ½ teaspoon salt
    ½ cup cocoa   1 teaspoon vanilla
    1 stick margarine   ½ cup peanut butter
    ½ cup milk   3 cups oatmeal

Cook together sugar, cocoa, margarine, milk, and salt until well blended. Remove from heat. Add vanilla, peanut butter, and oatmeal. Mix well. Drop from spoon onto waxed paper. Cool.

Pocket Game

This is a very good activity for matching colors and combinations of colors. Cut a piece of poster board to measure 28" by 7". Glue six library card pockets on the poster board. Make six poster board cards 3" x 6". Put a different colored gummed circle on the top half of each of the six cards and a matching gummed circle on each of the library card pockets.

To play the game, the child matches the colors by placing the cards in the appropriate pockets.

Variations:
1. Put two gummed circles on each card and each pocket.
2. Put a number on each library pocket and the appropriate number of gummed circles on each card.

Zipper Thermometer

Make a zipper thermometer from a large zipper (the kind that can be purchased at any fabric store). Mark the temperature on the sides of the zipper. Have the children zip the zipper to the correct temperature each day. Which way will it go?

Christmas Tree Puzzle

Cut out pictures of Christmas tree ornaments from magazines. Mount them on tagboard. Paint a Christmas tree on heavy tagboard or chipboard. Trace the outline of the ornaments on the tree. Cover both the Christmas tree and the pictures of ornaments with clear adhesive paper.

Have the children match and place the ornaments on the Christmas tree.

Christmas Sort

This activity will help the children learn to classify according to categories. Cut Christmas trees out of green construction paper, one for each child in the class. The trees should be approximately 12" from top to bottom. Glue a picture of a family member (for example, mother, father, brother, sister, baby, grandparent) at the top of each tree.

Have the children look through magazines to find pictures appropriate as Christmas gifts for the persons on their trees. They can cut out the pictures and glue them on their trees.

My Holiday Book

Tell the children to look through magazines and to select pictures that they would like to include in their very own picture books. Have the children cut the pictures out and glue them onto 9" x 12" pieces of construction paper—one picture to a page. Secure all the pages together in book fashion.

Have the child "read" the book by talking about the pictures. The children will enjoy bringing these books home to share with their parents.

Variations: During the month of December, have the children make these books with a holiday theme (Christmas or Hanukkah). During other times of the year, the books can be made for a wide variety of themes: families, animals, children at school, community helpers, etc. Books with nonsense and silly pictures are fun, too. (This is a great quiet activity for toddlers.)

Special Granola Cookies

Baking cookies during the holidays is a tradition in many homes. Here is a fun and easy recipe that the children in your room will enjoy creating. If possible, provide a small box for each child so that the children can take some cookies home to their parents.

½ cup honey	1 cup peanut butter
1 cup powdered milk	granola cereal

Mix honey, powdered milk, and peanut butter together. Roll into balls and roll balls in granola cereal. Makes two dozen.

Latkes (Potato Pancakes)

Latkes are served during the eight day celebration of Hanukkah.

4 large potatoes	3 tablespoons flour or matzo meal
1 medium onion	½ teaspoon baking powder
1 teaspoon salt	vegetable oil or other fat for frying
1 egg, well beaten	

Peel and grate potatoes. Grate onion and add to potatoes. Add salt, egg, and flour or matzo meal mixed with baking powder. Beat all ingredients well into a smooth batter. If batter seems too watery, add a little more flour. Drop by tablespoons into hot fat. The fat must be deep enough to almost cover the cake. Brown on one side, then turn over and brown the other side. These are delicious when served with applesauce.

School Spirit Week

School Spirit Week will energize you and all the children during the long month of January, and it can help chase away cabin fever, too.

Here are some additional ideas that can add fun to your school spirit week:

- Have the children vote for an official school mascot. Don't limit their choices to real animals—include animal story book characters, too. When I was teaching, our school mascot was "Tigger" from the Winnie-the-Pooh books.
- Let the children form a school marching band. Give them all instruments or improvise instruments from pots, pans, spoons, etc. The children can parade around the school singing their school song and accompanying themselves with their instruments.
- Have an "Awards Day." Each child should receive an award, and the awards should be personalized. For example, you can give awards for the best "rester," the best at taking turns, the best at coloring, etc. It is extra fun if the teachers create special awards for themselves, too. The children will think it's wonderful if the teachers also get awards.

Alaska and Eskimos

For your preparation on the Alaska unit, here is a summary of the information that is taught about Alaska and the Eskimo people.

- The word Alaska came from the language of the Aleuts (Al-Ay-Es-Ka) and means "Great Land" or "Main Land."
- New vocabulary words: hooded coats are called "parkas;" fur boots are called "mukluks;" a one-person boat is called a "kayak;" a 30-foot whaleboat is called a "umiak."
- Alaska has some very special animals: walrus, seal, polar bear, kodiak bear, fish (salmon, halibut, king crab, shrimp), moose, whale, raccoon, elk, caribou, deer, reindeer, bald eagle. Young children may be unfamiliar with some of these animals.
- Igloos: Most Eskimo people do not live in igloos, and have probably never seen one. Igloos are only built when there is no wood or stone to be found or bought.
- There are no snakes in Alaska. This is a fun fact that children seem to really enjoy.
- Some people in Alaska use dog sleds as a means of transportation. Two of the most popular breeds of dogs used are the Alaskan Malamute and the Siberian Husky. Both these breeds of dogs carry their tails curled up to keep them from becoming hardened with frozen snow. Usually five to nine dogs are used to pull a sled. They are harnessed by two's, with one dog as the leader.

Martin Luther King Jr. Day

January 15th is the day that we as a nation have set aside to remember Martin Luther King Jr. Even very young preschoolers can begin to develop an understanding of equal rights and the values that Martin Luther King stood for.

We naturally teach equal rights to preschoolers daily. We are giving them such examples as, "It is better to tell someone that you are upset rather than to hit them." We show the peaceful ways of solving differences rather than violence. Preschool teachers are continually setting good examples of equal rights by their equal treatment of children, by their teaching of the concepts of sharing, taking turns, and fair play, and by their fairness in judgements made in the classroom.

Help for Playing Outside

Teachers seem to develop wonderful systems for getting everybody buttoned, zipped, snapped, tied, and out the door in a reasonable amount of time (one of the most hectic moments of the day!).

Here are some extra developmental activities that will help very young children and those children who may need some additional practice to increase their fine motor skills, so that they can get themselves dressed more easily.

1. Buttoning, Snapping, and Zipping
   a. Have the child button or snap the sweater, shirt, coat, etc. on a doll.
   b. Have the child use a button board, a snapping board, or a zipper board for practice.
   c. Zip a coat that is on another child. Have the child zip his/her own coat.
   d. Attach a diaper pin to a child's zipper, so the child has something larger to grab onto when zipping.
2. Lacing and Tying
   a. Have the child lace a large adult shoe.
   b. Have the child lace his/her own shoe when it is off his/her foot.
   c. Lace and tie the first knot in a bow knot. (Tying is often too difficult for children under the age of five.)
3. Twisting and Tightening Bolts and Nuts
   (Excellent eye/hand coordination practice)
   a. Collect many different size bolts and nuts. Have the child remove the nuts.
   b. Have the child replace the nuts on the bolts. (Start with largest nut and bolt.)
   c. Have the child select the proper size nut for the bolt from an assortment.

Our Snowpeople

Provide each child with a large, a medium, and a small white circle. To build the snowperson, the children should paste their three circles together.

Using diluted white glue and a paintbrush, brush glue all over the snowpeople shapes. Cover the snowpeople with bits of cotton, and they will really look like they were made of snow.

Use scraps of fabric, felt, or construction paper for buttons, hats, scarves, and bow ties.

The Resolutions

New Year's resolutions are often a difficult concept for preschoolers to understand. I have found it helpful when talking about the New Year to present New Year's resolutions as "Things we would like to learn how to do this year," or "I'm going to be so good this year, that I'm not going to _____ anymore!" It is always fun to hear the original responses from preschoolers.

Write down what each child says on a piece of paper. Tape or glue the white piece of paper onto colored construction paper for a frame. Let the children decorate the frames.

Changing Seasons

The "Changing Seasons" bulletin board will take four days to complete—one day for each season. Divide the wall or bulletin board into four sections. In each section, put the trunk of a tree.

Day One (Winter): Add snow to the first section, a snow person, and other things that represent winter.

Day Two (Spring): Add some green and blossoms to the tree. Put up grass and some small flowers.

Day Three (Summer): The tree should be all green. Add lots of flowers.

Day Four (Autumn): Add multi-colored leaves to the tree. Have some on the ground, also.

After each day, have the children discuss the season and some of the different things that people can do during that season. Read the "Thirst Quenchers All Year Long" activity (*Learning Games/Experiential Activities,* page 156). Each day after you have completed a section of the bulletin board, follow the directions in that activity.

Alaska

Last month you made a bulletin board of the North Pole. Use the background of that bulletin board. Add pictures of the Alaskan animals that the children have learned about. You could also add pictures of people who are wearing parkas and mukluks.

Bulletin Board City

Have the children cut out pictures of all different kinds of houses and buildings. Paste the pictures on paper, covering a bulletin board or wall. Draw in the streets after the houses and buildings have been put up. The children can add trees to the city.

Each child should choose a house as his/her own. Put up a tiny mailbox with the child's name on it. Have the children make up a name for their city, and display the name as a caption on the bulletin board.

My Teachers and I Are Friends

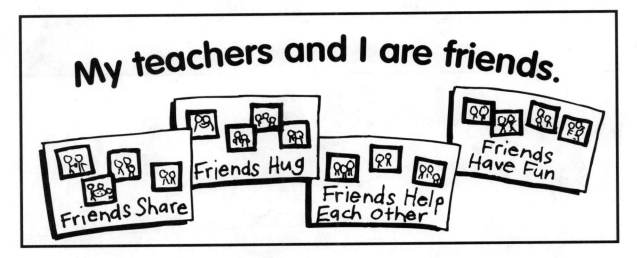

A few days before you are going to assemble this bulletin board, take instant pictures of the children and teachers in your classroom, working at their various activities. Prepare the bulletin board by putting up the caption, "My Teachers and I Are Friends," along with four boxes titled: "Friends Share," "Friends Have Fun," "Friends Hug," and "Friends Help Each Other."

Show the pictures that you have collected to your class. Let the children decide into which box each picture should be put.

Footprints in the Snow
(a flannel board story)

Little Brave and his father Crooked Arrow were going hunting for deer. Snow covered the ground, so Little Brave and his father had to find the deer in a particular way. Do you know how? That's right, they looked for footprints in the snow.

Now Little Brave and Crooked Arrow saw several types of footprints. You can help them find the footprints for deer.

The first prints they saw looked like this (*put rabbit prints on flannel board*). Do you know what animal made these prints? This animal is small and sleeps underground. Some can hop great distances. Yes, these are the footprints of the rabbit. (*Place picture of rabbit beside prints.*)

Little Brave saw these prints next (*put squirrel prints on flannel board*). Can you help Little Brave decide who made these prints? This animal is small, lives in a tree, and stores nuts for the winter. Who can tell me what animal made these prints? Correct—these are the footprints for a squirrel. (*Put picture of squirrel next to prints.*)

Next Crooked Arrow found another set of footprints (*put prints of fox on the flannel board*). The animal that made these prints has a long bushy tail and is a swift runner. Do you know the name of this animal? It is a fox. (*Put picture of fox next to prints.*)

Finally, Little Brave and his father saw these prints (*put deer prints on the flannel board*). Crooked Arrow was happy. Do you know why? Yes, these are the prints of the deer. (*Put picture of deer on flannel board beside prints.*)

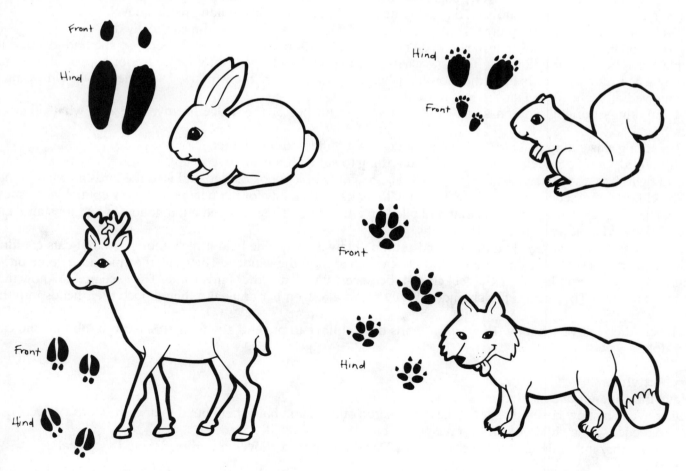

The Snow Lady Who Wanted a Job

Dick and Sharon stood back to admire the snow lady they had just finished.

"Say, she's fine!" Dick cried.

Sharon squared her shoulders. "I'm glad we worked hard making her," she said, "because now she looks almost real! You can tell that she wasn't put together in a hurry!"

And that was true. Everything about the snow lady showed careful work. She was strong and smooth. Her arms had been carved with a spoon. The children had patted a ring of snow around her neck, so that it looked as if she wore a collar. A bright strip of orange peel made a very smiling mouth. Chunks of coal made shining eyes and buttons. There was a black hat on her head, and a piece of red cloth from the rag bag had been poked into her side. That made it look as if a hanky were sticking out of her pocket.

Mr. Davis came by from his shopping. "My!" he smiled. "What a fine snow lady! She looks so friendly I feel as if I've known her all my life! What's her name?"

"Her name is Doris," the children said.

"Well, I'm glad to have met you, Doris," Mr. Davis nodded before he went on his way.

Before long everyone in the neighborhood had grown fond of friendly Doris. Dick and Sharon loved her so much that they decided to keep her all winter. "If a warm day comes and melts her around the edges," they said, "we'll be doctors and fix her up again!"

There was only one thing that troubled the children. Doris looked healthy and proud. She looked like the sort of person who would want a good job instead of just standing still!

"Why don't you give her a broom?" Mr. Davis asked. "Then maybe she'd feel as if she had a job."

The children gave Doris a broom. That didn't seem to help, because Doris couldn't really sweep. She could only pretend that she was sweeping.

"Why don't you give her a shovel?" suggested the mail carrier.

The children gave Doris a shovel. That didn't help either, because she couldn't really shovel.

"She wants a job that isn't pretending," Sharon said. "She wants a job that she can really do."

They thought and thought, but they couldn't think of a job Doris could really do, because she had to stand in one place all the time. It had begun to snow when the children finally went into the house for supper. It was still snowing when they went to bed. In the morning when they looked from the window, Dick cried, "Oh! Oh! It must have snowed all night! Poor Doris is half buried!"

"Everything's buried!" Sharon said. "You can't see the bushes or the hedge or anything! And what's that on Doris?"

Something was sitting on Doris' shoulder! Suddenly it fluffed out its feathers.

"It's a bird—a chickadee! I'll bet it can't find a thing to eat with the snow so deep!"

And right then, they knew just the job for Doris. She could hold a box of food and feed the birds all winter long!

The children dressed warmly and went outside to make Doris ready for her new job. They swept the loose snow off her. They shoveled away the drifts that had piled up around her. They scooped out a hollow in her arms and into it they set an old candy box filled with crumbs.

Doris held the box so tightly that the wind couldn't blow it away. She held it high enough so that cats couldn't bother the birds. Later in the day Sharon and Dick watched from the window. They saw the chickadee come back. It found the box of crumbs. "Chick-a-dee, chick-a-dee-dee!" it called. Other birds came. They seemed to know that Doris was friendly. They sat on her shoulders. They sat in a row on her arms and they dipped their heads into the box.

The children felt very happy. They said, "Doris doesn't have to pretend any longer! She has a job that she can really do!"

Story Activities

1. Have the children draw a picture of Doris.
2. If you live in a snow-covered region, take the children outside and have them build their own "Doris." Give Doris a bird feeder so the children can observe winter birds.
3. Turn this story into a flannel board story. Make Doris, a broom, a shovel, a bird feeder, and a chickadee.

The Three Little Pigs
a modern version

Once upon a time, there was a mother pig who had three little pigs: Peter, Patrick, and Percy. As the little pigs grew up, the mother pig sent the young ones out into the world to make their fortunes.

One fine morning the three little pigs started out into the wide world, each choosing a different road. Peter became a doctor, and he lived in a condominium. Patrick became a sculptor and he lived in a solar house. Percy became a teacher and he lived in a brick colonial.

Peter had just moved into his condominium when a big bad wolf came along. "Little pig, little pig, let me come in!" the wolf called.

"Not by the hair of my chinny, chin, chin." answered Peter.

"If you don't," said the wolf, "I'll drive my bulldozer through your front door!"

But Peter wouldn't let the big bad wolf in, so the wolf bulldozed down the front door of the condominium. Peter ran away to Patrick's house just as the front door was crashing in.

Patrick had just moved into his solar house when Peter ran in, with the big bad wolf close behind him. "Little pigs, little pigs, let me come in!" the wolf called.

"Not by the hair of our chinny, chin, chins," answered Peter and Patrick.

"If you don't," said the wolf, "I'll drive my bulldozer through your front door!"

But Peter and Patrick wouldn't let the big bad wolf in, so the wolf bulldozed down the front door of the solar house. Peter and Patrick ran away to Percy's house just as the front door was crashing in.

Percy had just moved into his brick colonial when Peter and Patrick ran in, with the big bad wolf close behind him. "Little pigs, little pigs, let me come in!" the wolf called.

"Not by the hair of our chinny, chin, chins," answered Peter, Patrick, and Percy.

"If you don't," said the wolf, "I'll drive my bulldozer through your front door!"

But Peter, Patrick, and Percy wouldn't let the big bad wolf in, so the wolf started to bulldoze down the front door of the brick colonial. But he ran out of gas and the bulldozer stopped.

Percy called the police and they arrested the big bad wolf for bulldozing front doors. And the three little pigs, Peter, Patrick, and Percy, lived happily ever after in the brick colonial.

(Use as a flannel board story. Make three pigs, the wolf driving a bulldozer, a condominium, a solar house, a brick colonial, and a police officer.)

Pine Cone Bird Feeders

Each child will need a pine cone, some peanut butter, bird seed or bread crumbs, sticks or spoons to use for spreading the peanut butter, string, and paper clips for hanging.

1. Tie string around the cone.
2. Spread peanut butter over the pine cone.
3. Roll the covered cone in birdseed or crumbs.
4. Hang the pine cones outside near a window, so the children can observe the birds eating the crumbs.

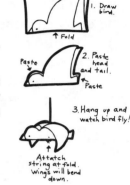

Bird Cut-Outs

This is a good art project in which all the children may participate. Each child's painted or decorated bird can be hung from the ceiling, perhaps over his/her cot location at rest time.

Cut large birds that can be folded double at the bottom. The children can brush paint, sponge paint, string paint, blow paint, or decorate the birds with feathers, tissue paper, curled paper, or any collage materials. Attach string to the center fold and hang from the ceiling so that the wings "float" freely.

Icicles

On the top of a piece of dark paper, paint a line of white tempera paint. Let the children blow gently with straws so the paint will run. The result will look like icicles. This is a wonderful art activity even for the smallest of preschoolers.

Window Paint

Ingredients: equal parts of Bon Ami, Albastrine (another name for glass paint—it comes in powder form and can be purchased in a hardware or paint store), and dry tempera paint.

Procedure: Mix ingredients. Add enough water to make a creamy paste. Paint on a window with a small brush or clean rag. This paint wipes off easily with a damp cloth and the mixture will not mar the window in any way.

Paper Mittens

Prepare two paper mittens for each child. Let the children create designs on their mittens with color crayons. The children should be encouraged to design a **pair** of mittens—the design of each mitten should be the same.

Tie the mittens together with a piece of colored yarn.

Puzzle Birds

The teacher will need to prepare small circles for heads, beaks of yellow, wings, bodies, and tails. Make some of the heads, wings, bodies, and tails red and make some blue. The children can then make cardinals and blue jays. Make several examples ahead of time so the children can see that all these shapes really do make a bird.

Provide the children with glue and large pieces of construction paper. The children can then pick out the shapes they need and paste them on the construction paper to make their birds.

Noise Makers

To celebrate the New Year, have the children make noise makers. Cover empty pop cans with construction paper. Decorate the construction paper by coloring, painting, or gluing on scrap materials or glitter. Fill the pop can with popcorn, seeds, small rocks, salt, etc. Put tape over the can's opening.

Play-Dough Snowpeople

Here is a fun recipe for making play-dough. Don't use food coloring and the play-dough will stay white.

1 cup salt	2 cups sifted flour
6 teaspoons alum	2 tablespoons salad oil
1 cup water	

Mix together until smooth. The play-dough will stay soft for several weeks if it is kept in a plastic bag.

Show the children how to form balls with the play-dough to make the snowpeople. Use small stones, fabric, etc. to add facial features, buttons, hats, and scarves.

Stuffed Kodiak Bear and Polar Bear

Use brown bags and white bags for this activity. Cut two bear shapes for each child. Staple the bear shapes together along the edge, leaving the top of the head open. Have the children stuff the bears with newspaper or tissue paper. After the bears are stuffed, staple the tops of the heads shut. Add facial features with a black crayon.

Some children can use the brown grocery bags and make Kodiak bears, while other children can use the white bags to make polar bears. You can also staple a brown bear shape to a white bear shape and have the children draw facial features on both sides. They now have a reversible Kodiak/Polar Bears.

Igloos in the Snow

Give each child a white paper circle and scissors. Have the children cut their circles in half. Each now has two igloos. Paste the igloos on a light blue sheet of paper. With a black crayon, color the opening of each igloo. Children with fairly good fine motor skills may want to draw black lines representing the individual ice blocks in the igloos. Use white chalk for coloring snow at the bottom of the paper.

When telling the children about igloos, it is important to tell them that most Eskimo people do not live in igloos. Igloos are only built in northern Alaska when there is not any wood or stones to be found.

Dog Sleds

There are many people who travel by dog sled in Alaska. There are several breeds of dogs that are used. Two of the most popular are the Alaskan Malamute and the Siberian Husky. Both these animals carry their tails curled up to keep them from becoming hardened with frozen snow. The team of dogs is harnessed by two's to the sled, with one dog as the leader. Five to nine dogs are usually used.

Give each of the children a copied picture of a dog sled. Follow the example on the right. When you are preparing the picture, eliminate the dogs' tails. Have the children color in the dogs' tails curling around to their backs.

Pan of Snow

There are many days in the winter (especially in northern climates), when it is too cold to play outside. Bring in pans of snow and let the children draw shapes and lines with their fingers in the snow. Use cookie cutters or other kitchen utensils to create drawings in the pans of snow. (Filling the water table with snow is a lot of fun, too!)

Popsicle Stick House

Give each child five popsicle sticks or tongue depressors. Have each child paste the sticks onto a sheet of construction paper in the shape of a house. Windows and a door can be colored in after the paste is dry.

Sponge Paint Windows

Give each child a piece of construction paper with a large rectangle drawn on it. Tell the children that these are big apartment buildings. Provide each of the children with paint and sponges cut into small squares. Have the children sponge paint windows on the apartment buildings. After the paintings are dry, the children can color in trees, people, clouds, etc.

Who is in the Apartment?

Draw the outline of an apartment building on a very large sheet of paper and tape it to the wall. Have the children cut out pictures of people from magazines, then paste them in the apartment building. This will help the children understand that many people live in an apartment building.

Happy Birthday, Martin Luther King Jr.

Tell the children who Martin Luther King Jr. was and why we remember his birthday. Talk about friendship and why it is important.

Then have each child trace the shape of one of his/her hands on a piece of construction paper. Help the children cut out the traced hands. Tape up all the cut-outs on a wall in your classroom, overlapping them so it looks like they are holding hands. Create a caption to put over the line of hands.

Our Duplex

Discuss duplexes and townhouses with the children. Then tell them to each choose a friend with whom they would like to live in a duplex. Give the partners a large piece of construction paper. Have each child draw one side of a house.

Write the names of the two children who are sharing the duplex on top of the piece of paper. Ask the partners to take turns telling the rest of the class about their house. Which side belongs to which child? What makes their house special?

Window Shade City

Discarded plastic window shades are wonderful for a large variety of projects. Never throw one away.

For this project, you should first draw in the streets of a city on a window shade. Then have the children take turns drawing in their own houses or apartment buildings. (Use permanent magic markers and watch the kids carefully.) The children will enjoy creating the city where they all live. Stores, gas stations, etc. can be added.

Keep the window shade city in your classroom. It is great fun on which to drive cars and trucks during play time.

The Snowman

Trace and color the snowman.

The Mouse and the Snowman

Directions:
The children cut out and paste the pictures in the order in which they happen.

Bean Bag and Hoola Hoop Fun

Each child, depending on age or skill level should have his/her own bean bag or hoop.

Bean bag: The children walk around the floor, throwing the bean bags up in the air and catching them as they move. On the teacher's signal, they drop the bean bags on the floor. They proceed to jump, hop, or leap over the many bags located all over the floor. When the teacher signals again, each child picks up the nearest bean bag and begins to play catch with him/herself again.

Hoops: The children spread out and use the hoops in various ways, such as rolling them, twirling them around their bodies, spinning them, etc. On the teacher's signal, the children place the hoops on the floor and proceed to jump with feet together or hop in and out of as many hoops as possible until the teacher gives the next command. Each child then picks up the nearest hoop and resumes the first activity.

Fly in the Window

Find pictures of winter birds, such as the chickadee, tufted titmouse, sparrow, hawk, owl, cardinal, quail, wild turkey, pigeon, blue jay, snow goose, etc. Let the children choose which winter bird they would like to be. Choose one child to be the person "in the house."

The person "in the house" raises his/her arms, pretending to open a window. When the person has his/her arms up, the birds may fly. When the person has his/her arms down, the birds must stop.

Keep It in the Circle

You will need an 8½" playground ball or soccer ball.

The children sit in a circle. They attempt to keep the ball from leaving the circle by stopping it with their feet and kicking it toward another child. They may not use their hands. The children should lean back on the hands to insure proper foot power and non-use of hands. If the children become proficient, they may stand and play the same game of keeping the ball in the circle.

Snow Trail

If you are fortunate enough to live in a climate where the ground is now frozen and covered with snow, your class can have a lot of fun making snow trails. Choose several children to run around the playground making trails in the snow. Let the other children try to follow the snow trails.

If you do not live in a climate that is now snow covered, let the children pretend to make snow trails by using leaves or sticks as a trail.

Snowflakes

Discuss how softly snowflakes float to the ground. Could we float down that softly? Establish boundaries in the room and have the children dramatize the movements of the snowflakes.

The Soldier's Line

Have 5–9 children line up facing the far end of the room. They each have a target on the far wall that they must look at. On the command **walk,** they walk towards their targets without looking to their left or right. The object is for the children to walk in as straight a line as possible.

Vary by having the children bunny-hop, walk heel-to-toe, hop, skip, jump, etc. Have the other children judge which group formed the straightest "Soldier's Line."

No Snakes in Alaska

Children are fascinated with the fact that there are no snakes in Alaska. Here is a fun "snake" game that is similar to Musical Chairs.

Place cards on the floor in a circle—one card for each child. All the cards should be blank, except for one card with a picture of a snake on it. Have the children walk around the circle to music. When the music stops, the child standing on the snake card must return to his or her seat, because he/she cannot be in Alaska. After all, there are no snakes in Alaska.

Each time a child leaves the circle, remove a blank card. Play the game until all the children have landed on the snake and have had to leave Alaska.

Hoola-Hoop Igloo

Tell the children that the hoola-hoops are igloos. Have the children run around the igloos, crawl through the igloos, jump up and down in the igloos. Use your imagination to come up with a variety of movement directions.

Build a Tower

Have the children pretend that they are in Alaska and are building an ice block tower. You can use empty cans, milk cartons, boxes, dominoes, spools, wood blocks, etc. Have each child take a turn placing a block on the tower. See how high the children can build the tower as a group before it falls.

Variation: Divide the children into small groups. Have each group build a tower. Which group can build the tallest tower before it falls?

Pull the Sled

It is discussed in the dog sled activity on page 137 how the team of dogs is harnessed by two's to the sled, with a lead dog at the front.

Using a long jump rope, choose a driver and a team of dogs. The team of dogs stands together with the jump rope around them. The driver holds the jump rope.

Give the children directions to follow, such as go slow, go fast, stop, go around the table, etc. See if the driver and the team of dogs can work together and follow the directions. This is a fun activity to do outside in the snow.

Athletic Contest

Traditionally, the Eskimo people are very peaceful. When a quarrel would arise, it was often settled by an athletic contest.

Have the children run races, two by two, to show how the Eskimo people might settle an argument. Talk about arguments with your children. Stress all of the different ways people can settle a disagreement without fighting.

Crawl Through a Tunnel

All young children enjoy the motor skill of crawling. Crawling is especially fun when you have something to crawl through. Provide the children with things to crawl through, such as an open-ended large box, a barrel, or use sheets or blankets to cover tables and chairs.

Have the children pretend that they are in northern Alaska, and that they are crawling through an ice tunnel. The sides of the tunnel are very cold, so the children should try not to touch the sides of the tunnel as they crawl through it.

Find My House

Choose one child to hide and one child to be "it." "It" covers his/her eyes. The other child hides and whispers, "Come find my house." "It" must find the hidden child. "It" then gets to be the child that hides, and a new "it" is chosen.

The Elevator Is Broken

Use playground equipment or the ladder on the slide, and have the children practice their climbing skills. For fun, tell the children that they live on the top floor of an apartment building. They usually take the elevator up to their floor, but today the elevator is broken. They must climb many flights of stairs before they reach their apartment.

Make the Circle Grow

After you have discussed Martin Luther King Jr., play this game. Choose two children. Have them hold hands and walk around in a circle to music. When the music stops, have one of the children invite another child to come and hold hands in the circle. Now there are three children walking around in the circle, holding hands. The third child can then ask a fourth child to join the circle. Keep the game going until every child has joined the circle.

Hide the House

Prepare small pictures of houses, one for each child in your classroom. Have the children close their eyes, then hide one of the houses. Tell the children to look for the house. The child who finds it can keep it—it is his/her house. Keep doing this until all the children have a house.

For some extra fun, let the children hide a house for you to find. Children really enjoy it when teacher plays the game, too.

Follow Me to My House

This activity is like "Follow the Leader." Have the children form a line. The first child in the line will lead the way, and everyone in the line must move as the leader moves. After a time, the leader stops and says, "This is my house." The second child in line now has a turn as the leader, and the first child moves to the end of the line.

Carpet Squares

Carpet squares are valuable pieces of equipment for any preschool. They can be used for a variety of games and activities—matching textures and colors, for sitting on, etc. Let the children use carpet squares as "scooters" on an uncarpeted floor.

Hoola Hoop Catch

You will need a hoola hoop suspended from the ceiling with a rope, and bean bags or small rubber balls.

Have the children play catch by throwing a ball or bean bag through the hoop while a partner catches it. The children can throw overhand or underhand. If the activity is too difficult, the children can let the ball bounce once before they catch it.

My School's Flag

Designed by _____

The United States has a special flag. My state has a special flag. My school should also have a special flag. This is what I think it should look like.

Build-a-House

Name_____

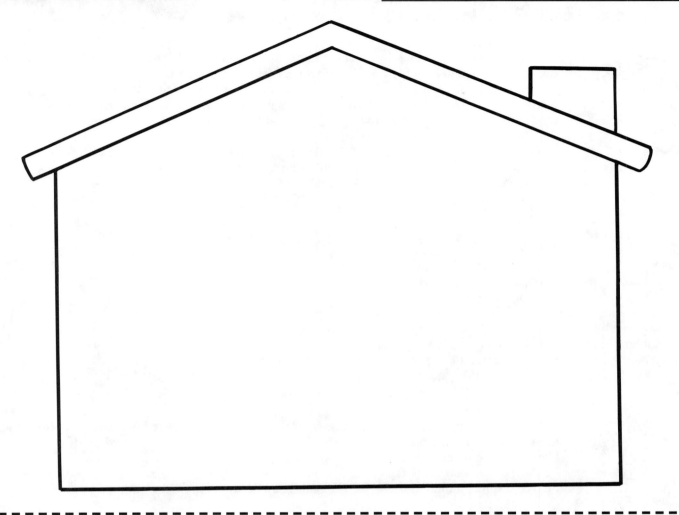

Cut out the door and the windows. Paste them on the house any way you would like. Color your house.

The Snow Fairy

Dress up a doll to look like a snow fairy. Dress the doll in white, and sprinkle on some glitter. You can also draw a picture of a snow fairy, but it is more fun to use the doll.

Place the doll on a chair and tell the children that the snow fairy has come to your class and wants to listen to wishes. Have each of the children make a wish. Explain the word "wish" to those children who may not understand the word. Make some wishes yourself, before you ask the children to make their wishes.

Preschoolers are such wonderful believers. You should be sure to explain that the snow fairy is not real—she is just pretend. Wouldn't it be fun if she really was real and could make wishes come true?

What Do You See?

Place several small familiar objects on a table covered by a cloth or paper. Remove the cover and expose the objects for a few seconds so the child can see them. Replace the cover and ask the child to name as many objects as he/she can recall. Gradually increase the number of objects.

Variation 1: Place several objects under the cover. Expose the objects for a few seconds. Have the children close their eyes while one object is removed. Rearrange the remaining objects. Expose again while the children try to recall which object is now missing.

Variation 2: Expose a picture containing a number of items. Remove and have the child tell as much as he/she can about the objects he or she remembers seeing in the picture.

Alaskan Animals

There are many wonderful animals in Alaska. The children may be unfamiliar with some of these animals. Locate pictures of the animals listed below to show your children. If possible, find two pictures of each animal so the children can match the ones that are the same.

You could also show the children three pictures at the same time. Have two of the pictures be of the same animal and one picture of a different animal. Ask the children to find the animal that is different.

| Walrus | Seal | Polar Bear | Kodiak | Bear | Fish | Moose | Raccoon |
| Elk | Caribou | Deer | Reindeer | Whale | Beaver | Bald Eagle | |

New Words

Young children always enjoy learning new words, especially if it is a word for something that they already understand. Here are four words that are used in Alaska that the children can learn.

PARKA: Hooded coat
MUKLUK: Fur boots
KAYAK: One-person boat (little boat)
UMIAK: 30-foot whaleboat (big boat)
The word Alaska (Al-Ay-Es-Ka) means "Great Land."
Make pictures of the new words and have the children learn the new words.

Ice Fishing

Many people earn a living in Alaska by fishing. Some of the different types of fish they catch are: salmon, halibut, king crab, and shrimp. Ask the children if they have ever eaten any of those fish. Someone in Alaska might have caught a fish that they have eaten.

Prepare paper cut-outs of fish. Make the fish all different sizes and colors. Place a paper clip on each fish. Put the fish in a box with a hole in the top. The children are going to go ice fishing. Place a magnet on a string to fish with. Have the children describe the fish that they catch.

New Year's Resolutions

Explain to your class what a New Year's resolution is. Ask each child to think up a New Year's resolution for him/herself. Write the resolutions down, and send them home for the parents to see. It's so much fun to hear what the children think would be a good resolution.

Where Do You Live?

Tell the children that everyone's home has a special address. That is how the mail carriers can find our homes with the mail. Then have the children listen carefully, and say one of the children's addresses. See if the children can recognize their own addresses.

Most preschoolers won't know their addresses, but a child may be able to recognize his/her address when he/she hears it. This is the first step in learning addresses. You may wish to try this with the children's phone numbers, too.

Square and Not Square

Fill a bag with many objects of various shapes. Have the children take turns picking out an object from the bag. They should decide whether the object is square or not square. If the object isn't square, see if the children can identify what shape it is.

Building Blocks

Have the children build houses and tall apartment buildings with building blocks. Point out which of the blocks are square. (Milk cartons covered with contact paper make excellent and inexpensive lightweight building blocks.)

Many/Few Windows

On a large piece of paper, draw a small square (to represent a house) and a large, tall rectangle (to represent an apartment building). Cut out many white paper squares. These will be windows.

Have the children take turns pasting windows on the house and the apartment building. Talk about how there are just a "few" windows on the house, but there are "many" windows on the apartment building.

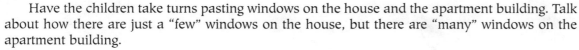

Tall/Short Homes

Find many pictures of houses, apartments, duplexes, townhouses, mobile homes, etc. Have the children sort the pictures by deciding whether the building is tall or short.

I Live "Next To" You

After you have discussed townhouses and duplexes, place two chairs side by side. Choose one child to come and sit on a chair. Tell that child to choose a friend to come and sit on the other chair. Encourage the child to say, "I live next to you." Every child should have a turn.

Walrus Puzzle

Directions: Cut out the puzzle pieces. Paste them together on a sheet of paper. Color the walrus.

January Snow

Here comes the month of January.
We are excited and happy and merry.   *(clap three times)*
From a big gray cloud in the dark, dark sky,
A crowd of snowflakes is starting to fly.   *(hands raised, fingers lowered)*
And so what will we do when snow covers the ground?
Should we tiptoe around and not make a sound?   *(children say "no")*
Should we get into bed like an old sleepyhead?   *("no")*
Should we dress in warm clothes and go out of doors?   *("yes")*
Shall we make a snowball and hit the brick wall?   *("yes")*
Shall we laugh? Shall we shout and roll all about?   *("yes")*
As we feel the wind blow, shall we pile up the snow?   *("yes")*
What shall we do with that big pile of snow
When it reaches our window? Does anyone know?   *(children respond)*
We will roll it and roll it and roll it and then
We will make two snow ladies and two fat snowmen!   *(show two fingers on each hand)*
Yes! Two snow ladies and two fat snowmen!

Snow Is On . . .

Snow is on the housetop,
Snow is on the ground.
Snow is on the mountain.
Snow is all around.

Five Snowmen

Five happy snowmen, standing in a row.
The sun melted one, so very slow.
Four happy snowmen, having lots of fun.
One ran indoors to hide from the sun.
Three happy snowmen, jumping up and down.
One ran away without a sound.
Two happy snowmen sliding down a hill.
Both fell over and lay very still.
(Use flannel board cut-outs of five snowmen with this rhyme.)

Little Nose

Where did you get that little red nose?   *(point to nose)*
Jack Frost kissed it, I suppose.   *(nod head)*
He kissed it once, he kissed it twice.   *(hold up one finger, then two fingers)*
Poor little nose, it's as cold as ice.   *(hug self and shiver)*

Tap, Tap, Tap

Tap, tap, tap goes the woodpecker,   *(tap with right pointer finger on inside of left wrist)*
As he pecks a hole in a tree.   *(make circle with pointer finger and thumb)*
He is making a house with a window
To peep at you and me.   *(hold circle made with pointer finger and thumb in front of eye)*

Three Little Penguins

Three little penguins, dressed in white and black,
Waddle, waddle forward, and waddle right back.
Three little penguins, in a funny pose,
They are wearing their evening clothes.
Their suits are black and their vests are white.
They waddle to the left and they waddle to the right.
They stand on the ice and they look very neat,
As they waddle along on their little flat feet.
(Ask: "Where might we see penguins? Where have you seen one? How are penguins different from other birds?" The children can act out this rhyme. Ask them to draw penguins.)

Time for Bed

In summer when it is time for bed,
It isn't dark—it's light instead.
In winter when I go to bed,
It isn't light—it's dark instead.

The Apple Tree

In spring, the apple tree was pink
And white all round about;
And somewhere, near the very top,
A pair of robins, in and out.
In summer, the old apple tree
Had fruit and leaves of green;
And hungry little baby birds
Among the branches could be seen.
Upon the tree in autumn time
Were apples big and gay.
We could not hear the robins sing,
They left and sadly flew away.
Cold winter time is here again.
The apple tree must rest,
With snow upon its spreading boughs
And snowflakes in the robins' nest.

Happy New Year

On New Year's Day, on New Year's Day,
This is what I always say:
"Happy New Year, Daddy,   *(hold up pointer finger)*
Happy New Year, Mother,   *(hold up ring finger)*
Happy New Year, Sister,   *(hold up small finger)*
Happy New Year, Brother."   *(hold up thumb)*
On New Year's Day, on New Year's Day.
This is what I always say:
"HAPPY NEW YEAR!"

Popping Corn

In January, cold winds blow.
Let's make five snowballs out of snow.   *(hold up five fingers)*
And next, we'll walk out to the barn.
Inside we'll shell four ears of corn.   *(hold up four fingers)*
We'll put the popcorn in a cup,
And then we'll fill the popper up.   *(cup hands)*
(Have the children pop popcorn in the classroom.)

Five Fat Walruses

Five fat walruses were at the North Pole.   *(hold up five fingers)*
One climbed upon the ice and fell into a hole.
Four fat walruses swam toward the ice.   *(hold up four fingers)*
One bumped an iceberg which wasn't very nice.
Three fat walruses had whiskers on their faces,   *(hold up three fingers)*
One got bored and went to sleep; he didn't like the places.
Two fat walruses went to look for food.   *(hold up two fingers)*
One swam far, far away; he wasn't in the mood.
One fat walrus was tired of the play.   *(hold up one finger)*
She flipped a good-by with her tail and then she swam away.

Snowflakes

We are ten little snowflakes,   *(move hands in sprinkling motion)*
Floating to the ground.   *(point to ground)*
"Sh," says the fairy,   *(put finger to lips)*
"Do not make a sound."
Children are sleeping,   *(clasp hands behind tilted head)*
But when they open their eyes,   *(point to eyes)*
The lovely white snow
Will be such a surprise.   *(spread hands as if making a blanket)*

I Am a Snow Person

I am a snow person, made of snow.
I stand quite still at ten below.   *(stand tall)*
With a big potato for a nose,   *(point to nose)*
And worn out shoes to make my toes.   *(point to feet)*
I have two apples for my eyes,   *(point to eyes)*
And a woolen coat about this size.   *(measure)*
I have a muffler warm and red.   *(circle neck with hands)*
And a funny hat upon my head.   *(put hands on top of head)*
The sun is coming out. Oh, dear!   *(make circle with arms)*
The sun is melting me, I fear.   *(sink slowly to floor)*
Oh, my, I was so nice and round,
Now I'm just a puddle on the ground!   *(curl up on floor)*

ᘯᘯ Finger Plays/Poetry ᘯᘯ

What Jack Frost Taught Me

Jack Frost paid me a visit,
On a January night.
He painted funny little shapes
On windows—What a sight!
He made a picture of a square,   (draw a square in the air)
And of a circle, too.   (draw a circle)
He made a pointed triangle;   (make a triangle with 2 index fingers)
Oh, these were just a few!
There was a curve just like an S;   (make an S in the air)
Some big waves went this way.   (make a series of W's in the air)
Some humpy shapes looked like an M;   (make small M movements)
I saw some tails like a J.   (make 1 large J)
There were four fence posts standing straight; (draw 4 straight lines)
I counted them, you see.
And then there were some slanted lines. (draw 3 slanted lines)
I think that there were three.
So many shapes! So many shapes!
Some different; some the same.
I learned them all, and then I found
That some were in my name!
(Write the names of several of the children on the board and discuss the various shapes in those names: tails, round letters, tall lines, humps, etc.)

The Little Mouse

There was a little mouse,   (hold up fist)
Who lived in his house.   (cover fist with opposite palm)
He wiggled his ears,   (wiggle fist)
He wiggled his nose,   (wiggle nose)
Then he wiggled his toes!   (point to toes)
He crept toward the dog,   (creep fingers)
He crept toward the cat,   (creep fingers)
He even crept toward me!   (point to self)
He stared at the dog,   (stare, wide-eyed)
He stared at the cat,   (stare, wide-eyed)
But he just wiggled and giggled,   (wiggle, smile, giggle)
When he got to me!   (point to self)

Windows

This house has many windows,
And some are very wide.   (measure with hands)
This one looks cross and frowning.   (frown)
You shouldn't look inside.
This window looks quite happy.   (look happy)
This window looks quite sad.   (look sad)
This window is so beautiful,
It makes us all feel glad.   (look glad)
This window has bright curtains.
This window looks so bare.
This window looks inviting.
I wonder who lives there!
(This rhyme can also be used as a finger play. Suggest that children draw pictures of the windows with various expressions.)

Painting

Paint the ceiling, paint the door,
Paint the walls, and paint the floor.
Paint the roof—slush, slush, slush!
Paint the doorstep with your brush.
Now my house is done, you see.
You may come and visit me.
I've been working very hard,
To paint my playhouse in the yard.
(Pantomime the action of painting. Ask, "What else would you paint if you were painting a house?")

Hands on Hips

Hands on hips, now turn around.
Plant your feet here in the ground.
Twist your hips, now stretch and bend.
Turn around, smile at a friend.
Bend your body, sway and sway.
That is all we'll do today!
(Read very slowly so that the children will have sufficient time to perform each action.)

Houses

This is a nest for the bluebird.   (cup hands, hold palms up)
This is a hive for the bee.   (put fists together, palm to palm)
This is a hole for the bunny rabbit.   (make a hole with fingers)
And this is a house for me.   (hold fingertips together to make a peak)

Guess Who

Secrets are fun, aren't they? Guess the secret in my song.

Suggestion: Pretend you are Jack Frost. With your "brush," "paint" in time to your singing.

Jack Frost Dance

Play music in 6/8 tempo, suggestive of running steps and quick, jerky movements. To indicate the time for the sun to come out, change to a waltz tempo.

Talk about how Jack Frost comes out from hiding at night and with a brush and paint pot, quickly makes windows frosty and sidewalks slippery. He pinches people's fingers. When his work is done, he dances gayly until the sun comes out—and then slyly and quietly creeps back into his hiding place for the day.

Warm Mittens

No matter how cold the weather is, our hands are snug and warm in mittens. Sometimes mothers or grandmothers knit them for us. What is brighter than a pair of red ones! It is fun to take a skein of yarn, wind it into a ball, and watch someone knitting a mitten from one little loop to the end. Children can help roll balls of yarn ready for knitting.

How did the child in this song help? Who got the mittens?

Suggestion: When you come to the end of this song, hold up your hands like mittens and show both sides of them, when you say "both to you."

On a Dog Sled

Wherever people live in the world they have ways of traveling around. Up in the far north countries, Eskimos get around over the ice and snow on dog sleds. These sleds are long and low with a back like the back of a chair. Several dogs in pairs are hitched up to the sleds. There is a leader dog out in front. This dog understands all the calls of the driver and leads the team over the snow and ice, running as fast as the wind.

I should like to ride, I know, With a lit-tle Es-ki-mo,

Thru the win-ter winds that blow, Dressed in fur from head to toe,

Sail-ing o-ver ice and snow On a dog sled. Oh, ho, ho!

Suggestion: Sit on the sled and drive your team while you sing. Sing and ride smoothly.

Playing in the Snow

What is more fun than to play out-of-doors after a snowstorm? If you are warmly dressed, you can lie down and roll in the snow as much as you like. There are so many things to do. Tell me about the fun you have when you play in the snow.

HAPPILY

I rolled and tum-bled in the snow, In my fun and play.
I made a tun-nel to the tree, Round and ver-y low.

I was white from head to toe, A cold and win-try day.
Pic-tures ev-'ry one could see, I drew up-on the snow.

Suggestion. Now that you know the song, could you think of a different name for it? With one finger, draw a picture in the snow as you sing.

If You Can't Be the Sun, Be a Star

(This is a wonderful song to be sung in a round.)

Music Boxes

Bring in several music boxes. Ask the children to bring one from home, if possible. Play each music box and have the children guess what the song is. Talk about music boxes.

Our School Song

Tell the children that they are going to help you write a song especially for your school. Choose a melody that the children already know, for example a college song like "On, Wisconsin," or a patriotic song. Guide the children to help you choose the words for their school song.

Here is an example of a school song that we wrote when I was teaching at a Day School and Research Center called "Sheltering Arms." The melody is the patriotic song, "The Caissons Go Rolling Along."

> Red and blue, red and blue, red and blue, our colors true.
> We're the Tigers from Sheltering Arms.
> In our work, in our play, we are glad that we can say,
> We are happy at Sheltering Arms.
> We're proud of you, our colors red and blue,
> And our school is the very best by far. Rah, rah rah!
> And wherever we go, you will always know,
> We're the Tigers from Sheltering Arms.
> Yes, the Tigers from Sheltering Arms.

Hot Chocolate and Donuts

January in many parts of the United States is a very cold month. Let your children help you prepare hot chocolate.

Donuts are always a nice addition to hot chocolate. Here is an easy recipe (you will need a donut maker machine):

1 cup flour	½ cup milk
½ cup plus 1 level tablespoon sugar	1 egg
1 tablespoon baking powder	¼ cup oil
½ teaspoon salt	½ teaspoon vanilla

In a bowl, combine flour, sugar, baking powder, salt; mix thoroughly; add milk and egg and beat together; add oil and flavoring; bake 5 minutes in donut maker.

Winter Booklet

This is an ongoing activity that can last as long as you would like. During the unit on "Winter," let the children draw pictures illustrating wintertime. You may include a snow scene on black paper (use white chalk), white chalk drawing on light blue paper, snowflakes, trees without leaves, children building a snowman, skiing, etc.

Martin Luther King Jr. Day

January 15 was established to honor a great American black leader who practiced peaceful demonstration for equal rights. Martin Luther King Jr. was born in the South and grew up to become a Baptist minister. His work for equal rights was supported by people of all races, and he was given many awards for his efforts. He was shot and killed on April 4, 1968 in Memphis, Tennessee, and our whole country lost a great leader.

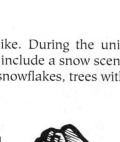

Discuss this holiday with the children. Correlate equal rights to sharing toys and taking turns, and explain how discussion and cooperation (peaceful means of problem solving) are more effective than fighting and violence.

Snow and Icicles Experiment

Will they both make water? Will they both make a cloud (steam)? Melt both in a pan on the hot plate and continue until the water boils away.

What is a snowflake? Look it up. What is an icicle?

Magnifying Glass

Divide the class into small groups and give each group a magnifying glass. Catch snowflakes on pieces of black paper and look at them under the magnifying glasses.

Who Is Awake? Who Is Asleep?

Borrow a world globe if you do not already have one. Using a flashlight, show how it is nighttime in part of the world while it is daytime in the other part. Let the children locate the country where they live. What is the name? What are the names of the towns where they live? Does any child know the name of his/her street?

Mitten Match

Cut four pairs of mittens from each of four colors of construction paper (sixteen mittens). Glue one mitten from each pair on a large cardboard background, placing them either as left or right and facing up or down. Leave a space next to each mitten large enough for the matching mitten.

Mount each of the remaining mittens separately on pieces of black or white construction paper. The children then try to match up the pairs of mittens, placing the separate mitten so that its thumb position matches the thumb position of its mate glued on the large piece of cardboard.

Thirst Quenchers All Year Long

This activity is meant to be used in conjunction with the activity "Changing Seasons" (*Bulletin Boards/Wall Displays*, page 131), but it could be done separately, too.

When you are discussing the four seasons with your class, and adding a section a day to the bulletin board, conclude each section by letting the children help prepare and taste a drink that represents that season.

WINTER: Hot chocolate and marshmallows. It is always nice to have something warm to drink on a cold day.

SPRING: Strawberries and orange juice. Put strawberries (fresh or frozen) and orange juice in a blender. This makes a foamy, healthy drink. Talk about how different fruits come into season in the spring.

SUMMER: Lemonade. Use frozen lemonade, or if you are more ambitious, squeeze your own lemons.

AUTUMN: Apple cider. Warmed and with cinnamon, apple cider is especially good.

Match Seasonal Pictures

Look through old magazines and find a wide variety of pictures that depict seasons. Have the children look through all the pictures and sort and match them according to the seasons.

Eatable Play-Dough

This is a really fun activity for any time of the year—fun to play with AND fun to eat.

1 cup peanut butter	1¼ cup nonfat dry milk
1 cup corn syrup	1¼ cup confectioner's sugar

Have children wash hands thoroughly. Mix, then knead the ingredients. Let each child do his/her own thing. After completing the project, let the children eat their dough.

Snow Ice Cream

Snow ice cream is a taste sensation with which children are delighted. Gather fresh, clean snow. Add milk, sugar, and vanilla to taste. Put in the freezer. It is also fun to freeze the ice cream in small individual paper cups.

Let's Get Dressed

You will need Pellon, assorted colors of marking pens, glue, and a shallow box.

Make figures of a boy and a girl out of pellon to fit in the box. Draw appropriate faces with marking pens on the figures. Glue one figure on the box bottom, and the other inside the lid. Make boy's and girl's clothing out of pellon and color them with marking pens. (Coloring books are a good source from which to trace figures and articles of clothing.)

The children can then sort the clothes into the appropriate section of the box and dress the figures. When the game is not in use, store the articles of clothing in the box. Make clothes that depict each season, so that you can use this activity when the children are learning about the four seasons.

Scavenger Hunt

Have a traditional and entertaining scavenger hunt. The hidden objects might be organized by color, shape, size, etc.

School Spirit Week

In this section, you will find ideas for organizing a School Spirit Week. Refer also to the school song activity on page 154, and the suggestions in the January information section found on page 129. Read through all the ideas before beginning School Spirit Week.

Send home a letter to the parents beforehand, explaining School Spirit Week. Include a schedule of the week's activities so that the parents can plan ahead and organize the things that the children will need to bring or wear to school.

MONDAY—Hat Day

Have each child wear a hat of his/her choice to school—silly hats, baseball hats, fancy hats, etc. Children love being able to do something that isn't always allowed.

TUESDAY—School Colors

Have the children wear clothing that is in the school's colors. If your school doesn't have school colors, have the children vote on what they would like to have as their school colors.

WEDNESDAY—Stuffed Animal Day

Many schools discourage children from bringing toys to school, since this can create chaos. But tell the children that this is a special day, and they can each bring a special animal to school. Use the animals for a language experience, a "show and tell" time, and as models for an art project. Children love to draw pictures of their favorite things. Display the drawings of the stuffed animals.

THURSDAY—Dress-Up Day

Have the children come to school wearing their best clothes. Be sure that the parents understand that dress-up day means party clothes, not costumes.

FRIDAY—Spirit Week Party

This is a nice time to sing your school song and have fun cheering with the school cheer. Here is a fun cooking activity that all the children can make to have at their School Spirit Week party:

one 5⅛ ounce box instant pudding (any flavor)
3 cups milk
Cool Whip (if desired)
colored sugar or chocolate sprinkles (if desired)

Put 1 tablespoon instant pudding in a baby food jar for each child. Add ¼ cup milk. Screw lid on tight. Shake jar 50 times. Wait 5 minutes. Top with Cool Whip and colored sugar or chocolate sprinkles if desired. Makes 9 ½-cup servings.

Scavenger Hunt

Let the children in your class have a real scavenger hunt. The list of things that they should find can include: an object the color of your school colors, something that is hard, something that is soft, something that is made of wood, something that is made of plastic, something that is rough, something that is smooth, something that is tiny, something that is big, something that is long, something that is short. There are many descriptions that you can give the children.

School Cheer

Teacher: Where do kids have lots of fun?
Children: Yeah! *(your school's name)*
Teacher: We all play and laugh and run.
Children: Yeah! *(your school's name)*

Teacher: All the kids here are happy.
Children: Yeah! *(your school's name)*
Teacher: We're the best, as you can see.
Children: Yeah! *(your school's name)*

Special Days

Although February is a short month, it is an extremely busy one! There are several special events and holidays that occur during the month of February which are of special interest to young children.

The month begins with *Groundhog Day*. The groundhog is an animal with which most preschool children may be unfamiliar. If so, find photographs of groundhogs so the children have a better understanding of what you are talking about. "Seeing one's shadow" is also a difficult concept for young children. Take the children outside and point out various shadows. The story of "Peter Pan" is a fun story to read to your class when you are discussing Groundhog Day. (Remember, Peter loses his shadow and Wendy must sew it back on.)

Presidents' Day is a holiday in February, a day in which we remember Abraham Lincoln and George Washington. It is nice to begin teaching some history and current events at the preschool level, but they are difficult for children to grasp because they are so abstract. Story telling is an effective technique to use when talking about Abraham Lincoln and George Washington. Talk about our current leaders, also. Who is our President and who is our Vice President today? Where do they work? What do they do?

And of course, February contains *Valentine's Day*, one of my favorite holidays. Valentine's Day can serve as a nice reminder to us all to remember to say all the good and kind things that we may be thinking about other people. It is a good holiday to remind children about being good friends, sharing, and taking turns.

Health and Nutrition

There are many fun activities that can be done in the classroom to promote a better understanding of all the things people should do to take care of their bodies. It is amazing how much information young children can understand about "staying healthy."

Below are some of the key points of the Health and Nutrition unit, along with some additional teaching suggestions for you, and some ideas the parents of your preschoolers may appreciate.

1. **We All Need Exercise and Rest.** Most preschoolers do not need any additional encouragement to exercise, but they may need some help learning about the importance of rest. Naptime and bedtime are often moments when adults and children have a difference of opinion. A radio with soft music often helps keep a preschooler in bed. A quiet story will help, too. Encourage a routine before nap or bedtime. If the child sees that the routine before going to sleep does not change, he/she will know that the "going to sleep now" routine will also not change.

With my own daughter (who does not like to nap or go to bed), I have used a chart made up of many little beds. Each morning after she has gone to bed nicely the night before, she is able to put a sticker of a little animal in one of the beds on the chart. When she has filled up a certain number of the beds, she earns a special activity. It works wonders. The bed chart would work for naptime at a preschool, too!

2. **We All Need Good Food.** (The Food Pyramid.) You have all heard the old adage, "We are what we eat." Explain to the children that our bodies are like houses. Relate this to the story of the three little pigs. A house made of straw will not stand for long. Good materials will make a good, strong house. Bodies fed with good food will be strong. Bodies fed with junk food will not be as strong. When we eat well, we also feel well. A fun healthy snack to make at school (or home) is granola. Use up small portions you may have left in a variety of boxes of raisins, peanuts, cereals, etc. Mix these together and serve in paper cups. This is a nice way to empty a box and a nice way to fill up children with something healthy.

3. **We All Need to Be Clean.** Cleanliness, grooming, brushing teeth, bathing, combing hair, general neat appearance—these are all important needs that must be met. People who look their best feel their best. I believe that is true for very young children, too. Just watch a three-year-old in a new outfit. There is no denying the fact that the three-year-old feels great, because the child thinks he or she looks great!

Brushing teeth can be a trying moment for parents. Here is a successful idea that worked for the parents of a child I used to have in my classroom. Every night after this child brushed his teeth, his father would rate the job he did on them. A "3" was wonderful—a perfect job! A "2" was so-so—passable, but let's try harder tomorrow night. A "1" meant the teeth had to be brushed again. This became a game every night for this father and son. Both enjoyed it and the child's teeth were always brushed without a battle.

Bathing is another area that some children may complain about. A little girl is often easier to talk into taking a bath. Bubble bath (for little boys, too), a few drops of perfume, funnels, basters, measuring cups, spoons, anything which pours well is fun in the bath.

Love Is . . .

Ask each of the children what they think love is. Record each of their responses on a white heart-shaped piece of paper, with the caption "Love is . . ." above it.

Let the children mount the white hearts on red construction paper. Doilies and glitter can be used to decorate the "Love is . . ." hearts even more.

Bubble Gum Fun

Children really enjoy this project. On a blue piece of construction paper, glue a black triangle (this is the base of a gum ball machine), and a white circle (this is the top of the gum ball machine).

Have many pre-cut circles of many colors (these are the gum balls) ready for the children to paste on their gum ball machines.

Older children may want to paste each gum ball individually on the machine. With younger children, I have found it successful to paint white glue all over the white circle, and then let the children put on the gum balls.

This is a good project for teaching the circle shape and the concept of "round," and for comparing sizes big/little and large/small.

Valentine's Day Mailboxes

Construct an awning at the top of the bulletin board or wall display and label it "Valentine's Day Mailboxes." Have each child decorate a white paper bag with hearts, doilies, wall paper, foil, felt, scrap fabric, etc. Throughout the week as children bring their valentines to school, they can go to the bulletin board and drop one in each bag. Tell the parents to have the children sign their names to their valentines, but not to address them. That way the children can put any valentine into any of the bags.

Good Food/Good Pep

Cover the bulletin board or wall display with a large piece of white paper. With a magic marker, mark the paper into four sections. At the top of each section, write the name of each food group.

Provide the children with pictures of food or empty food containers (egg cartons, milk cartons, frozen vegetable boxes and bags, cans, etc.). The children can then take turns putting these items up on the bulletin board.

Put pictures of people at the bottom of the bulletin board. The people should look active and full of pep.

Valentine Tree

On the background of this bulletin board, the teacher should draw a very large tree with no leaves. Have the children make valentines to display on the tree. Let them use as many fun materials as they can find in the scrap box. (If your scrap box is low, send notes home to the parents and ask them to help supply you with lots of interesting art materials.)

The Five Senses

Prepare the background of the bulletin board, following the above example. Draw the five senses chart, label each section, and draw in the body part that represents the sense. Then have the children go through magazines and catalogs and cut out many pictures. Collect all the pictures.

Show the children the pictures one at a time. Ask the children to decide if the picture represents something that you can see, taste, hear, smell, or touch. Many things will fit several or all of the senses. Let the children take turns taping up the pictures under the categories where they think the pictures fit best.

Wilbur Woodchuck

(The children can pretend to be Wilbur Woodchuck and crawl on hands and knees. Some can be Mother Woodchuck. It may be necessary to define "hibernation" and "woodchuck " or "groundhog.")

Wilbur Woodchuck (or groundhog as he is sometimes called) was **sleeping** soundly in his large burrow. It was winter and like many animals he was hibernating, having eaten tremendous amounts of food in the late summer. This extra food turned into fat in his body which nourished him during his long winter sleep.

In the compartments or rooms of the burrow, the woodchuck family was waking up. Mother Woodchuck was curious about the weather outside, for it was February 2, Groundhog Day.

Mother Woodchuck went into Wilbur's room and gave him a nip on the nose. Wilbur **woke slowly** and **shook his head.** He **rubbed his eyes,** and **crawled** out of bed. He **stretched his front feet forward** and his **rear feet backwards.** He **yawned. Squatting** on his rear legs he looked at his mother and then at his warm soft bed. The young woodchuck **bent down** to lay on his side. But Mother Woodchuck nipped him harder on his toe and he cried. Mother wanted Wilbur to go outside and check the weather. Wilbur didn't want to go, and he tried to get away by **crawling** into the other rooms hoping to find protection from his family. But Mother was persistent. She **chased** him up to the burrow opening. Wilbur had to use his sharp claws to **dig** at the entrance for it was full of leaves and snow.

Now Wilbur really didn't want to go outside. What if it was cold and snowy? He tried **moving in all sorts of wild ways** to make his mother think be was too sick to go out. He **stood up tall and bent to the floor, touching it with his front paws.** He **did this five times.** Next he **squatted and turned all around at his waist with his front paws up in the air.** That didn't work. Wilbur tried **laying down and bending at the waist, coming up to a sitting position (sit up) five times.** He **stood tall with his arms above his head and his feet together.** Suddenly he **jumped, throwing his arms over his head and spreading his legs apart (jumping jack) ten times.** Nothing seemed to work. Wilbur **tried laying down and swinging his legs wildly as if he were riding a bicycle.**

That did it! Mother Woodchuck nipped him hard on his nose and he **sat up quickly, rubbing his sore nose and breathing deeply.** He wanted to rest a minute.

Mother told him why it was so important to check the weather. People depended on the woodchuck on February 2 to tell them about spring. If the sun was shining and the woodchuck saw his shadow, he was frightened and crawled back into his hole. That meant there would be six more weeks of winter weather. But if the day was cloudy and the woodchuck could not see his shadow, he stayed out, meaning spring was coming soon.

Wilbur **stood up tall** and brave. He **marched** toward the opening. He didn't want to be frightened by his shadow but it was better than getting nipped by his mother again. Slowly he **crawled** with his **eyes closed.** He was afraid to look. Wilbur **opened one eye, then the other.** Something moved behind him! Like a flash the woodchuck **zoomed** down the tunnel into the burrow, into his bed, and **buried his face.** He was **shaking.** Mother Woodchuck came after him and nipped him on the tail.

Again poor Wilbur **marched** through the burrow and **squatted** at the opening. He had to be sure of what he saw to tell his mother, so he **kept both eyes open.** Slowly he **stretched his head out, his neck, two front paws, stomach, back paws, and tail.** He **turned in every direction** but saw nothing frightening. The sun came out from behind a cloud and Wilbur saw his shadow, but it didn't scare him. The woodchuck **sniffed** the air and his shadow.

He **climbed backwards** into the opening and down into the tunnel. He **scurried** into his warm bed and **turned around and around** for a comfortable spot. Mother Woodchuck followed him and wanted to know what happened. He explained how brave he was for he saw his shadow. That meant six more weeks of winter so Wilbur was going back to sleep. He **yawned and closed his eyes.**

A Visit to Good Food Town

Billy was in bed. He had eaten too many sweets and had a tummy ache.

"Billy," his mother had said, "You must learn to eat foods which are good for you." His father said, "I'll give you something to settle your tummy and then you can lie there and rest." So here Billy was, lying in bed and wishing he had not eaten so much candy.

When he went to sleep, he dreamed he was in Good Food Town. At the entrance to the town was a sign which read: "Welcome to Good Food Town, the Home of Healthy Boys and Girls."

Billy entered Good Food Town and started down Vegetable Lane. The first house he came to belonged to the carrot family. "Hello," said Billy. "I know you. You're Mrs. Carrot. You are a vegetable that's good for my eyes."

"You're so right, Billy," said Mrs. Carrot. "You need yellow vegetables like me every day. I give you vitamin A and C."

Billy waved goodbye to Mrs. Carrot and continued on his way. He soon came to a group of lettuces playing ball. "Hello," said Billy. "May I play, too?"

"Sure," said the lettuce children. "We play ball here every day. Along with good foods, exercise helps to keep our bodies healthy."

When Billy began to tire of the game, he said goodbye to his new friends and went down Dairy Street in search of something to drink. He was very thirsty after playing so hard. Soon he came upon a refreshment stand. "May I serve you something cool to drink?" said the Orange who was behind the counter.

"What do you have?" asked Billy.

"We have delicious cold milk, orange juice, grape juice, pineapple juice, and the specialty today is cranberry juice," said the Orange.

"No soda pop?" said Billy.

"We serve only those drinks which are good for the body and keep us healthy," said the Orange. "Our drinks give you calcium and vitamins."

"I'll try the cranberry juice," said Billy. Billy took a couple of sips. "Hey, this is good. It tastes good and is good for me, too. That's great."

Billy was discovering a lot of interesting things during his visit to Good Food Town. When he finished his drink, he decided to walk down Meat Boulevard. He said hello to Mr. Fish who was rocking on his front porch; he waved to Mrs. Chicken who was feeding her chicks; he nodded his head when he passed by the Hamburger family who was taking an afternoon stroll.

Billy knew about the value of meats. His mother had told him that meats help build strong muscles. Since Billy wanted to play ball in Little League next summer, he always ate his meat at dinner.

Before leaving Good Food Town, Billy took a stroll down Bread Alley. At the first house he heard laughter and talk, so he peered through the window. It looked like a family reunion. He saw all the bread family: White Bread, Rye Bread, Whole Wheat Bread, and Raisin Bread. There were cousins to the bread family there, too. The cereals, rice, macaroni, and grits were all there, having a good time.

"Please join us," called Mr. White Bread.

"Thank you," said Billy. "I'm on my way home. I've learned a lot about good foods since I've been in your town. I've learned that I should eat vegetables for vitamins and minerals, dairy foods for calcium and vitamins and meats for protein."

"What about the bread family? Don't forget about us," said Mrs. Macaroni. "We supply carbohydrates to keep you from getting tired as well as iron and vitamin B. You should eat us every day, too."

"I'll remember that," said Billy. "I must go now."

Billy waved goodbye to his friends. Suddenly he felt someone shaking him. When he opened his eyes, he saw his mother and father. "How do you feel, son?" his mother asked.

"Much better," said Billy.

"Do you feel like eating dinner?" his father asked.

"Oh, yes," said Billy. "I want to eat all the good foods that you have fixed for me. I know that I must eat these good foods to build a strong and healthy body. I'm not going to eat any more sweets. Oh, maybe just a little now and then!"

Lovely Liquids
(Physical Science)

Have ready an overhead projector, water in clear cups or baby food jars, and food coloring. As you tell the story, demonstrate color mixing on the overhead projector. Be sure to begin with clear water each time.

Once upon a time there were three good friends, Larry, Luke, and Linda. One day Larry asked Luke and Linda to come over to his house and paint with him. Larry had blue paint, Linda brought red paint, and Luke brought yellow paint. They started to paint, but soon discovered they couldn't paint grass because they had no green, and they couldn't make a pumpkin because they had no orange, and they couldn't make violets because they had no purple.

Accidentally, Luke spilled a drop of blue paint onto Linda's yellow sun. What do you think happened? Let's see what happened. *(Make green by adding blue food coloring to yellow food coloring.)* The three children were very surprised to see a green sun. But now they knew that if they mixed yellow paint with blue paint, they would get green paint. The children started painting everything green: green leaves, green lollipops, even green lions!

But then Linda got mixed up and put her red brush in the yellow paint jar. Linda said, "Look what happened!" *(Have the children predict what Linda saw. Make orange by adding red food coloring to yellow food coloring.)* The children learned that if they mixed yellow with red, they would have orange.

Then Larry said, "Hey, let's see what happens when we mix blue and red!" *(Have the children predict what will happen. Mix blue food coloring and red food coloring.)* The children learned that when they mixed blue and red, they would get purple to draw grapes, or violets, or cars, or anything.

So before the day was through, Larry, Linda, and Luke had six colors to paint with instead of three. They started with red, yellow, and blue, and they used those colors to make green, orange, and purple. What a fun day they had painting!

Ned, the Night Owl
(Earth Science)

Have the children close their eyes and then read the following story to them. Encourage the children to visualize all of the things that are mentioned in the story.

Hi! I'm Ned, the Night Owl. I'm going to take you on a tour of my world at night. Close your eyes, everybody, and think very, very hard, and listen to what I say. We're going to fly around and find out what goes on at night. Look up at the sky. We can see the moon coming up, and we begin to see the stars as the sky grows darker.

First, we'll fly over the forest. Many of my friends who live here are awake at night. Night is when they look for food and do their other activities. Look, and you can see the bats flying out of their caves. The bats come out to eat insects. Over there is a family of raccoons. They are washing their food before they eat it. The baby raccoon is holding a shiny piece of aluminum foil that he must have found in the trash. Raccoons love shiny things.

Now we have made our way to the city. Look at all the lights. There aren't as many cars and trucks on the streets as there are in the daytime. All the cars and trucks that are out have their lights on, so the people can see to drive. We can see lights on in some of the buildings, but most of the houses are dark. The families must all be asleep. The building down there is a factory, where people work during the night. Some factories don't stop their machines at night. There is our friend, Ms. Nettle, the police officer. She works at night to help keep us safe. The nurses and doctors at the hospital work through the night, too. Do you see the nurses and doctors coming and going at the hospital?

Well, I'm getting tired now and it's beginning to get light. The night is almost over. Did you notice all the insects everywhere we went? They bother me. Did they bother you?

The sky is turning pink in the east and I'm getting very, very sleepy. It's time for owls to go to bed. Thank you for keeping me company on my trip.

Groundhog Picture

Color and cut out a picture of a groundhog. Mount the groundhog on a craft stick. Cut a slit in a piece of paper—this represents a hole in the ground. Now the children can push their groundhogs in and out of the holes.

Potato Print Valentines

Cut a potato in half and cut a heart shape on one of the cut ends. Paint the heart shape a bright red color and press it on white paper to make a Valentine. Several similar valentines can be printed with the same heart shape cut on the potato.

Valentine Mailboxes

Ask each child to bring a shoe box to school. The teacher will need to cover each of the boxes with construction paper.

Provide the children with cut-out hearts of various sizes and colors, glitter, and glue. Now let them create.

The boxes can be arranged so you have a Valentine's Day Post Office. The children will enjoy delivering their valentines as well as receiving them.

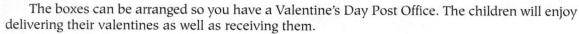

Silly Putty

Silly putty is always exciting to make and to play with. Take two parts white glue and one part liquid starch. Mix together. If the putty is too sticky, add more starch until the texture is workable.

Lincoln's Bracelet

Ask the children to bring 3 to 6 pennies. Let them shine the pennies with copper cleaner. (Vinegar and salt or an eraser will also clean pennies.) Cut a piece of clear adhesive paper and press in half, enclosing the pennies. Adjust this bracelet to slip on the child's wrist.

Cherry Tree

Give each child an outline of a tree. Let the children cut cherries from red construction paper and paste them to the tree. Younger children who are unable to use scissors could paste on pre-cut cherries.

Rip and Tear

Let the children make a torn paper collage using the colors red, white, and blue. After it is completed, you can leave it as is, or you could paste on top of the collage a black silhouette of George Washington.

Bubbles Are Circles

Children from infancy on up enjoy blowing bubbles. It is very easy to make your own. Here is one very successful recipe.

    ¼ cup glycerin
    ½ cup water
    1 tablespoon liquid detergent

Mix all ingredients in a jar and let the child use a bubble pipe or straw to blow bubbles.

Pipe Cleaner People

Each child will get three pipe cleaners. One pipe cleaner is used for the body and the head, one pipe cleaner is used for the legs, and one pipe cleaner is used for the arms. Follow the illustration on the left to see how the pipe cleaners are put together. After the pipe cleaner people are made, the children can move the people into different positions. Talk about how our bodies need exercise to stay healthy.

Valentine Dolls

Valentine dolls can be made with a small heart for the head, glued onto a tongue depressor or craft stick for the body. A small lace doily can be used for a dress. Have the children add facial features with a crayon or felt pen.

Valentine Cards

These valentine cards are made by the children to take to their parents. Fold red construction paper. Cut out a white heart or use a white doily and paste it on the front. The teacher should have a copy of the following verse for each child to paste on the front of their card.

Someone loves you,
Do you know who?
Take a look inside and see,
The one who loves you is me!

Inside the card paste a picture of the child. (Use a school picture or an instant picture.)

American Flags

Use a white piece of construction paper, 9" x 11". The children should cover the paper with paste or glue, and then paste red, white, and blue pieces of paper to the flag. For younger children, the teacher may want to draw the lines on the construction paper where the different colors should go. Have a real American flag on hand for the children to see. After the red and white stripes and blue square are finished, the children can add small white pieces to represent the stars.

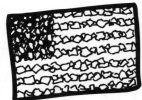

Our Good Meals

After discussing what foods are good for you, have the children cut out pictures of foods from magazines. Have the children decide ahead of time if they are going to plan a breakfast, lunch, or dinner. Give each of the children a 15" x 18" sheet of construction paper that has a plate and silverware drawn on it. Have the children paste on their plates the pictures that they found. Have each child take a turn showing the others what meal he/she has planned.

Healthy Stick Puppets

Make stick puppets of various objects that have been discussed in the Health and Nutrition unit (foods, soap, toothpaste, toothbrush, comb, people resting, people exercising, etc.). After each child has made one, go around the group and have each child tell you why his/her stick puppet is important for staying healthy. Have some extra stick puppets on hand.

Mr. Groundhog's Shadow

Tell the children the story about Mr. Groundhog and his shadow. Cut out a large groundhog (about 18" tall), and glue a tagboard rectangle on the back for a stand.

Place the groundhog in direct sunlight at different times of the day. Trace the shadows on paper. Paint, then cut them out.

Repeat this activity a month later and observe the changes in the shadows.

Heart Designs

You'll need various colors of construction paper, scissors, and glue. Prepare many cut-out hearts ahead of time. If you have children who are able to use scissors fairly well, you can teach them how to cut out hearts.

After the hearts are prepared, have the children glue them onto construction paper to form a design.

Valentine Fish

Each child will need one very large heart, one large heart, three middle-sized hearts, and one little heart. Have the children glue the six hearts together to form the fish, following the illustration on the right. The valentine fish will look nice hanging in the windows in your room or suspended from the ceiling.

Valentine Boxes

Ask each child to bring a tissue box to school. It doesn't matter what size or shape tissue boxes the children bring. Your Valentine's Day Post Office will look even cuter if the children bring a variety of boxes. Send notes to the parents well in advance of this activity so there is plenty of time to accumulate the boxes.

Have the children paint the tissue boxes red, pink, or white, using thick tempera paint.

After the boxes have dried, the children can cut out valentine decorations and glue them onto their boxes. Use a variety of interesting scraps: foil, wallpaper, fabric, glitter, sequins, etc. Write the children's names on their boxes.

Valentine Kids

Have each child in your classroom decorate a construction paper heart. The heart should be large enough so a photograph of each child will be able to fit onto it.

Take a picture of each child in your classroom. The children should glue their pictures to the hearts that they decorated. Display the hearts as shown in the illustration at the left. On February 13th, the children can take home the hearts and give them to their parents as valentines.

Yankee Doodle

Have the children make paper hats from large pieces of plain newsprint. You may need to help those who find it difficult to fold the paper correctly. The children can then decorate the hats with red, white, and blue crayons. A feather made from blue paper can be pasted to one side. Marching and singing "Yankee Doodle" while wearing their "Yankee Doodle" hats is so much fun.

Valentine Tracing

Name_____

Directions: Have each child trace the dotted lines and then color the picture.

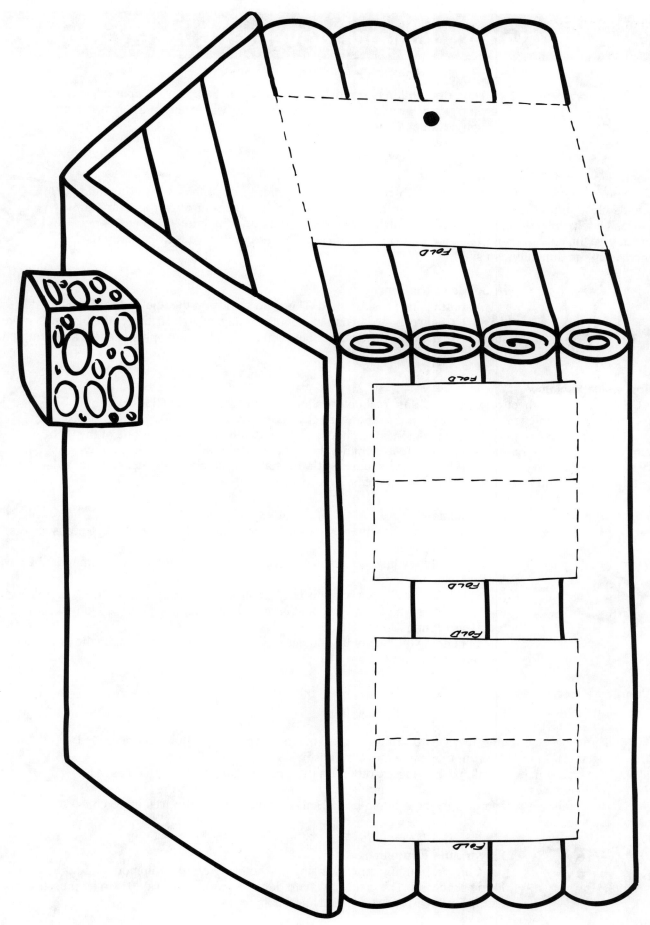

Color the cabin. Cut out the door and windows along the dotted lines. Fold along the solid lines so the door and windows can be opened. Attach the picture to another sheet of paper. The children can then draw pictures behind the door and the windows.

Lincoln's Log Cabin

Crawling

Have the children stand in a line with their legs wide apart. Let each child take a turn crawling under everyone's legs. The children will really enjoy this activity—it is like crawling through a tunnel.

Bean Bag Heart Toss

You will need to prepare a board with cut-out hearts (or circles) of various sizes. The child stands close to the board and throws bean bags, attempting to get them through the hearts or circles. Each time a bean bag goes through, the child moves back a little further. Do not encourage the child to move back too quickly. Success and gaining confidence is as important as increasing the difficulty of a skill!

In Between the Pins

A starting line is established. The child stands on the line and rolls the ball down the floor so it will go between two pins set about six feet apart. As the child becomes more and more successful, increase the distance between the child and the pins, and decrease the space between the pins.

Toss-a-Shape Game

Divide a large sheet of paper (such as washable wallpaper) into 8" squares. Glue a cut-out geometric shape in each square. Cover the shapes with clear adhesive paper.

Four children can play this game. Each child chooses four matching bean bags in one of the shapes depicted on the paper. From a pre-determined line, the children take turns tossing their bean bags, trying to get the bean bags in the squares with the matching shapes. The first child to get all his/her bean bags in the matching square is the winner.

Alert Game

You will need to prepare lines, circles, and other shapes of various colors, cut out of construction paper.

The children line up on a straight line. On the teacher's command, they walk rapidly, following instructions.

Examples: Walk to a straight red line; touch something wood; walk to a straight blue line; touch something metal; walk to a square; touch something made of cloth; walk to a black circle; touch something rubber, etc.

Depending on the ability and age of your children, you can make the directions as easy or as difficult as you want.

Running Races

Running races are always a lot of fun for children.
Examples:

1. Three-legged running races (two children each put one leg in a bag or have legs tied together). In order to run, they must move in unison.
2. The crab run, horse gallops, and tag are other fun running movements that can be used for running races.
3. Run pulling a wagon or pushing a hoola-hoop. This can make running races more challenging, also.

Playground Equipment

Climbing, sliding, and swinging on the playground equipment should be a daily happening for preschoolers. The greatest way to develop gross motor skills is to let preschoolers experiment with what their bodies are ready and able to do.

Aerobics

Put on a tape or CD which has a variety of energetic music. Recordings from the 50's are great. Lead the children in some simple aerobic movements and exercises, such as running in place, stretching in rhythm to the music, jumping jacks, arm circles, etc. Use your imagination. Children really enjoy this type of movement. (It is good for the teacher, too!)

Shadows

Use a projector screen which is free standing, or hang up a sheet. Set up a filmstrip projector or a lamp behind the screen. Turn off all the other lights. Have the children sit in front of the screen. Let the children take turns going in back of the screen. The children in front of the screen will be able to see the child's shadow. The child behind the screen can dance or move in any way he/she wants.

A fun variation of this is to have the children in front of the screen close their eyes. The teacher chooses one child to stand behind the screen and move. The other children open their eyes and try to guess who is behind the screen.

Over Relay

The children line up in a straight line. At a signal, the first child passes a 9" ball over his/her head in a relay fashion to the person behind, and so on down the line.

Under Relay

The children line up in a straight line. They bend over at the waist and spread their legs. The person in front of the line then rolls the ball between his/her legs to the person behind and so on until the ball is successfully rolled between the last child's legs.

Hoola-Hoop Roll

Use a plastic hoola-hoop or tire, and have the children perform these activities (all rolls should be executed with only one push):

1. Roll the hoop as far across the room as possible.
2. Roll the hoop straight.
3. Roll the hoop and run ahead to a designated line to catch it.
4. Roll the hoop and try to run around it as many times as possible.
5. Roll the hoop to a certain target area.
6. Roll the hoop while running alongside.
7. Roll the hoop to a partner, who then rolls it back.

Rat and Cat Game

With the exception of two players, all the students join hands and form a circle. One person is chosen as the cat and stands outside the circle. The other person is the rat and stands inside the circle. The object of the game is for the cat to catch the rat. The players in the circle can raise or lower their arms to allow the rat to enter or leave the circle. By lowering their arms, they will not allow the cat to follow and catch the rat. If the rat is finally caught, the rat and the cat each return to the circle after choosing their replacements. If the cat does not catch the rat by the time the circle group has counted to 50 slowly, then a new pair is selected.

Circle Stride Ball

Use a large ball. The players stand in a circle with feet touching on both sides. One child is "it" and stands in the center. He or she tries to roll the ball between the feet of any child in the circle. If the child is successful, he/she takes the place of the child who had the ball go between his/her legs, and this person in turn becomes "it." The children in the circle can only use their hands to stop the ball; they should not move their legs.

Dancing Dolls Dramatic Play

Tell the children that you are going to pretend to be a wizard. When you wave your magic wand and say the magic words "diddledy do, diddledee dum," the children should pretend to be dancing dolls. Read the following story to them, and begin the dramatic play:

- Once upon a time there was a wizard who could make electricity. With her electrical powers, she could turn children into dancing dolls. To turn on the electricity in her wand, she used the magic D words "diddledy do, diddledee dum."
- The wizard could turn the children into all different kinds of dolls. Can you help the wizard? On the count of three, say the magic words. One, two, three—"diddledy do, diddledee dum." Now pretend to be rag dolls, and dance around until I say the magic D's again!

Repeat, having the children act out different kinds of dolls (Teddy bears, "Cabbage Patch" dolls; "He-Man" dolls; "Princess of Power" dolls; "Barbie" dolls, "Beanie Babies," etc.).

Valentine Game

Staple a 2" piece of yarn to a heart cut out of tagboard. Hide the heart while the children sit with eyes closed. The valentine may be covered, but the yarn must be left showing.

Tell the children that they should all search for the valentine, but when they see it, they shouldn't pick it up or say anything. They should just go back and sit quietly in their places. (This way each child must find the valentine.) The first one back in place will be the next one to hide the valentine.

Find Your Valentine

Have the children stand in a circle. Choose one child to be blindfolded. The blindfolded child walks around in the middle of the circle. The first person that the blindfolded child touches is his/her valentine. Repeat so all the children have a turn.

ᴧᴧᴧᴧ Language Activities ᴧᴧᴧᴧ

For What Is This For?

Fill a box with pictures and objects with which the children are familiar. Show the children the pictures/objects one at a time, and have them tell you for what the objects are used. (*Examples:* Bed for sleeping; Shoes, you wear on your feet; Stove, for cooking food; Pencil, for writing.)

What Is This?

Place in a box a piece of chalk, a small toy car, a doll, an eraser, a crayon, a coin, a balloon, a book, and a block. Have a child choose something from the box and describe it to the class. The child who guesses what is being described gets the next turn to choose from the box.

Truth or Fib

Tell the children the story about George Washington and the cherry tree. George Washington was an honest man—he told the truth, not a fib. Now tell the children short phrases, and ask them to tell whether the phrase is the truth or a fib. Here are some examples:

The moon is made of green cheese.	All the children in the room are girls.
We get light from the moon.	There are girls and boys in our class.
People should eat five meals a day.	
People should eat breakfast, lunch, and dinner.	

Groundhog Play

Children really enjoy dramatizing the story of the groundhog. Find a picture of a real groundhog and explain the story about the groundhog's shadow and when spring is to begin. Let the children dramatize, discovering their shadows (or not discovering their shadows).

The Mood Mobile

Children sometimes need help in recognizing and discussing their moods and emotions. This mobile of many faces can bring a wide variety of feelings to the surface where they can be identified, accepted, and channeled into socially accepted actions.

Draw facial expressions on both sides of tagboard discs using felt pens. Suspend the discs from crossed dowel sticks.

Ask a child to look at the mobile with you. Ask the child to tell you how he/she feels right now, and to show you the face that he/she thinks feels the same.

You can also try making disc pictures in matching pairs and have the child find the two that are alike; or make all "happy faces" except for one "sad face" and ask the child to find the one that is different. These would be appropriate for 2- and 3-year-olds, while the mobile described above is more appropriate for 4- and 5-year-olds.

Feeling Balloons

Blow up one balloon for each child. Twist and fasten to 6-inch long feet. See the drawing on the right for an example of how to make the feet.

Each child should be given the opportunity to draw with magic markers how he/she feels this day. On the back of the balloon the teacher writes, "Johnny feels happy/sad/loving/angry/thoughtful, etc. today."

When tossed in the air, the balloons always land on their feet.

(Miriam H. Manfied, Edina, Minnesota)

Talking About Love

The teacher brings a pretty valentine candy box of old valentines to school. The children discuss love—whom they love, how they show their love, etc. The teacher leads the discussion into showing love to others and the importance of loving people. This is a good human relations lesson—accepting a new child, not excluding certain children in play, and not making fun of someone who is different.

Listen Carefully

For a change of pace when the children need to move about, sing the following:

"If your name is Mary, wink your eye.
If you are a boy, jump up high.
If you are a girl, wave hello.
If you have a dog, say 'Bow-wow.'
If you have a cat, say 'Mew.'
If you have a fish, swim around," etc.

Children like to make up their own lines for the others to act out. Encourage them to do so.

Top/Bottom

You will need to prepare strips of felt that will be used to represent shelves on the flannel board. Let each of the children take turns placing flannel board cut-outs on either the top shelf or the bottom shelf.

Abraham Lincoln

Read the following story to the children:

February 12 is an important date on our calendar. Sometimes it is printed in red. It is one of our special days because it is the birthday of one of our greatest presidents, Abraham Lincoln.

"Abe," as he was called, was born in a little log cabin in Kentucky. His parents were very poor. When Abe was just a little boy, perhaps as big as you, he worked hard to help his family make a living in the wilderness. Food was cooked in a large kettle hung over a fire, and on the cold winter days, it took much wood to keep the little cabin warm.

Abe slept on a bed of leaves in the loft, which he reached by climbing a ladder. Often the snow would blow in, between the logs, and on his bed.

There was not much chance for him to go to school, but his mother helped him to read books and to study. After his work was finished, he would read far into the night. Abe didn't have paper and pencils. He wrote on a wooden shovel with a piece of charcoal. The only light was from the fire in the fireplace.

He studied very hard, and when he became a young man, he was a very fine lawyer. Later he was elected to be President of the United States.

One of the most important things he did when he was President was to sign a paper called the "Emancipation Proclamation," which made all the slaves free.

Today the whole world remembers Abraham Lincoln for his kindness, his wisdom, and his honesty.

Have the children try to make some comparisons between Abe Lincoln's life and theirs. Abe lived in a log cabin; where do they live? Dinner was cooked over a fire; where is their dinner cooked? Abe slept on leaves; where do they sleep?

Parent/Child Role-Playing

Let the children take turns playing the part of a parent. The teacher can play the child. The "child" should ask the "parent" what they are going to have for breakfast, lunch, dinner, etc. Encourage the children who are playing the parent's role to try and make good choices for the meals.

Good Health Chart

Let the children keep a daily record (for one week) of their health habits. Include washing face and hands, brushing hair, brushing teeth, eating a good breakfast, etc. Mark the chart with stars or "smile faces."

Dirty/Clean

Talk about the importance of cleanliness—clean hair, clean clothes, bathing, washing hands and face, brushing teeth, combing hair. Show the children pictures of various clean and dirty objects and/or people. Have the children label the pictures either clean or dirty. Encourage the children to make statements about the pictures using complete sentences. Have the children speculate how the objects or people in the dirty pictures became dirty.

Daytime/Nighttime

Discuss with the children the importance of brushing their teeth (decreases cavities, makes healthy gums, keeps breath fresh) in the morning and before bed. Brushing teeth is often a task about which preschoolers need reminding.

Show the children pictures depicting daytime and nighttime (pajamas, breakfast, sun, moon, stars, rainbow, lamp on, lamp off, child sleeping, child awake, and playing). Have the children label the pictures.

What Did You Do This Morning? Name _____

Directions: Give each child a copy of this page. Use it as a guide for a discussion about all the "healthy" things people should do in the morning to get the day off to a good start. What other things do the children do in the morning that are not pictured on this page? After discussion the children may color the pictures.

Valentine Exchange

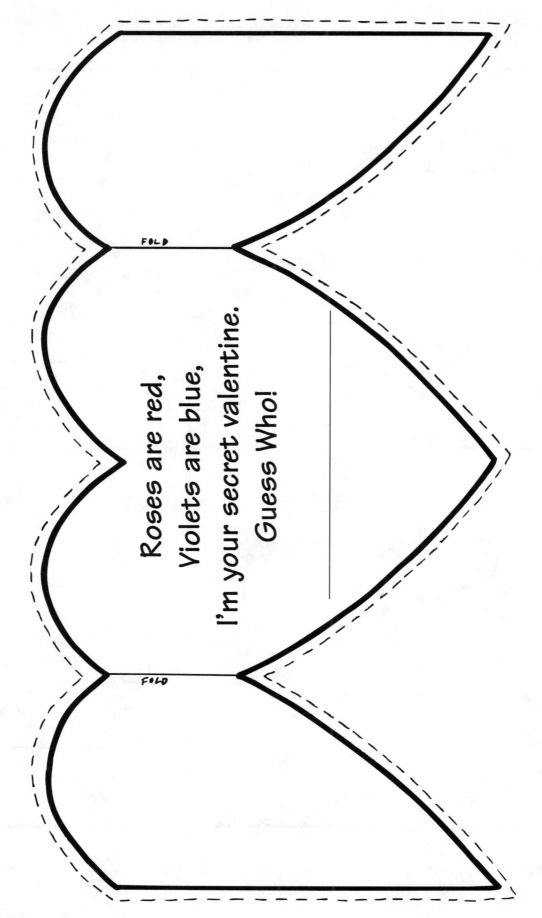

FOLD

FOLD

Roses are red,
Violets are blue,
I'm your secret valentine.
Guess Who!

Reproduce this page for each child in your classroom. Have the children color the valentines, sign their names under "Guess Who," and cut them out. Fold the valentines and seal them with stickers. Put all the finished valentines into a box. Let each child pick out a valentine. Once all the children have a valentine, let them open the valentines and discover who their secret valentines are.

Love Somebody

Love somebody? Yes I do!   *(nod yes)*
Love somebody? Yes I do!   *(nod yes)*
Love somebody? Tell me, who?
Love somebody, but I won't tell who!   *(shake head no)*

Mother Dear

Mother dear, can you guess
Who it is that loves you best?
I'll give you three guesses, 1, 2, 3.
There! I knew you'd think of me!
(This is a nice verse to include in a Valentine's Day card for the children's mothers.)

Shapes

Here is a big, round doughnut.   *(make large circle with fingers and thumbs)*
Here is a little, round hole.   *(make small circle with fingers)*
Here is a short little blade of grass.   *(crouch down)*
Here's a tall, tall telephone pole.   *(reach arms high and stand on tiptoe)*

Five Little Valentines

Five little valentines were having a race.
The first one was all covered with lace.
The second one had a funny face.
The third one said, "I love you."
The fourth one said, "I do, too."
The fifth one was sly as a fox,
He ran the fastest to your valentine box.
(This is a fun rhyme for the flannel board. Make five hearts and decorate one with lace, make one with a funny face, one with a fox face, and two that say "I Love You."

Groundhog Day

February second   *(hold up two fingers)*
Is Groundhog Day.
Will he see his shadow?   *(hands shading eyes)*
And what will he say?
If he says, "More cold,"   *(hug body)*
If he says, "More snow,"   *(raise arms and let fingers
Then into his hole   wiggle as they fall)*
He will surely go.   *(fist behind back)*

Special Valentine

(Prepare five valentines and five envelopes to use on the flannel board.)
Look at all these valentines,   *(put valentines on board)*
I made one for each friend.
I'll put them in some envelopes,   *(put envelopes on board under valentines)*
So each one I can send.
How many valentines do you see?
Start to count them now with me.
1, 2, 3, 4, 5,
One for _(name of child)_ ,
One for _____,
One for _____, too.
One for _____,
And here is one for YOU!   *(point to child)*
(Repeat until each child's name is mentioned.)

I Am Special

I am special,	*(point to self)*
I am special.	*(point to self)*
If you look,	*(put hand above eyes)*
You will see,	*(point to eyes)*
Someone very special,	*(nod head yes)*
Someone very special.	*(nod head yes)*
Yes, it's me.	*(point to self confidently)*
Yes, it's me.	*(point to self confidently)*

(This is a good poem to use to develop a positive self image and feelings of self worth. It may be sung to the tune of "Where is Thumbkin?")

Health

Let's pretend that we are sleeping,
Getting lots and lots of rest.
For good sleep helps all the children,
Helps us act our very best.
When we rise, let's eat a breakfast,
That will help us feel just right.
Let's drink our milk and eat our food,
And not leave a single bite.
Jumping rope and throwing soft balls,
Is a way to have great fun.
Playing, "Let's Follow the Leader,"
Makes us skip and jump and run.

Toothbrush Song

I jiggle the toothbrush again and again.	*(pretend to brush teeth)*
I scrub all my teeth for awhile.	
I swozzle the water to rinse them, and then	*(puff out cheeks to swish)*
I look at myself and I smile.	*(smile)*

Bedtime

When hands on the clock show it's time for bed,	*(hold arms like clock hands)*
And my parents say it's time for sleep,	*(put head on hands)*
I wash and scrub and jump in bed,	*(make washing motion, make jumping motion)*
Soon I'm breathing deep.	*(put head on hands and close eyes)*

Five Little Valentines

Five little valentines just for you.
The first one says, "My love is so true."
The second one says, "You have my heart."
The third one says, "Let us never part."
The fourth one says, "Won't you please be mine?"
The fifth one says, "'Til the end of time."
(Use fingers, holding up one for each line of the poem. Five valentines, cut from felt, make a nice flannel board activity.)

Groundhog Day

This furry friend might come out once a year,
To see his shadow if the day is clear.
And on this very special Groundhog Day,
If his shadow is seen, winter will stay.
For six more long weeks we'll have to keep warm.
We'll thank the groundhog for his quiet alarm.
(Explain the story of the groundhog to the children.)

Five Little Mice

Five little mice went out to play,
Over the field and far away.
Mother Mouse said, "Squeak, squeak, squeak."
Four little mice came out to peek.
Four little mice went out to play,
Over the field and far away.
Mother Mouse said, "Squeak, squeak, squeak."
Three little mice came out to peek.
Three little mice went out to play.
Over the field and far away.
Mother Mouse said, "Squeak, squeak, squeak."
Two little mice came out to peek.
Two little mice went out to play.
Over the field and far away.
Mother Mouse said, "Squeak, squeak, squeak."
One little mouse came out to peek.
One little mouse went out to play.
Over the field and far away.
Mother Mouse said, "Squeak, squeak, squeak."
No little mice came out to peek.
No little mice went out to play.
Over the field and far away.
So Mother Mouse said **"SQUEAK, SQUEAK, SQUEAK."**
Five little mice came out to peek.
(Make five little mice and one Mother Mouse from patterns on page 11. Attach paper clips to mice. Set up a shallow cardboard box straddling two tables, allowing enough room around the box for the children to be able to reach under it. Teach the children the rhyme, and then have them act out the rhyme, using magnets under the box to make the mice move.)

The Second of February

There's only one day the whole long year,
That I hope and pray the sun won't appear.
The second of February, you all know,
The groundhog goes searching for his shadow.
If he should find it, the story is told,
We'll have six more weeks of winter's cold.
But if it's cloudy, his shadow's not there,
There'll soon be warm weather and days will be fair.
So please, Sun, for just this one day,
Find a big dark cloud—**and stay away!**

Making Valentines

In February, what shall I do?
I'll make some valentines for you.
The first will have a cupid's face;
The second will be trimmed with lace;
The third will have some roses pink;
The fourth will have a verse in ink;
The fifth will have a ribbon bow;
The sixth will glisten like the snow;
The seventh will have some lines I drew;
The eighth some flowers—just a few;
The ninth will have three little birds;
The tenth will have three little words—
I Love You!
(The odds and ends box will contain materials to inspire creativity in making valentines. Read the poem a second time and ask the children which valentine they would like to make.)

The Valentine Shop

There is the nicest valentine shop.
Before I pass, I try to stop.
Inside the shop, I always see,
Valentines for my family.
Brothers, sisters, aunts, and cousins,
Friends and classmates by the dozens.
A tiny one, a nickel buys.
A dime is for a bigger size.
A quarter for a much bigger size.
A dollar for the biggest size.
(Have a valentine box where children can drop in valentines for their friends. Have the children draw small to large valentines to learn seriation.)

A Valentine from Grandma

A little girl's grandma lived in another city, many miles away. Not very often could Grandma visit her, but she always came at Christmas and in summer vacation. What fun they had—shopping, making cookies, sewing doll clothes, and reading stories! When Grandma went home, she wrote letters and often sent surprises to the girl.

What was the girl expecting from Grandma in this song?

SMOOTHLY

I'm look-ing out of the win-dow. Where can the post-man be? A

Val - en - tine I know will come From Grand - ma dear, to me.

A Valentine March

Every child will cut out a big heart from a piece of red construction paper 6" x 9". Point out a line of march and place all but two of the hearts anywhere on the floor in the line of march.

Play a march. The children march until the music stops (at an unexpected place) and the two children not finding a heart to stand by will be eliminated. Proceed to the end of the game. Let the last two "march it out" to find the champion.

Younger children may simply enjoy the fun of marching on the hearts, rather than playing the game.

Making a Valentine

I will make a Val - en - tine,

Send it off to you. A

heart of red with lac - es fine!

You will like it, too.

Stay Healthy

(Sing to the tune of "Row, Row, Row Your Boat")

Wash, wash, wash your face,
Before you come to school.
Wash, wash, wash your face,
That's our good health rule.
Sleep, sleep, sleep each night,
You need to get your rest.
Sleep, sleep, sleep each night,
You'll look and feel your best.
Play, play, play each day,
Outdoors in the sun.
Play, play, play each day,
Healthy children having fun.

Brush, brush, brush your teeth,
Brush them every night.
Brush, brush, brush your teeth,
Keep them shiny white.
Brush, brush, brush your hair,
One hundred strokes at night.
Brush, brush, brush your hair,
You'll keep it clean and bright.

A Valentine

(Sing to the tune of "Skip to My Lou")

I have a valentine just for you.
I wrote on the card, "I love you true."
I wrapped it and mailed it yesterday.
Close to your heart I hope it will stay.

Roses are Red

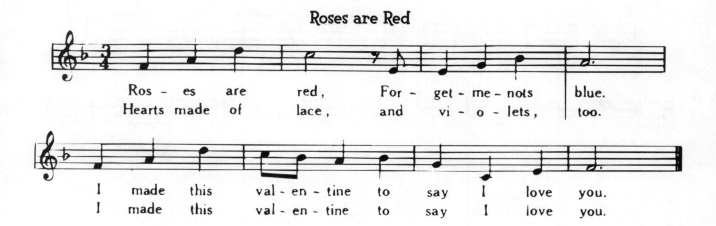

Great Americans

Will You Be Mine?

(Sung to the tune "Jack and Jill")

Valentine,   Valentine,
Will you be mine?   Please be mine,
This card I made for you. We're good friends, we two!

Pedro, Pedro

The following song tells a true story about a volcano that grew from a cornfield in Mexico. The name of the volcano is Paricutín. It erupted in 1943, and a center cone over five hundred feet tall was built up in six days. In nine years it grew to 1345 feet high.

Teach the song to the children, then add the movements after they are familiar with the words.

Chorus

faster

1. There once was a boy named Pedro.   *(put thumbs under arms)*
    He worked in his parent's cornfield.   *(make spreading motion with hands)*
    One day as he hoed this cornfield,   *(make hoeing motion)*
    A rock hit him on the leg.   *(slap leg on word "rock")*

    Chorus
    Pedro, Pedro,   *(skip in a circle, holding hands)*
    What did you think that day?
    Pedro, Pedro,
    Were you afraid that day?

2. He picked up the rock that hit him,   *(pick up "rock")*
    Then dropped it upon the cornfield.   *(throw "rock" down)*
    The rock was too hot to handle,   *(shake hand as if hurt)*
    And Pedro was awfully seared.   *(hold yourself and shudder)*
    Chorus   *(skip in a circle, holding hands)*

3. The ground began to open,   *(put arms together above head, then spread arms)*
    Black smoke came from the cornfield.
    It seemed like big black snowflakes,   *(wiggle fingers)*
    Were falling all around.
    Chorus   *(skip in a circle, holding hands)*

4. The ground began to shudder,   *(shake knees)*
    As it grew all around them.   *(extend arms, bring arms upward)*
    The cornfield was no longer.   *(shake head "no")*
    It now was a volcano.   *(spread legs, bring arms straight up)*
    Chorus   *(skip in a circle, holding hands)*

Groundhog Ideas

Be sure to explain what happens if the groundhog sees his shadow.
Let the children go outdoors and see their own shadows.
Make shadow pictures with hands using a projector light.
Use the projector light to illustrate the idea of the groundhog seeing his shadow.

Finger Jello

2 envelopes unflavored gelatin   2 cups hot water
2 packages "Jello" gelatin   2 cups cold water

Combine "Jello" and gelatin with hot water. Stir until gelatins are dissolved. Add cold water, pour into pan. Chill. Cut into squares with knife or use cookie cutters to cut shapes. (Save for your Valentine's party.)

Sidewalk Games

Make "sidewalks" from discarded strips cut from the edges of window shades (usually available at stores for the asking).

Tape strips together to make the desired length. Divide the "sidewalk" into squares and glue on colored geometric shapes.

Walk along the "sidewalk" and name the color and shape.

Variations: Put shapes of the same color on the "sidewalk" and name the shape only; or make other "sidewalks," using numerals, the color words, etc.

Queen of Hearts Tarts

1 cup flour   pinch of salt
⅓ cup + 1 tablespoon shortening   preserves
2 tablespoons water

Cream flour and shortening together. Add water and salt. Mix well. Roll into small balls. Press down into muffin tin with thumb. Bake at 350° for 8–10 minutes. Cool and fill with preserves.

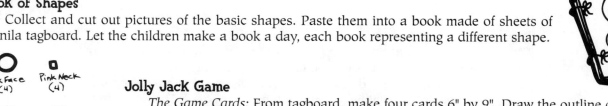

Book of Shapes

Collect and cut out pictures of the basic shapes. Paste them into a book made of sheets of manila tagboard. Let the children make a book a day, each book representing a different shape.

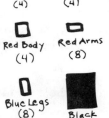

Pink Face (4)   Pink Neck (4)

Red Body (4)   Red Arms (8)

Blue Legs (8)   Black Storage Board (1)

Game Card (Make 4)   Jolly Jack Spinner

Jolly Jack Game

The Game Cards: From tagboard, make four cards 6" by 9". Draw the outline of the figure on each with a marking pen. Cover with plastic or clear adhesive paper.

The Felt Pieces: Cut pieces for the game from felt: Face—four pink circles, 1¾" diameter; Neck—four red rectangles, ¼" x ¾"; Body—four red squares, 2" x 2"; Arms—eight red rectangles, 2½" x ½"; Legs—eight blue rectangles, 1" x 3"; storage board for felt pieces—one black rectangle, 6" x 9".

The Jolly Jack Spinner: To make the spinner, cut a six-inch circle from tagboard. Divide into six equal sections. From construction paper, cut shapes as shown. Glue one shape in each section. Cover with clear adhesive paper. Cut an arrow from tagboard and attach it to the circle with a paper fastener.

To Play the Game: Four players each receive one card. They take turns spinning, and add a corresponding felt shape to the figure with each spin. The winner is the first to complete his/her figure.

Valentine Cookies

Here is an easy method for creating some very fancy valentine cookies. Purchase some pre-made rolls of sugar cookie dough—the type of dough that comes wrapped in long plastic rolls and needs only to be sliced before baking. Slice the dough and then cut out with a small heart-shaped cookie cutter. Bake the heart-shaped cookies. After baking the cookies, let the children frost them using pre-made canned frosting. Small candies or colored sugar can be added to make them look very fancy. Save the cookies until the Valentine's Day party.

Valentine Bingo

Prepare four or six heart-shaped cards, 9" x 12" with "I Love You" printed on them. For each player, print a set of alphabet letters, I, L, O, V, E, Y, O, U, on 1½" hearts. Make a heart-shaped spinner that has these letters printed on it. Players take turns spinning. The one to cover his/her letters first is the winner.

Valentine's Day Party

You and your class have already prepared the valentine cookies. To accompany the cookies, prepare a red juice. Before the party, you should freeze ice cubes made from the same type of juice that will be served at the party. Children think that juice ice cubes are rather like popsicles floating around in their drinks. Many parents send candy to school on Valentine's Day, so you probably don't need to prepare anything else for the children to eat or drink.

After eating, have the children go through their valentine mailboxes. It is to hard to wait to get home to look at your valentines. Let the children open them at school. If some are lost before the children are picked up to go home, well, that is the price that has to be paid for enthusiastic excitement.

"Pin the Kiss to the Valentine" is a fun Valentine's Day party game. Use bright red lips made from construction paper and a rolled piece of masking tape.

Pennies and Nickels

Show the children coins and bills with pictures of Abraham Lincoln and George Washington. Have the children sort pennies and nickels.

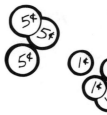

String-a-Long

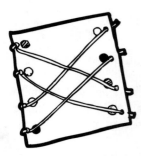

This board can be made to teach a wide variety of concepts. For the purpose of the Health unit in this issue, show the four different food groups on the board.

Here's how you make the string-a-long board. Cut a piece of poster board to measure 9" x 12". Stick four different seals down the left side of the poster board. Then stick four identical seals on the right side of the poster board, but not in the same order as on the left side. Cover the poster board with clear contact paper. Punch a hole by each seal on the left side of the poster board. Tie 15" lengths of string through these holes, and dip the other end of the strings into glue to make them stiff. Punch a hole by each seal on the right side of the poster board.

The children can then match the seals by putting the string through the correct hole on the right side of the board.

Here are some fun variations:
1. Use workbook pictures rather than seals.
2. Have a child match identical shapes.
3. Have a child match identical colors.
4. Have a child match like numbers and sets.

Valentine Jello

Here's an easy and fun cooking activity for your Valentine Party. The day before the party, prepare red Jello. Pour it into small paper cups and let it set. The day of the party, turn each cup of Jello out onto a small paper plate. Decorate with a dab of whipped cream.

Magnets *(Physical Science)*

You'll need large and small magnets; a variety of small objects such as paper clips, nails, buttons, bottle caps, wooden beads, etc.; a piece of construction paper; and a glass of water.

Allow the children to experiment with the small objects and the magnets. Which ones will the magnet pick up? Arrange the paper clips on the piece of construction paper. Let the children move a magnet under the paper. What happens? Put the paper clips in a glass of water. Have the children move a magnet around the outside of the glass. What happens? Place a large magnet and a small magnet the same distance from an object that will be attracted. Move the magnets closer to the object. Compare the distance at which the object will be attracted. Give each child a magnet and have the children find things in the room that the magnets will attract.

How Do Plants Grow? *(Life Science)*

Sandwich assorted seeds between paper towels inside a "zip-lock" plastic bag. Pour enough water into the plastic bag to soak up into the paper towel. Staple the seeds into position inside the bag. Seal the top of the bag and place it on the bulletin board or in a sunny place.

The seeds will soon start to grow, the roots growing down toward the water and the stems growing up toward the sunlight. Compare the growth of the different plants daily.

Make the Dolls Dance *(Physical Science)*

Read the following explanation of electricity to the children:

Electricity is very important. All kinds of things in our houses use electricity: lamps, washing machines, stoves, televisions, radios, telephones. Electricity can help keep us warm in the winter and cool in the summer.

There are two kinds of electricity. The kind that we just talked about is called "current" electricity. It is extremely dangerous. Children shouldn't play with things that use current electricity.

The other kind of electricity is called "static" electricity. It isn't as dangerous. Static electricity happens when two things are rubbed against each other. We are going to do an experiment where you will see how static electricity can make paper dolls dance.

You will need a cardboard box, a clear cellophane folder cover, a string of paper dolls cut slightly smaller than the depth of the box, and a handkerchief or tissue.

Cut the clear cellophane folder cover to make a cover for the box. Stand the dolls up in the box. Cover the cardboard box with the cellophane lid. Rub the top of the box with the handkerchief or tissue. The dolls will "dance" because of the static electricity created by the rubbing.

Floating Fish *(Life Science)*

Here is a fun experiment that will actually make a fish move in water. Cut a piece of tagboard into the shape of a fish. Cut a slit in the tail of the fish. Punch a hole at the end of the slit, and put a drop of cooking oil in this hole. Place the fish on the surface of the water. The fish will move forward under its own power.

Comparing Rocks *(Earth Science)*

You will need an assortment of rocks and a nail. Have the children compare the rocks, looking at several different features:

1. Is this rock hard or soft? Can you scratch it with a nail?
2. What color is the rock?
3. How big is the rock?
4. Is the rock rough or smooth?
5. What shape is the rock?

Only Odors *(Life Science)*

Read the following explanation of the sense of smell to the children:

Being able to smell odors is very important to people and animals. The air carries odors. When we breathe in air, odors are carried into our noses and from there messages about the odors go to the brain.

The senses of taste and smell work together. Some foods wouldn't have any taste if you couldn't smell them. Try this experiment. Hold your nose and eat a piece of potato and a piece of onion. Can you tell the difference between the two?

The sense of smell is also very important to animals. Some animals use odors to recognize where they live and where food will be.

For the experiment, you will need things for children to smell, such as an onion, a lemon, perfume, etc. Let the children smell the things you have collected. Then have them walk around the room, smelling objects they normally wouldn't smell, such as blocks, chalk, color crayons, the pencil sharpener, etc. Have the children tell what was their favorite smell or their least favorite smell.

Here are some other fun ideas:

1. Put a variety of things to smell in baby food jars. Have the children close their eyes, smell what is in the jar, and try to identify it.
2. Have the children make an odor book, cutting out pictures to illustrate favorite smells, "yucky" smells, sweet smells, etc.

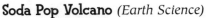

Indoor Jets *(Physical Science)*

Read the following explanation of jets to the children:

All of you have probably seen jet airplanes fly over your house or school. Jet airplanes work a special way. The engine of the jet airplane blows air out the back of the airplane. When this air shoots backward, it bumps into the air around the airplane, and the reaction pushes the airplane forward.

Then perform this experiment to demonstrate jet propulsion. String fishing line between two chairs. Thread a straw onto the fishing line, and tape an oblong balloon to the straw. Blow up the balloon partially, then hold until ready. When ready, let the balloon go. The balloon will propel the straw down the fishing line.

Soda Pop Volcano *(Earth Science)*

For this experiment, you will need a bottle of soda pop and a plastic tub or sink. Shake the bottle vigorously, holding it over the plastic tub or sink. Open the bottle. The soda pop will spew from the top of the bottle.

Explain to the children what happens in this experiment. When the soda pop is in the bottle, the glass keeps the liquid quiet, even when the bottle is shaken vigorously. But when the lid is removed, the gas in the soda pop escapes and pushes the soda pop out of the bottle. This is similar to the way volcanoes happen.

Daytime/Nighttime *(Earth Science)*

Make a sun made from yellow tagboard and a moon made from white tagboard. Then choose two children, one to hold the sun and one to hold the moon. Have these two children stand on opposite sides of the room.

Tell the rest of the children to form a circle between the sun and the moon, facing out. Have them walk counterclockwise. The children who can see the sun should role-play normal daytime activities, such as eating, dressing, walking, etc. The children who see the moon should pretend to be sleeping.

Create Your Own Circus

The Circus Parade

Make a ring (as large as the room will permit), using the kindergarten blocks. The children parade around the ring. Play marching music on the piano or use a recording.

The Performance

THE RINGMASTER announces each act with a loud, shouting voice. Many circus songs and poems are available, and the group may sing a song or recite a poem before each act begins.

THE LIONS: "The lion is a fierce beast.
    His roaring makes me hide.
    I'm glad he's locked up in his cage,
    And we are safe outside."

The lions roar and act fierce, but at the crack of the lion tamer's whip, they take turns jumping on their stools, and finally, single file, they leap through the fiery ring.

THE ELEPHANTS fold their hands to form their trunks, and bend over so their trunks almost touch the floor. They then pretend to waltz in a clumsy fashion, swing their trunks in time with the music, and very slowly walk across the balance beam. For a bow, they stand on their hands and kick their feet in the air.

THE CLOWNS tumble on a mat, do tricks, and act silly. Some may do juggling.

THE STRONG MAN puffs and struggles, then very slowly lifts his "weights" above his head, and lowers them slowly. He then quickly picks them up and walks out of the ring.

THE CIRCUS PONIES gallop around the ring, sometimes by two's and sometimes single file. They close with a bow made by crossing their feet and standing tall.

THE TIGHTROPE WALKERS walk slowly across the balance beam, forward and backward. They then jump off and curtsy or bow.

THE ACROBATS wear leotards. On a mat, they turn somersaults, hand springs, and cartwheels. They also do "rock chair" (sit on each other's feet and rock back and forth) or any other acrobatic stunts they have learned.

(Simple ideas for making costumes and props are on page 191.)

Finale

Two children pretend to prepare to be shot from a cannon. With a drum roll, they bow several times, then crawl into the "cannon." Two other children are dressed similarly and hide behind a screen which is placed near the "net." With another drum roll, these two children jump into the net, then stand up and bow while the audience applauds. (The first two children remain hidden in the "cannon.")

For a treat, small bags of popcorn or "circus peanuts" are passed to the performers and the audience.

The Jungle

"Jungle Animals" is always an exciting unit to teach. Young children (even toddlers) delight in learning about animals: how they move, feel, sound, eat, live, and care for their babies. You may wish to use the following information for a March Language Activity.

ELEPHANT: The elephant is the largest animal found in the jungle. Some elephants have huge ivory tusks. They use the tusks for digging up roots to eat, or for digging water holes. Elephants have very large ears. They use their ears like fans to keep cool. An elephant's ears can also tell you when they are angry. When they are angry, their ears stand out straight. Elephants are very peaceful animals.

HIPPOPOTAMUS: A hippo is a very large animal, too. Hippos love the water. They stay under the water so only their eyes, ears, and nostrils show. Sometimes they like to walk on the bottom of the water. A baby hippo will ride on its mother's back. Hippos live in large groups. All the hippos help take care of each others' babies.

RHINOCEROS: The rhino looks like it is wearing a coat of armor. It also has a huge horn on its nose. A mother rhino will move her baby along by poking the baby with her nose.

GIRAFFE: Giraffes are the tallest animal in the jungle. Their necks are very long. They need their long necks, because they eat the leaves off the top branches on the trees. Giraffes can look over everyone's heads. They are often the first to know if there is danger near by. When they sense danger, they start to run. When a giraffe runs, all the other animals start running.

ZEBRA: The zebra looks like a short, fat, black and white striped horse. When a baby zebra is born the stripes are a very light color. As the baby grows older, the stripes get darker. Zebras live together in large groups. Because they stay in such large groups, they are very hard to catch.

MONKEY: Monkeys have very long, strong arms, legs, and tails. They use them for hanging, climbing, and swinging in the trees. Monkeys have four fingers and a thumb, just like we do. They also have four fingers and a thumb on their feet.

Monkeys take very good care of their babies. A baby will hold onto its mother's fur and ride as she swings through the trees.

TIGER: Tigers are orange and white with black stripes. They are beautiful to look at, but are very fierce. If a mother tiger has to move her baby, she will pick the baby up with her mouth. If you have seen a mother cat, she will do that, too. The tiger is one of the very largest animals in the cat family.

LION: Most animals in the cat family live alone, but not the lions. They live together in a family. A lion family is called a pride. The father lion is called "the king of the beasts." He has lots of long, thick fur around his head and neck. His roar is very loud. It can be heard for miles.

The mother lion (lioness) works very hard. She does most of the hunting. All the lionesses look after each others' cubs. The lion cubs are very playful, like kittens.

The End of the Rainbow

The background of this bulletin board or wall display should be a light blue to represent the sky. The rainbow can be made from construction paper or if you are very ambitious, let your children take turns (with supervision) painting the rainbow. The caption can be made in any color and put inside a cloud.

The pots of gold are made by the children. Following the "pot of gold" pattern, the children who are able to can cut it out and either staple it or glue the sides together. The children can then cut coins from yellow construction paper.

Here Come the Circus Clowns

Give each child an oval piece of white paper 9" x 6". Have them use colored scraps of paper or pieces of scrap material to make the features and the hair, hat, and collar of a clown. Use red and white crepe paper streamers hung alternately for the top of the bulletin board or wall display. Create the caption in red letters.

Let's Go Fly a Kite

Before beginning this bulletin board, have a discussion with the children about the March winds. March is a very windy month for many parts of the United States.

The background of the bulletin board should be blue. A white cloud, puffing like Mr. March Wind, goes up in the left-hand corner. Kites folded from different colors of construction paper with colored yarn strings cover the sky. A wide border of curled green grass at the bottom frames the picture. Kite tails have pieces of colored paper taped to them for bows.

If My Wish Came True

Ask each of the children in your class, "If you could pretend to be anything that you wanted, what would you be or where would you go?" Encourage the children to be imaginative.

Once the discussion is done, have the children draw pictures to illustrate their wishes. Make frames for the pictures and a label under each picture describing the wish. Add the caption at the top of the bulletin board.

How Do Animals Feel?

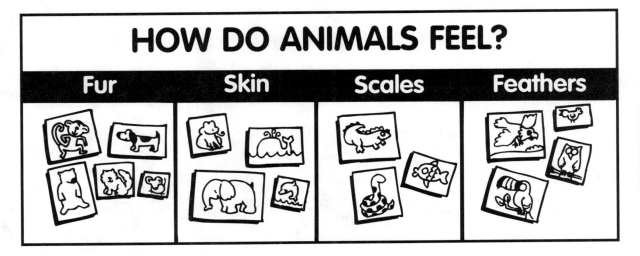

Divide your background paper into four sections: fur, skin, scales, feathers. Collect many pictures of animals. As a group lesson, show the children the pictures of the animals. Have them decide how the animal feels. What texture covers the animal's body? Let the children take turns taping up the animals' pictures under the proper categories.

Dragon Kite

The background of this bulletin board should be light blue to represent the sky. Have each child in your classroom make a kite out of construction paper. The children may color and decorate their kites in any way they would like.

Display all the kites on the bulletin board as illustrated. The teacher should make the head of the dragon. If possible, bring a dragon kite to school. Take the children outside and fly the kite. In the spring, many department stores or drug stores carry dragon kites that are very inexpensive.

The Circus Performance Costumes

Below you will find suggestions for making costumes and props for your grand circus performance.

Ringmaster

Measure construction paper to form a tube to fit the child's head. Staple. On another sheet of paper, draw around the tube to form a circle, then draw another circle about two inches larger. Poke a scissors through the center of the small circle. Cut wedges to the line of the small circle. Fold the wedges upward and paste to the inside of the tube to form a hat with a brim.

Lions

Fringe a strip of brown crepe paper to fit around the child's face. Decorate small tubs or wastebaskets for the stands. Staple triangles of red and yellow crepe paper around a hoola hoop to make the "Fiery Ring."

Lion Tamer

Make the hat the same as for the Ringmaster. Make a "whip" from a strip of crepe paper, about 10" x 20", which has been tightly rolled. Fringe the edges. Wind the whip with string or tape to the fringe.

Elephants

Measure a headband to fit the child's head. From a piece of 12" x 18" grey construction paper, cut a heart shape. Cut to make two ears as shown. Fold the straight edge back about one inch and staple to the headband.

Clowns

Form a cone-shaped hat and add a crepe paper frill. The ruffle is a 4" wide strip of crepe paper gathered to fit around the child's neck. Tie in the back.

Strong Man

Use rubber balls, or form balls from strips of tagboard, covered with crepe paper. Fasten a ball on each end of a dowel.

Circus Ponies

Use paper bags, cut as shown. (They may need to be tied under the chin.) For the mane, use a 6" wide strip of construction paper. Fold back 1" of the strip, lengthwise, and glue to the horse's head. Paste on eyes, triangle ears, and if desired, some brown or black spots. Add a plume.

Measure a band to fit around the child's waist. Staple a crepe paper tail to the band, made the same way as the Lion Tamer's whip.

Tightrope Walkers

The tightrope walkers wear leotards with a gathered crepe paper skirt. Add foil "spangles." They can each carry a child-size umbrella.

Use a balance beam for the tightrope. At each end, place a cardboard tube with a piece of yarn or rope fastened to the balance beam to give the illusion of a rope high in the air.

Cannon

Cover a clean trash can or large wastebasket with grey or black paper. Add a decorated cardboard circle "wheel" to each side. About 15' away, place two cardboard poles with a fish net attached.

The First Umbrella

Once an elf-child went out to play. He was an odd little fellow who wore a queer little coat. The bottom of this coat was cut into sharp points. The elf-child wore a pointed cap and tiny pointed shoes. Even his little ears and nose were pointed.

The elf-child was having a good time playing. He rang the bluebells and blew the trumpet flowers. Then he tied a spider's thread to a bit of thistledown and made a kite.

He ran after his kite until by and by the elf was far from home. Then the rain began to fall. The big drops came thick and fast. "This is a new cap and coat," said the elf. "I do not want to get them wet. What shall I do? Oh, I know what to do! I will hide under a big leaf."

So the elf hunted for a leaf big enough to keep him dry. But he could not find one. Then he saw a toadstool. "Oh, this toadstool is better than a leaf," he said. "It will keep me snug and dry."

So the elf crept under the toadstool. But someone else was already there. It was a little mouse, fast asleep. Now the elf was afraid of the mouse. "If I stay here, that great beast may eat me up," he said. "But if I go away, my new cap and coat will get wet. What shall I do?" The elf peeped around the stem of the toadstool. The mouse had not seen him; she was still fast asleep.

Then the elf thought of something. He smiled to himself. "I know what to do to keep my coat and cap dry!" he said. He began to pull at the stem of the toadstool. He put both arms around it, and pulled and pulled. It was very heavy, but at last it came up. The elf-child ran off with the toadstool over his head.

The mouse was left out in the rain. She got up and shook herself. "Squeak, squeak!" she said. "How very wet I am! Where is that toadstool?"

The toadstool was far away. The elf-child was holding it over his head. He was snug and dry, and his new cap and coat were safe. "Now I know what to do when it rains!" he said.

And that was the first umbrella.

The Mouse and the Thunder

Once there was a little mouse who was afraid of thunder. When he saw thick dark clouds in the sky, he would run and hide. "Thunder! Thunder scares you!" the other mice would cry. They would chase him and cry, "Thunder! Thunder! Run!" And it scared the little mouse, so he ran and hid.

One day the little mouse went for a long walk. He was far, far away. It was hot. "I'm thirsty," said the mouse. "Oh, I want a drink. I am so thirsty!" Just then it began to thunder, but the little mouse was so thirsty that for a moment he didn't hear the thunder. Then a great thunder rolled out of the sky. It scared him and he cried and began to run. Then the little mouse saw a frog.

"Thunder!" the frog said. "I'm glad. Now my pool won't dry up." The frog liked thunder. Then the little mouse saw a duck. "Thunder! Hurrah!" the duck said. "Mud is nice." The duck liked thunder.

"Why, they are glad it thunders," said the mouse. He thought and thought. "I know! When it thunders, we have rain," the mouse said, "and rain is good. If it rains, I can have some water. And I'm so thirsty!"

The mouse was right. Soon it rained. He got his drink of water and thunder didn't scare him after that.

Enlarge these pattern pieces to turn the stories into flannel board stories.

The First Umbrella   *The Mouse and the Thunder*

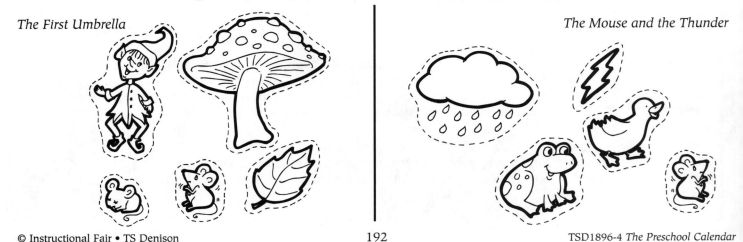

Poor Mr. Lion

1. The lion climbed into the barber's chair,
   And ordered, "Somebody cut my hair!
   It's far too shaggy and much too thick,
   So bring on your scissors and cut it quick."

2. The room was empty, with not a sound;
   The lion growled as he looked around.
   "Will someone tell me what's going on?
   And where have those monkey barbers gone?"

3. Behind the curtain, beyond the door,
   The monkeys shook as they heard him roar;
   But never a one would ever dare,
   To cut the angry creature's hair.

4. And that is why, whenever you look,
   At a lion's picture in a book,
   You will see his head is shaggy still.
   He has yet to find a friend who will
   Give him a haircut or a shave,
   For there isn't a barber quite that brave!

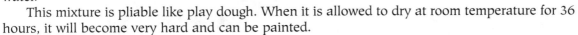

Fine Motor/Art Activities

Lions and Lambs

At the beginning of the month of March, discuss with your children the old saying, "March comes in like a lion and goes out like a lamb." Explain to them what that means.

After you have done this, give each child in your class the outline of a lamb on cream manila paper. The children can draw curly shapes on the lamb with a white crayon. Cut out the lamb and paste it on green paper.

Magic Clay

Heat 2⅔ cups water over low heat until bubbly. Remove from heat and add 1 cup cornstarch dissolved in ½ cup cold water. Stir quickly. Mix with hands if necessary. If too dry, add a bit more water.

This mixture is pliable like play dough. When it is allowed to dry at room temperature for 36 hours, it will become very hard and can be painted.

Stringing Beads

Bead stringing is an ancient and colorful art, along with being an excellent fine motor skill. There are many good manufactured kits of beads and strings. Unfortunately, children are never able to take home their finished products when they use a manufactured kit.

You can use macaroni and straws that have been cut for children to string. They can practice the fine motor skill of stringing beads and will be able to take their creations home.

Leprechaun Hat and Ears

Hats are very easy to make out of large sheets of newsprint. The children can decorate their hats with one large shamrock, or they can put many small shamrocks on them.

You can make pointed ears from green construction paper. Staple the ears to the outer edge of the hats.

Circus Train

The children may draw any animal they wish, (or the teacher can provide an outline of an animal). The children should color their animals.

Paste each animal onto a Styrofoam meat tray. (Many grocery stores will donate new Styrofoam trays.) Make the bars of the cage with pipe cleaners.

The animals in their cages can be displayed on the wall as if they were in a circus train. Add black circles at the bottom of the cage if you want it to look even more like a circus train.

Brown Bags

If you are planning to serve popcorn to your guests at the circus, it would be nice to have something special to put the popcorn in.

Take small brown bags and let the children decorate them with color crayons. The children can just make scribble designs or they could draw circus animals or clowns on the bags.

Lambs/Lions

Give each child a copied piece of paper with a lion's head and a lamb's head on it. Include the caption, "March comes in like a lion and goes out like a lamb."

Have the children glue cotton on the lamb's head and gold yarn (for a mane) on the lion's head. Discuss with your class the meaning of the caption.

Rainy Days

Have the children draw a picture of a cloudy day. Be sure to tell the children not to draw any raindrops on their pictures. The picture is just to be of a cloudy day.

Once the children's pictures are completed, tell them that you are now going to turn their "cloudy days" into "rainy days." You will do this by putting drops of white glue on the pictures. When the white glue dries, it will be clear and will look like raindrops.

Rainbow Colors

Discuss rainbows with your children. Has anyone ever seen a real rainbow? When do you see rainbows? What colors are in rainbows?

What makes rainbows so much fun are all the colors. Here is a fun project that will create a lot of different colors that blend together, just like the colors of a real rainbow blend together.

You will need white paper towels, food coloring, and muffin tins. Dilute the food coloring with water and put the various colors in the different compartments of the muffin tin. Fold paper towels in fan formation. Dip the paper towels into the food coloring. Unfold the towels, and permit them to dry. This project will seem almost magical to the children.

Eggshell Collage

Make a collage from crushed eggshells. The eggshells may be colored or white. Brush diluted glue into an outlined shape, and then place the eggshells into the shape.

The children may create their own designs or you may wish to provide them with the shapes of a rabbit or chick to fill in with the eggshells.

Walking Ducks

This activity has been entitled *Walking Ducks*, but it is a great project to do anytime of the year with any animal. Fold a piece of stiff paper in half, and cut out the outline of the body of an animal. Then cut a wheel for the feet out of stiff paper and attach it to the bottom part of the animal opposite the fold with paper fasteners. Decorate the animal and the wheel with paint.

Bunny Baskets

Cover a child's shoe box, or make your own box by folding and taping construction paper. Draw paws on the box with a crayon. Add a matching circular head. Paste on ears. Add facial features and a cotton ball tail. Pipe cleaners make cute whiskers, too!

Egg Hunt

Ask your children to each bring in a large plastic egg. Cover the egg with contact paper, or decorate any way you wish. After the children have completed decorating their eggs, the teacher takes them and secretly puts a surprise in each egg.

Hide the eggs around the classroom. Each child must find his/her own egg. Once the eggs are all found, the children may open them and find the surprises.

Cereal Box Elephant

You will need an oats box for each child in your classroom, construction paper, toilet paper rolls, tape, and scissors.

The oats box is the body of the elephant. Cut out the trunk and ears from construction paper. Tape them to the body. Tape a piece of yarn to the bottom of the oats box for a tail. Use the toilet paper rolls for legs. Eyes can be added with color crayons or markers.

Pipe Cleaner Giraffe

The giraffes will be able to stand up when they are completed. The children should bend the pipe cleaners in half for the legs. The legs and one long pipe cleaner for the neck should be stapled to stiff paper. Pipe cleaner ears and tail can also be added. The bottoms of the legs can be bent into feet, and stapled onto a stiff piece of construction paper as a base.

Lion Mask

Select paper bags that are big enough to be slipped down over children's heads. Cut holes in them for their eyes, noses, and mouths. Then decorate them with crayons or paint. Also, yarn may be pasted or glued to the tops of the bags for the hair.

Use these masks when you read the children the story of "Poor Mr. Lion," found on page 193, Story of the Month. The children will enjoy reenacting the story as you read it. Be sure that some of the children also play the role of the monkeys.

The Jungle Scene

Each child is going to make a jungle animal. The teacher should draw many different animals on 5" x 7" index cards. Older children may wish to draw their own. The children should color the animals and cut them out. The animals will stand up when their feet are placed in a small amount of clay or play dough.

Cover a table with green paper. Take a large piece of poster board and have the children decorate it, by drawing trees and plants. Bend the poster board into three sections. The jungle scene that the children have drawn will stand up. Place the jungle scene on the table. Arrange the animals in their natural habitat.

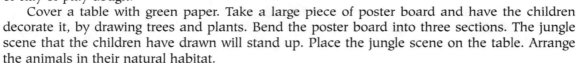

Shamrocks

Give each child a shamrock, cut out of an 8½" x 11" piece of green paper. Glue the shamrock on a piece of white paper. The children can draw a face on the shamrock and add legs and arms. A hat and a bow tie are nice additions, too.

Clouds

Give each child a piece of light blue construction paper. Have the children draw a picture of spring. Tell the children NOT TO draw any clouds. They will add "real looking" clouds to their pictures when they are done drawing. When the children are finished, let them glue cotton balls on their pictures to represent the clouds.

Tulip Cups

Have each child make a tulip. Glue a cut-out of a tulip on the top of a craft stick. Cut a slit in the bottom of a Styrofoam cup. The slit should be large enough for the craft stick to go through. Pull the craft stick down far enough so you cannot see the flower in the pot. Talk about how the flowers need sun and water to grow. As you talk about the things that plants need, slowly push the craft stick up and the tulip will be growing.

Shamrock

Directions: Color the shamrock.

Some Animals Are Real; Name _____
Some Animals Are Pretend.

Color all the animals. Talk about which ones are real and which ones are pretend.

Pass the Hot Potato

The children stand at arms' length apart in a circle. First using a 10" playground ball, they pass it quickly from one person to the next. They then move to a 8½" playground ball, then finally a 6" playground ball. Remember to reverse the direction of the passes after each cycle is completed.

It is also fun to have the children sit close together in a circle and use a real potato!

Clothespins

Children for years have enjoyed the traditional birthday party game of dropping clothespins into a container. (Many different types of containers work well—wastebaskets, coffee cans, quart jars, etc.) The children can take turns kneeling on a chair and using the chair back to steady their hands while dropping the clothespins into the container.

This game is very good for developing eye-hand coordination. Your older children will enjoy doing this activity blindfolded.

Name the Balloon

You will need a round party balloon. (I suggest having more than one on hand, just in case of a pop!)

The children stand in a circle. The teacher stays in the middle of the circle and bats the balloon to different children, who in turn bat it back to him or her. The teacher then can name a child after batting the balloon in the air. That child bats it up and calls out another child's name. Do not eliminate any children, but rather make it a fun game.

Pouring

In an empty salt carton or measuring cup, put rice, beans, or gravel. Have the children practice pouring from container to container. Rice and beans are easier to clean up than a liquid is. The children love the sensation of pouring too!

Act Like an Animal

Encourage the children to pantomime the ways that different animals move:

- stretch like a giraffe
- walk like an elephant
- run like a bear
- gallop like a horse
- perform like a seal
- walk like a monkey
- prowl like a lion

Walk on Stilts

You will need strong cord or rope and large juice cans or small coffee cans.

The stilts can be made by tying the strong cord through holes in opposite sides of large juice cans and then tying them over the children's feet. The side ropes must be tied so as to reach up to the child's hands. The child attempts to walk on the stilts, while grasping the right rope in his/her right hand, and the left rope in his/her left hand.

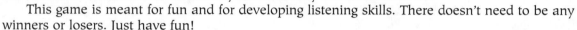

Real Kites

Hopefully your school has enough space outdoors so that you can offer the children the experience of flying real kites. Bring in one or two kites and fly them outside.

Children are fascinated by watching and chasing a kite. In all my years teaching, I was always surprised by how many children had never seen a real kite up in the air. It is such a wondrous sight, especially if you have a nice windy day.

Remember to discuss kite safety and power lines.

Stay Out of the Rain

"Stay Out of the Rain" is a great game on a rainy day. Have several tables in the room with the chairs moved away and stored in the corner of the room. Put on a tape or CD. Tell the children to walk around the room as if they were on a walk on a beautiful, sunny spring day. When the music stops, that means that it is starting to rain. All the children must take cover (hide under the tables) when it starts to rain. Everyone must stay out of the rain.

This game is meant for fun and for developing listening skills. There doesn't need to be any winners or losers. Just have fun!

Can You Make Your Face Smile?

Have the children follow directions. Ask, "Can you make your face smile? Show me that you can make your body do all these things: frown, whisper, hum, breathe, smile. Now wink one eye, and then wiggle your eyebrows, ears, chin, nose, toes, fingers, tongue, eyes.

"Now with your hands, find these parts of your body: nose, hair, eyelashes, eyebrows, chin, cheeks, ears, neck, shoulders, chest, tummy, seat, knees, legs, feet. Are they rough or smooth, soft or hard?"

Let's Pretend

Have the children pantomime the following things:
- Pretend to open the door and enter your home without making any noise.
- Pretend you are an ugly frog and suddenly you turn into a handsome prince or beautiful princess.
- Pretend you are walking in the rain and the wind is blowing hard.
- Pretend you are Mary and you are trying to get your little lamb to go home.

Give each child time to express his/her suggestions for things to pantomime. Choose someone to pantomime what the child has suggested.

Bunny Jump

Draw a hopscotch board, as illustrated. Instead of numbers, place a paper egg in each square and have a basket at the end of the hopscotch board. Let each child have a turn jumping on the squares. Each time the child lands on a square, he or she should pick up the egg. When the child reaches the end and has collected all the eggs, he/she can put the eggs in the basket.

For very young children, you will probably want to draw the hopscotch board with only five squares. Older preschoolers will enjoy picking up nine eggs.

Who Has It?

Choose a child to sit in a chair. The child's back should be to the class and his/her eyes should be closed tightly. Place an eraser under the child's chair. Point to someone, who quickly steals the eraser. The "thief" then returns to his/her seat and sits on the eraser. The child who is "it" turns around and tries to guess who has the eraser. If he/she is not successful after three tries, the child who has the eraser is "it."

Gross Motor/Movement Activities

Monkey Hunt

The teacher will need to prepare banana peels, made from long, narrow strips of yellow construction paper. Lay the banana peels in a varied path on the floor, under tables, on chairs, and around the other obstacles.

Tell the children that they are going on a monkey hunt. They must follow the trail of banana peels until they find the monkey. (Place a picture of a monkey or a stuffed animal monkey at the end of the trail.)

Tiger Walk

Tell the children about tigers. Tigers are very quiet animals. They move slowly and deliberately. The other animals in the jungle cannot hear the tiger when it moves.

Have the children take slow measured steps throughout the following rhyme. The repetitive words will be easy for the children to memorize.

Walk, walk, softly—slow—
This is the way the tigers go.
Walk, walk, get out of the way!
Tigers are coming to school today.

Creep, creep—softly—slow—
This is the way the tigers go.
Creep, creep, come and play.
Tigers are here at school today.

We Do As the Animals Do

Provide the children with the experience of pantomiming the movements of jungle animals (lion, elephant, monkey, giraffe, alligator, etc.)

Have the children pantomime answers to the following questions:
- How does an elephant move when she is taking a bath?
- How does a giraffe move when he is eating?
- How does a monkey move when she is scared?
- How does a hippo move when he is tired?
- How does a snake move when she is in a hurry?

Make-Believe Elf

- Pretend you are watching an elf dance on the lawn in front of your house. You watch the elf for a long time. The elf waves good-bye to you and lies under a tree to take a nap.
- Pretend you are a floppy rag doll with no bones. Flop like a rag doll.
- Pretend you are a tree with branches blowing in the wind. Make believe your arms and hands are branches.
- Be a snowperson melting to the ground. Show us how you would do that.
- Be a big block of ice. The sun comes out and you melt slowly.
- Pretend you just found a pot of gold at the end of the rainbow.

Blown by the Wind

The wind sometimes blows very hard and sometimes the wind blows very gently. Have the children pretend that they are sailboats, trees, clouds, and kites. The teacher makes the sounds of the wind. When the wind blows hard, the children should move as if they are being tossed about. When the wind blows gently, the children should move slowly and gracefully.

The Lion or the Lamb

This game is similar to Duck, Duck, Grey Duck. The children sit in a circle. The child who is "it" walks about the circle, touching all the other children on their heads. As "it" touches the children, he says, "tap, tap, tap." When "it" wants to choose the next child to be "it," instead of saying "Grey Duck," the child says either "lion" or "lamb." If the child says "lamb" the children must walk around the circle. If the child says "lion," the children must run around the circle.

Pot of
St. Patrick's Day Puzzle

Color, cut, and paste.

᭱᭱᭱ Language Activities ᭱᭱᭱

Let's Guess
Place a number of familiar objects in a box or bag (pencil, cup, crayon, paintbrush, comb, plate, doll, etc.). Let each of the children take turns being blindfolded. After the blindfold is put on, the child picks out an object and tries to guess what it is.

It is also fun to do this with wooden or plastic shapes.

Balloons
Using real balloons that are blown up to different sizes, have the children order and name the sizes of the balloons. Encourage these vocabulary words: "big, bigger, biggest; small, smaller, smallest."

Light/Heavy
Prepare many objects that are light and heavy in weight. This is a fun activity to do when talking about the strong man at the circus. Let the children compare the weights of the objects and use the vocabulary words "light" and "heavy." It is also fun to bring in a scale and let the children weigh the objects.

Tiny the Leprechaun (a story)

In Ireland, so folks say, there lived a tiny leprechaun. No one had ever seen him, but they knew he was there because of the mischievous things he did. Legend tells us that anyone who could catch him would get his pot of gold.

Every night the mischievous two-foot tall man played jokes on the townspeople. One time he stuffed cotton into everyone's shoes. When they got up the next morning, they couldn't put their feet into their shoes.

The leprechaun's favorite trick was to put salt in the sugar bowl. "Oh, how terrible my cereal tastes," the children would yell when they took a mouthful of salty flakes.

"This trickery must end," declared the mayor one day. He passed a decree that all the families of the town must make a special effort to catch the leprechaun. This was not easy, because the leprechaun never appeared until everyone was fast asleep.

The members of the families would take turns sitting in the living room at night to wait for the leprechaun to appear. Every night the leprechaun waited until the person on watch was asleep before he would come inside.

Each morning when the families awoke, they would know that the leprechaun had been there, for something mischievous had been done. There was no doubt that the leprechaun had been busy again.

One night Molly, the smallest member of the Irish town, decided to take her turn on watch.

"I'll keep my eyes open and catch the leprechaun," she promised.

"You're too little to sit up and wait for the leprechaun," said her mother. "Besides, you will surely fall asleep as soon as it is dark."

Molly would not give in. That night she waited and watched but the leprechaun didn't appear. Molly decided to pretend to be asleep and trick the leprechaun into coming inside.

She leaned back in the big armchair and closed her eyes. Sure enough, the leprechaun came out from his hiding place and started his mischief-making.

"I've caught you," said Molly, sitting up in her chair.

"Oh, no," said the leprechaun. "You have spoiled my fun and now you will have my pot of gold."

After that night, the leprechaun was never seen again. Molly was a hero of the town and shared her treasure with the other girls and boys.

Can You Help Me Get Dressed Today?

Discuss with your children that different weather conditions need different clothing—"Would you wear a snowsuit on a warm day? When do you need an umbrella?," etc.

Prepare a large figure cut from cardboard, with curly hair made from shirred gift wrap ribbon. Prepare a variety of clothes for different weather conditions. The clothes should have tabs on the top, so they can be put on the cardboard figure just like a paper doll's clothes. Give the children many different weather situations and have them decide what clothes the weather figure should wear.

Have your children name the over-sized paper doll. Keep the figure and make it a part of your morning circle time when you have your daily discussion of the weather.

Watch the Clouds

Watch the clouds move across the sky. Observe the kinds of clouds. See what "pretend" shapes can be seen in the clouds (shapes, animals, people, objects, and so on). Encourage the children to stretch their imaginations.

After you have observed the clouds, give the children paper and have them tear it into the different shapes that they saw. Paste the shapes on colored construction paper.

St. Patrick

Give the children some background on St. Patrick's Day. The following is some information for you.

Irish people throughout the world celebrate St. Patrick's Day on March 17. People from other countries also like to remember St. Patrick and the Irish people on this day. There are many stories about St. Patrick. One of the best-known tells that he rid Ireland of all the snakes. It is said that he charmed the snakes; they followed him down to the seashore, were driven into the water and drowned. To this day, the story tells, there are no snakes in Ireland. The shamrock is the national flower of Ireland. Many people wear shamrocks as pins or ornaments on St. Patrick's Day. The shamrock leaf is much like our clover. Perhaps best of all, we like the story of the leprechauns. These are the little people of Ireland. Stories say that they are shoemakers during the day, but mischievous little elves who play tricks on you at night. If you ever have trouble—or if things should go wrong—the Irish say, "Just blame it on the leprechauns!"

Talk with your students about playing tricks. Has anyone ever played a trick on you? Was it nice? Was it not nice? Was it funny? How did it make you feel?

Tiny/Giant

Draw a picture of a tiny fairy and a very large giant. Have the children think of things that are either tiny or giant. Use other words such as big, little, large, small. Let the children draw tiny pictures and giant pictures.

Alive/Not Alive

In many stories and fairy tales, children are exposed to a wide variety of objects that are not alive but do and say things as if they were alive. For example, brooms may dance, cookies may jump out of ovens, and furniture may talk.

Discuss with your children things that are not alive—chairs, tables, stuffed animals, etc. What makes something alive?—it breathes, eats, etc. What is alive in your classroom and what is not alive?

Hide the Fairy

Play "Hide the Fairy" the same way you would play "Hide the Thimble." Use a tiny picture of a fairy or a tiny doll instead of a thimble. Encourage the children to use positional words when describing where the fairy is, for example, behind, under, in, etc.

My Jungle Animal Book

Read the information about Jungle Animals, which is provided on page 187. In the article you will find some small paragraphs written about eight different jungle animals. For each animal, copy the paragraph on the bottom of a piece of paper. Make copies for each child in your room. Have the children illustrate pictures of the animals above the paragraphs.

After the children have completed drawing all seven animals, the pages can be punched with holes and put together in book form. Have the children draw covers for their books on construction paper. (A note of caution: This project should take seven days to complete, one day for each animal. The children will become bored and work too fast if they think they must complete all seven drawings in one day.) The children will enjoy "reading" their books to their parents.

The Animals Escaped from the Zoo

News flash! All the animals have escaped from the zoo! We must find them!

Hide pictures or toy animals in the classroom. Send the children on a search to find the animals. Help those children who are having a difficult time finding the animals. Make sure that every child has at least one animal when the search is over.

After the children have found all the animals, have each child tell the group what animal he/she found, where he/she found it, and why he/she thinks the animal ran away from the zoo.

Near/Far Noises

Use a CD player or a tape recorder. Turn the volume up or down to demonstrate the concept of noises that are near and noises that are far away.

To make this activity even more fun, have the children make a tape recording of jungle animal sounds. Play the tape for the children. Turn the volume up and down. Pretend that the animals are near you and that the animals are far away.

The Wind

Have a discussion with the children about the wind. What is wind? [Moving air.] Can air push? Have a child place a large piece of paper over the front of his chest and run across the room, letting go of the paper. What kept the paper in place against the child's chest? [Air pushing against the body.]

Discuss how the wind can help us. [Dry clothes, fly kites, sail boats, disperse seeds, etc.] The wind can be helpful. It is air in motion.

Can the wind also be harmful? [Blows trees down, blows nests from trees, makes tornadoes.] Conclude that the wind can be both helpful and harmful.

Loud/Soft Wind

Give each of the children musical instruments. Talk about the concepts of loud and soft. (This is also a good time to review "inside" and "outside" voices.) Use the musical instruments to demonstrate sounds that are loud and sounds that are soft. Give individual children an opportunity to demonstrate this for you.

Now have all the children play their instruments at the same time. Tell them that when the wind is loud, they must play loudly. When the wind is soft, they must play softly.

What Do You See in the Clouds?

When you were little, did you ever lay in the grass and pretend to see many different shapes and objects in the clouds? I think all children have seen incredible images in the clouds.

Draw cloud shapes on the blackboard. Have the children tell you what they see. Let the children take turns drawing clouds on the blackboard.

What Would You Need on a Rainy Day?

Color your answers.

Name_____

A St. Patrick's Day Elf

I met a little elf man once,
He wore a stovepipe hat.   *(place elf's green hat on flannel board)*
His face was round and mischievous.   *(place face under hat)*
He stopped awhile to chat.
I asked, "Why are your trousers green?   *(place trousers on board)*
Instead of red or blue?
Your coat is green and there I see   *(place coat on board)*
A buckle on each shoe."   *(place two shoes on board)*
I asked, "What are you doing here?"
And then I heard him say:
"Why, I have come to visit you
This fine St. Patrick's Day.
"I'm dressed in green from head to toe,
For I'm an Irish elf.
I wear a buckle on each shoe
Which I made by myself."
He said, "I've come to visit you
This fine St. Patrick's Day."
He sang a song and danced a jig,
And skipped far, far away.
*(Read the poem aloud before any action is taken.
Say, "Think of a St. Patrick's song the elf might
have sung. Paint a picture of him. Help me make
the parts of him for the flannel board. Show how he
would dance a jig." Cut all pieces from felt. Then
you are ready to present the poem as children take
turns placing the pieces on the flannel board.)*

Shamrocks

Shamrocks, shamrocks,
On Ireland's hills,
Greenest of green
Over rocks and rills.
Good luck they do bring,
For one and all,
On St. Patrick's Day
We can see them call.

Five Big Elephants

Five big elephants—oh, what a sight,
Swinging their trunks from left to right!
Four are followers, and one is the king.
They all walk around in the circus ring.
*(To pantomime, the children crouch over and clasp
their hands, then move arms left and right as they
walk. Choose four children to be elephants who follow
one chosen to be king. The "elephants "walk around
the room several times as the rhyme is recited.)*

The Balloon

Once I had a balloon   *(make circle with hands)*
That I held really tight to me.   *(bring circle close to body)*
There was a great big "pop."   *(clap hands)*
Now there's no balloon to see!   *(shake head, raise palms upward)*

This Circus Clown

This circus clown shakes your hand.   *(shake hands)*
This circus clown plays in the band.   *(pretend to play flute)*
This circus clown has enormous feet.   *(show foot)*
This circus clown dearly loves to eat.   *(pretend to eat)*
This circus clown has a round red nose.   *(point to nose)*
This circus clown has white teeth in rows.   *(point to teeth)*
This circus clown has very sad eyes.   *(look sad)*
He laughs, and frowns, and then he cries.   *(demonstrate)*
This circus clown bends away down.   *(bend down)*
What would you do if you were a clown?
*(Draw a large clown face on durable tagboard. Color in the features
and cut a large opening for the mouth. From a red scrap of felt or
colored paper, make a tongue. The children take turns moving the
tongue in and out as they make the clown talk.)*

Circus Time

Teacher: We will see a big parade.
All: The circus is coming to town.
Teacher: We'll have pink lemonade.
All: The circus is coming to town.
Teacher: The horses will put on a show.
All: The circus is coming to town.
Teacher: The clowns will march in a row.
All: The circus is coming to town.
Teacher: There will be some acrobats.
All: The circus is coming to town.
Teacher: There will be some tiger cats.
All: The circus is coming to town.
Teacher: There will be a buffalo.
All: The circus is coming to town.
Teacher: Come on! Let's go! Let's go!
All: The circus is coming to town.

Tall and Small

Here is a giant who is tall, tall, tall;	*(stand up tall)*
Here is an elf who is small, small, small.	*(slowly sink to floor)*
The elf who is small will try, try, try,	*(slowly rise)*
To reach to the giant who is high, high, high.	*(stand tall, stretch, and reach arms high)*

Ten Giants

Not last night,	*(shake head "no")*
But the night before,	
Ten giants,	*(hold up all fingers of both hands)*
Broke down my door!	
As I ran out,	*(make fingers "run out")*
They came in.	*(fingers "run in")*
And I hit one on the head,	*(make hitting motion)*
With a rolling pin!	

Five Little Bunnies

Five little bunnies, hopping all around,
The first bunny said, "I'm going to town."
The second bunny said, "I'll hide the eggs."
The third bunny said, "I will stretch my legs."
The fourth bunny said, "I'll eat a carrot."
The fifth bunny said, "I'll scare a parrot."
Five little bunnies, so soft and furry,
Ran around the yard in such a hurry.

I Saw a Rabbit

I saw a rabbit,	*(put hand up over eyes)*
I said, "Hello."	*(point to self and wave "hi")*
He didn't stop,	*(shake head "no")*
He just kept going:	
Hop, hop, hop.	*(make two fingers "hop")*

My Little Kite

I have a little kite—the best I've ever seen.
It has a long tail, colored white and green.
Dance, little kite! Wiggle and dance!
Along the ground you bounce and prance.
Up in the air my kite starts to go.
Up, up, up, swaying to and fro.
Fly, little kite! Fly and sail!
Dip and dive, and shake your tail!
It's fun to fly my little kite.
I hold the string, and hold on tight.
If I should let go—away you'd fly.
Good-bye, little kite! Good-bye! Good-bye!

The Elf's Coat

Under a toadstool, there sat a wee elf;	
He rocked to and fro and he sang to himself:	*(rock body back and forth)*
"A snippety-snappety, hi-diddle-dee!	*(say refrain)*
A clickety-clackety, one, two, three!"	*(clap hands on each count)*
He cut and he basted, this wee little elf;	
Because he was making a coat for himself.	*(hold up imaginary coat)*
"A snippety-snappety, hi-diddle-dee!	*(say refrain)*
A clickety-clackety, one, two, three!"	*(clap hands on each count)*
The little elf rocked and sang all the night;	*(rock back and forth)*
He stitched and he sewed till the morning light.	*(pretend to sew)*
"A snippety-snappety, hi-diddle-dee!	*(say refrain)*
A clickety-clackety, one, two, three!"	*(clap hands on each count)*
He borrowed some green from the grass on the ground;	*(cup hands)*
From a nut on the tree, he borrowed some brown.	*(put pointer finger and thumb together)*
"A snippety-snappety, hi-diddle-dee!	*(say refrain)*
A clickety-clackety, one, two, three!"	*(clap hands on each count)*
His coat was all done and he scampered away,	*(make fingers "run")*
Singing his song that was happy and gay.	
"A snippety-snappety, hi-diddle-dee!	*(say refrain)*
A clickety-clackety, one, two, three!"	*(clap hands on each count)*

∧∧∧∧ Finger Plays/Poetry ∧∧∧∧

Ten Little Elves

Ten little elves, dancing in a ring;   *(extend ten fingers and dance them back and forth)*
Ten little elves, hear them sing!
Oooooooooo—ooooooooo!   *(give cry)*
Ten little elves wave their arms high;   *(wave hands above head)*
Ten little elves give a loud cry;
Ooooooooooo—oooooooo!   *(give cry)*
Ten little elves in a hollow tree,   *(bring fingertips together to make point over head)*
Ten little elves quiet as can be!   *(fold hands)*
Shh!   *(finger at lips)*

Spoonful of Clouds

If I had a spoon as tall as the sky,
I'd dish out the clouds that go sliding by.
I'd take them right in and give them to cook,
And see if they tasted as good as they look.
(let the children draw chalk pictures of clouds)

Animal Shadows

Will you look and see,
Whose shadow this could be?   *(put up each animal shadow one at a time—remove when children guess correctly)*
Additional Rhyme
Elephant, elephant, what will you do?   *(put up elephant)*
Someone is standing in front of you   *(repeat with monkey, giraffe, and zebra, putting each in front of the other, then conclude with lion)*

Lion, Lion, what will you do?   *(put up lion)*
No one is standing in front of you.
"I'll lead the parade, that's what I'll do!"   *(Use as a flannel board rhyme. Make an elephant, monkey, giraffe, lion, and zebra. Color each a solid color, so the animals look like shadows.)*

Who Has Seen the Wind?

Who has seen the wind?
Neither I nor you;
But when the leaves hang trembling,
The wind is passing through.
Who has seen the wind?
Neither you nor I;
But when the trees bow down their heads,
The wind is passing by.

Kite Flying

Pick a windy day.   *(make wind noises)*
Pick a kite that's gay.   *(sketch diamond in air using hands and arms)*
Send it on its way.   *(lift hands high to hold imaginary string)*
Give it lots of play.   *(unwind more string)*
Watch it dip and sway.   *(dip and sway motion with hand and arm)*
Follow it. Follow it.
Don't let it get away.   *(run in place or around the room while holding string high)*

Rhinoceros

A rhinoceros, a rhinoceros
Sometimes he makes a dreadful fuss.
He has a big horn on his nose   *(extend pointer finger from nose)*
He snorts and rumbles as he goes.   *(children say, "Grrump!")*
He's very long and very wide.   *(measure length and width with hands)*
He has a very wrinkled hide.   *(wavy motion with hands)*
He has big hoofs on his four feet.   *(hold up four fingers)*
We feed him grass and hay to eat.
A rhinoceros, a rhinoceros
Is surely not a pet for us.   *(shake head negatively)*
(Show a picture of a rhinoceros. The rhyme may be written on a wall chart. Ask, "Why wouldn't a rhinoceros make a good pet?")

The Funniest Clown

Whenever I ask boys and girls what they like best in the circus, they always say, "Clowns!" Those funny actors do tricks that everyone loves to see. It is hard to imagine how they can think of so many, many things to do. Their faces are funny. Even their clothes are funny.

Listen to my clown song. Name the things the clown had.

Suggestion: Be a clown leading a make-believe dancing bear. March along to the rhythm of the song.

The Circus

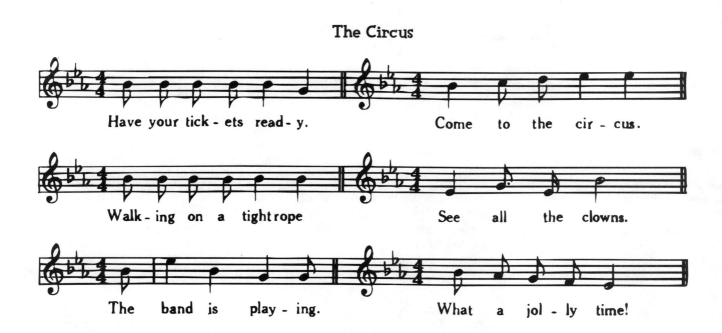

March Winds

"If March comes in like a lion, it will go out like a lamb."

The March wind roars, like a li - on in the sky, And makes us shiv - er as he pass - es by. When winds are soft, and the days are warm and clear, Just like a gen - tle lamb, when spring is near. (here)

Who's Afraid of Thunder?

(Sing to the tune of "Sing a Song of Sixpence.")

Who's afraid of thunder?   First the lightning flashes,
Thunder's just some noise.   Then the thunder crashes.
Just like a loud racket,   Tell me, who's afraid of thunder?
When children play with toys.   Not these girls and boys!

Treasure Hunt

(a "Let's Pretend" song)

Let's go, let's go. Let's look for a treas - ure - trove. Our map will show each moun - tain and stream and cove. Like pi - rates of old, with chests of gold, We'll seek for a place un - known. A Trea - sure Hunt. The prize will be ours a - lone.

Tarzan Lived in the Jungle

(Sung to the tune of "Old MacDonald Had a Farm")

Tarzan lived in the jungle. E-I-E-I-O.
In the jungle, he had a lion. E-I-E-I-O.
With a roar, roar, here.
And a roar, roar there.
Here a roar. There a roar.
Everywhere a roar, roar.
Tarzan lived in the jungle. E-I-E-I-O.

(Sing the verse several times. Let the children choose the jungle animals for the verses.)

Fly, Kite, Fly

We have fun with our ready-made toys, but sometimes it is more fun to play with toys we have made ourselves, such as kites. Early in March, windy days come along so we had better have our kites ready. With a good tail on the kite to steady it, and a long cord wrapped around a stick, up goes the kite little by little, up, up, into the air. Sometimes it flies so high that it looks very tiny, tugging away in the wind.

How high did the kite go in the song?

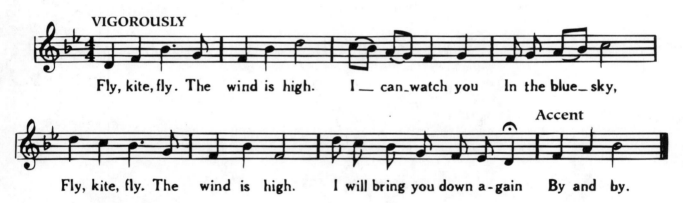

Bring your kite	Give it string
And come to the hill—	As much as you choose
To run in the wind	And hold your kite
And the March wind's chill	Or you will lose.
Raise your kite	Bring your kite
And then let it fly	And come to the hill—
Above your head	To run in the wind
In the cold, gray sky	And the March wind's chill

Suggestion: Hold your kite and unwind the string as you sing. Do it in rhythm.

St. Patrick's Day

This is a happy holiday in March that celebrates the myth of St. Patrick in Ireland. We celebrate this day on March 17th.

Tell the myth of St. Patrick chasing the snakes out of Ireland to bring good luck to the people there. Explain Ireland's legend of the little people and the good luck that follows them. Their pot of gold is found at the end of the rainbow, if anyone can ever get there before the rainbow fades.

Celebrate St. Patrick's Day

The teacher can be the leprechaun who visits the school at night, doing a little mischief. Print small green footprints around the room, mix up the puzzles, and leave out some games for the children to put away. On St. Patrick's Day, the leprechaun leaves a treat for the children, and a note explaining that he is returning to Ireland.

Find the Four Leaf Clover

Prepare cards with pictures of green clovers or use cut-outs of green clovers. Prepare enough for each child in your classroom. All the clovers should have three leaves except one which will be the four leaf clover.

The children can take turns passing around the clovers to music. When the music stops, the child who has the four leaf clover gets a special treat: a sticker, a hug from the teacher, etc. The person who has the four leaf clover is lucky—that is why he/she gets a special treat.

If passing the clovers to music is too difficult for your children, you can simply take turns passing the clovers out to the children, or they can each pick one out of a hat or a bowl.

Popcorn

Popcorn is always a fun treat for children to eat and equally as much fun to make. There is something magic about watching popping corn pop!

Make popcorn with your class. I suggest that you use it for a treat after your circus performance. After all, what is a circus without popcorn?

A *note of caution:* If you have 2½ year-olds in your preschool program, be careful with popcorn. Many children under the age of three are not able to digest popcorn. I would advise getting parental permission before giving popcorn to children under three.

Clown Circle Game

Children love matching colors and this clown will give them lots of experience and rewards while they are doing this matching activity.

You will need Pellon, assorted colors of felt, and assorted colors of marking pens.

Draw a large clown on the Pellon. Cut the clown out. Draw outlines of circles on the Pellon, using assorted colors of marking pens. The same colors can be repeated on different parts of the clown. Cut circles from felt the same size and colors as the circle outlines on the clown.

The children will enjoy laying the clown on a flat surface and placing the felt circles on the matching colors of circle outlines on the clown.

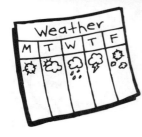

Classroom Weather Chart

When you are studying the weather, make a special, more complicated chart than is usually used. Follow the example on the left. Include charting the temperature, the conditions of the sun and clouds, rain, snow, fog, etc. Encourage the children to make comparisons of different weather conditions. Is it warmer when the sun is out? What does the sky look like before it is going to rain? Have the children take turns making and recording the various things on the chart.

Each child may like his/her own weather chart. The children could draw pictures on their charts each day to record what the weather looked like.

The Wind

Have the children fold a sheet of 9" x 12" paper into a fan. The phrase, "The air is all around us" could be printed on the fan. Staple the bottom closed and suggest that the child fan himself or herself. Can he/she feel that the air is all around us?

Listen to the sound made by an empty jar or large shell pressed against the ear. Air makes a sound. Fill the jar with water. Listen for a sound now that the air is gone.

Rain, Snow, Sleet, and Hail

Explain that rain, snow, sleet, and hail are all forms of water, and that the temperature of the air determines what form the water will take. Fill two ice cube trays with water. Put one outside and one in the freezer. Which one freezes faster? Why? Keep an ice cube tray filled with water in your classroom. Did the water freeze? Why or why not?

Weather Puzzles

Find pictures in magazines or draw your own pictures that depict different weather conditions (a sunny day, a rainy day, a cloudy day, a snowy day, etc.). Glue these pictures on cardboard or on tagboard. Cut the pictures into as many pieces as you think your children will be able to successfully master. Make some of the puzzles easier than others. This will ensure that all the children in your room will have a good experience.

Cover the puzzle pieces with clear adhesive paper, so they can be used over and over again. Put each puzzle in a separate envelope so they stay organized.

Leprechaun Lime Finger Jello

Finger "Jello" is always a big hit with young children and it is so easy to make.
> 4 envelopes unflavored gelatin
> 3 packages lime gelatin (3 ounces each)
> 4 cups boiling water

Add boiling water to gelatins. Pour into 13" x 9" pan. Chill until set. Cut into squares. Finger Jello does not melt at room temperature after setting. Makes 24 squares.

Lucky Rabbit's Lollipops

Making your own lollipops is a real treat for children—it's as much fun as eating them.
> 2 tablespoons margarine   ¼ cup light corn syrup
> 6 tablespoons sugar   few drops food coloring

Mix margarine, sugar, and corn syrup. Cook and stir until the candy thermometer reaches 270°. Stir in food coloring. Drop by tablespoons onto straws or craft sticks on waxed paper. Cool. (*Caution:* The syrup is hot when poured, so keep small fingers from touching.) Makes 10 lollipops.

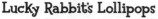

Banana Boats

This is a warm, sticky, delicious treat that the children will love making and a lot of little monkeys will love eating! You will need bananas, marshmallows, chocolate chips, and tin foil.

Peel back a long strip of banana peel on the inside of the curve, leaving one end attached to banana; scoop out some of the banana and fill with marshmallows and chocolate chips; replace strip of peeling; wrap in foil; bake at 350° until banana, marshmallows, and chocolate are melted.

Animal Concentration

You will need a set of animal pictures pasted on identically sized cards. You may choose to use either two cards of each animal or four cards of each animal. Lay the cards face down on a table top. Have the children take turns turning over two cards at a time. If a child finds a matching set he/she may keep the cards. If the animals do not match, the child must turn the cards back over.

Concentration is a wonderful game for developing memory skills. Play the game throughout the year using a variety of pictures.

Mixed-Up Animals

Find pictures of jungle animals. You may wish to draw your own if you are artistic. Tracing animals from library books works well, along with using animal pictures from old coloring books.

Once you have a collection of animal pictures, cut the animals out and then cut off their heads. Glue a piece of Pellon or sandpaper on the back of all the bodies and heads. They can now be used on the flannel board.

Mix up the animals when you display them for the children. Ask the children to identify the name of each animals' head and the name of each animals' body. Have the children put the animals back together in their correct forms. This is a fun way to teach animal name identification. The children will also think that it is very funny.

The Wind Is Moving Air

Explaining to young children what the wind is, is not an easy task. You can tell the children that the wind is air. You can't see air. But air is all around you—above you, behind you, over you. Even though you can't see the air, you can see what the air does and how the air feels. Try these experiments:

- BALLOONS—Air is what is inside a balloon when it is blown up. Air comes out of the balloon when you let it go.
- SOAP BUBBLES—Air is what is inside a soap bubble. Blow some bubbles with the children.
- STRAWS AND BUBBLES—When you blow through a straw into a glass of water, it is the air that makes bubbles.
- CANDLES—It is the air that blows out a candle.

Making a Cloud

Pour hot water into a glass jar. When the bottle becomes hot, pour out all but one inch of the water. Stretch a cloth over the mouth of the jar. Fasten. Place some crushed ice on top of the cloth. A cloud forms as the warm air meets the cold. Discuss the difference between hot and cold.

Spring "Inside" Playing

Cut-off some carrot tops and put each one in a dish with pebbles. Add just enough water to cover the bottom of the carrot. Place the dishes in a place where there is not too much sun. In just a few days, the carrot tops will begin sprouting and turn into beautiful plants.

Stars, Space, and the Moon

You will find activities for the children to pretend that they are astronauts or space people, equipped with space-ships and space suits. They will have lots of fun pretending, role-playing, and participating in space games. Some simple science activities have been included to demonstrate answers to questions about space.

When you are teaching the space unit, be sure to show the children in your class pictures and photographs of real spacecraft, astronauts, the moon, the stars, and other planets. With so many television cartoons and movies about space travel, the children will probably have lots of pre-conceived notions about what we have achieved in space travel. It is interesting to find out how much they already know and how accurate it is. Is the moon really made of green cheese?

House Pets

"House Pets" is a "warm fuzzy" unit. I do believe that it is important to stress the responsibilities that come with caring for an animal. If you do not already have a classroom pet (guinea pigs, hamsters, gerbils, mice, and rabbits make good classroom pets), this is a good time to get one. The children can learn how to properly care for a pet. A note of caution: Beware! Find out ahead of time if an animal is pregnant. Twice I purchased a guinea pig for my classroom. The first had five babies a month after I bought her. The second guinea pig had four babies within a couple weeks. And of course, I couldn't part with any of them. Everyone in my class learned how to help clean cages!

Weekends sometimes are problems if you have animals in your classroom. Some animals can be left for a couple of days with an ample supply of water and food, but other animals can't be left like this. If your classroom pet does need someone attending to it over the weekend, here is an idea. Have a parents' sign-up sheet. Ask the parents to take turns taking the pet home for the weekend. This has been very successful in many preschools. It is also very special for the children to have the responsibility and fun of caring for the classroom pet at home.

I Used to Be a Baby

Children love talking about babies, playing with babies (real and pretend), looking at pictures of babies (especially looking at their own baby pictures), and hearing stories about themselves when they were babies. My own children spend hours with their baby books and photo albums.

This unit can be so much fun, especially if you have parents who are willing to help you. Write the parents and ask them to help you with these things.

1. Send a baby picture of their child to school. Tell the parents that it will be returned safely.

2. Ask the parents to send a pair of their child's baby shoes to school. Children love looking at tiny baby shoes. It is hard for small children to believe that their feet were ever small enough to fit in the baby shoes.

3. Make copies of the following questionnaire for the parents. Ask them to fill it out and return it to you. Go over the questionnaires with your class. The information provided by the parents will entertain and delight all the children.

Dear Parents,

We are going to be working on a unit called "I Used to Be a Baby." To make this unit more personalized for the children, would you please fill out the following questionnaire?

1. Child's full name: (First, Middle, Last)
2. My child was born on: (Month, Day, Year)
3. My child was born in the (circle one): Morning, Afternoon, Evening, Middle of the Night
4. My child was this big when he/she was born: (Weight, Length)
5. These were some of my child's special words: (i.e., Blanket—"Ba-Ba"; Bottle—"Bobby"; Pacifier—"Paca"...)
6. My child's favorite baby activities were:
7. Tell us a "funny" story about your child when he/she was a baby.

The Rainy Day Blues

If you are experiencing a lot of rain or other weather that is keeping the children indoors more than they want to be, your classroom may have "cabin fever." Minnesotans have a great understanding of what "cabin fever" is. To help with your classroom's "cabin fever" or "rainy day blues," here are some "silly" suggestions that will perk you and your class up!

Make "Gunk." You will need a large bowl and a mixing spoon. Use 1 box of cornstarch, 1¾ cups water, and food coloring. Mix all the ingredients together, and let the children have fun playing and creating with their "Gunk." They will have as much fun telling their parents that they made "Gunk" at school as they did making and playing with it.

An **Indoor Picnic** is always a hit, too! Bring in blankets and a large picnic basket filled with a picnic lunch. Let the children sit on the blankets on the floor and really pretend that they are outside on a picnic. Be sure to remind them to keep an eye out for ants. Ants always come to picnics. I am sure if you are lucky, you will have some children who truly believe that they see ants. After all, pretend ants are the best type to see.

Make **Juice-Sicles.** This idea is not silly, but it is something that is guaranteed to perk up any child with the "rainy day blues." Some schools have commercial popsicle molds. If you do not, use an ice cube tray and fill it with any juice. Place a craft stick, tongue depressor, or even a toothpick into each section of the ice cube tray. This is a great healthy treat that children love.

Bunnies

The background of this bulletin board should be done in blue and green paper to represent the sky and the grass. A big, bright yellow sun adds nicely to the sky also.

The bunnies are pre-cut shapes (which may have to be done by the teacher). The bunny shapes should be cut out of tagboard. Dilute white glue with water and let the children "paint" the glue on their bunny shapes. The children can then stick cotton on the bunny shapes.

Pink construction paper can be glued on top of the cotton ears. Pipe cleaners can be used for whiskers, and black construction paper can be used for the other facial features.

April Showers

When you are done with your "Bunnies" bulletin board, all you need to do is take down the bunnies and the word "Bunnies." The green grass and blue sky can be left up for this bulletin board.

The teacher will need to make a very large umbrella out of construction paper, with the words "April Showers" on the umbrella. Make a sign for the bottom of the bulletin board saying "Bring May Flowers."

The children make the flowers. The stems are tongue depressors which are colored or painted green. The leaves are green construction paper glued on the stem. The petals are cut out of colored construction paper, glued to a small circle of paper and then added as a whole piece to the stem.

Pet Store

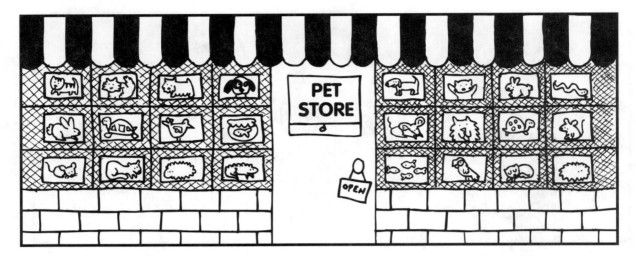

Each child may draw the pet of his/her choice on a piece of 9" x 12" manila paper. The background is 12" x 18" construction paper, lined to give the appearance of a wire cage.

Arrange the drawings in rows. Add an awning of scalloped construction paper with contrasting stripes. The foundation is construction paper, lined to form bricks.

Look What We Found on the Moon

The top of the bulletin board background is black. The bottom of the bulletin board is curved and designed to look like the surface of the moon. Have the children find pictures in magazines or draw their own pictures of things that they would like to discover on the moon. Their ideas can either be pretend or real. The bulletin board is much cuter if the children think up lots of things—the man in the moon, green cheese, rockets, astronauts, flying saucers, plant life, etc.

Look How We Have Grown

Children are fascinated by pictures of themselves as babies. (After all, it wasn't very long ago!) Have the children bring baby pictures to school. Show each picture to the entire class. Let the children guess who it is. Be sure to include baby pictures of yourself and some of the other teachers. It is so hard to believe that a teacher was ever a baby.

Mount the baby pictures on a bulletin board. Display a current picture of each child next to his/her baby picture. The children will love looking at this bulletin board and the parents will enjoy seeing it, too.

April Showers

The month of April is known for all its rainy days. Talk to the children about the rain. What should they wear outside on a rainy day?

Have each child in your class make a rain character for the bulletin board. Use a triangle for the body, small rectangles for arm and legs, circles for the head, feet, and hands. (Follow the illustration.) Tape or pin the characters up on the sidewalk on the bulletin board.

Each character will need an umbrella. Use wallpaper samples for an interesting effect. Cut out umbrella shapes. Glue construction paper handles to the umbrellas and position one over each rain character.

Benny Helps the Easter Bunny

(The children can pretend to be Benny, the baby bunny. It might be helpful to define "quail" and "pheasant.")

Benny was a tiny, teeny bunny who was only a few weeks old, but already he had heard of the Easter Bunny and his important job delivering Easter eggs. Benny was **sitting** in the tall grass of a field that was his home. He **hopped** a few steps further, trying to **munch** some grass. All the while, he was thinking why couldn't he help the Easter Bunny as some of the other rabbits did? After all, he was a bunny, too! He **stretched** and **scurried** through the weeds, **jumping** over a stick, and **stopping** quickly by a tree. Benny was trying to prove to himself how able he was for the job.

He **walked** around a tree and **sat frozen, wiggling his nose** and **turning his ears.** He smelled and heard a fox approaching. If he stayed frozen the fox might not find him, as his fur matched the color of the tall grass. The fox came closer and closer. Benny **shook** with fear. He **turned to the left, then the right** and **scampered** as fast as he could, **jumped** over a fallen branch, **leaped** across a nest of pheasant eggs, **crawled** under a stick, and **squatted** in some bushes. The fox had long given up the chase but Benny **sat, breathing deeply,** and still **shivered.** The little rabbit **walked** to his mother and **sat** by his own nest.

There the Easter Bunny was passing out the eggs that the other bunnies would help deliver. Benny wanted to help but the Easter Bunny told him he was too young. Next year he would be an adult and could help. The tiny bunny **crawled** into his soft nest in the tall grass and **curled up in a ball** to sleep.

Next morning he **woke** very early, before all the other rabbits. He **stretched out his front paws,** then his **back paws,** and washed his ears by **licking his paw** and **rubbing it over his ears.** He had an itch on his back so he **rolled** in the grass several times to scratch. Benny **sat down** to think. His cottontail **wiggled.** He was hungry, so he **hopped on one foot, then on the other, then on both,** to the other end of the field to try the grass. He found some tender pieces, **pulled them up,** and **ate them.** He **chewed slowly** and **wiggled his nose.** As he moved through the grass, he noticed twelve speckled eggs laying in the weeds. Benny **turned his head in every direction,** looking for the owners of these eggs. No one was around! Someone forgot to deliver these eggs. Here was Benny's chance to help the Easter bunny.

Bending down to pick up the eggs, he **carefully piled them** in his arms. Slowly he **walked, stepping** over rocks and sticks. He left four eggs at Mr. Woodchuck's burrow and **skipped** on to Mrs. Muskrat's den, where he left four more eggs. **Scampering,** he **tripped** over a stone. Luckily the eggs rolled to the ground. Benny **got up slowly, rubbing his sore knees and toes. Bending down,** he **picked up** the remaining eggs for Mrs. Raccoon. He was so happy!

Benny **raced** back home to tell the Easter Bunny of his deed. When he returned home, he **sat to rest.** There was great excitement, for Mrs. Quail was screaming and crying. Someone had stolen her twelve speckled eggs from their nest by the tall grass where Benny had breakfast.

The little bunny realized he had made a mistake. He had picked up Mrs. Quail's eggs from her nest where she was trying to hatch them. He thought they were Easter eggs. Benny had to save those eggs! He **raced** to Mrs. Raccoon's and found the four eggs untouched, since no one was awake yet. Carefully carrying the eggs, he **ran** to Mrs. Muskrat's den and **picked up** the next four. Benny was worried that he would be too late! He **scampered** to the Woodchuck burrow to find only two eggs laying by the opening. Benny was frantic! He **dug** and **crawled** down the tunnel of the burrow. There lay the last two eggs. They must have rolled down the hole. He **picked up** the eggs and **skipped** back to the Quail nest; he **bent down** and **put all twelve back** in their place.

Hurrying, he **hopped** back to his home to announce to Mrs. Quail that her eggs were safe in their nest again. Benny **sat, resting** and **breathing deeply.** He told the Easter Bunny about his mistake. The little bunny was sorry he had not asked about the eggs, but at least Mrs. Quail's eggs were safe.

Rocky, the Rocket Mouse

I am a little white mouse. My name is Rocky. I live in a small glass house in a big room called a "laboratory." There are many houses in the laboratory, and in each one lives another little white mouse. Every day a woman in a white jacket comes in, opens my door, and gives me a slice of cheese and three dandelion leaves. I used to be just an ordinary mouse. I had never done anything brave or important or exciting. But now I am a very special mouse, because I have been on a very exciting adventure.

One day, as I was taking a nap in the corner of my glass house in the laboratory, I heard footsteps. When I looked up, I saw two scientists I had never seen before, a man and a woman. They were walking from one little house to another, looking into each. "If I sit quietly in the corner," I thought, "perhaps they won't notice me." Oh, how frightened I was. My heart pounded faster and faster as the people came closer. I shut my eyes and waited for them to go by. But when I opened one eye and peeked out, there were two faces, looking at me through the top of my glass house! Suddenly, the man opened the door. He took me out and held me in his hand. "Here is a nice healthy mouse," said the man. "He would be perfect," said the woman. "He is not too big or too small. This will be a very important job, and we must have the best mouse we can find."

"What important job could the scientists have for me?" I thought. Then I heard the man say, "The rocket will be blasting off for the moon at five o'clock tomorrow afternoon. Will you have him ready to go?" "He will be ready," said the woman, and the man put me back into my house. Think of it! A trip to the moon! How excited and happy I was! I had dreamed about going to the moon ever since I had learned that the moon is made of green cheese. There is nothing in the whole world a mouse likes better than green cheese! "Perhaps when it's time for the rocket to leave the moon, I'll hide behind a big lump of cheese," I thought. "Then I can stay there and eat green cheese and more green cheese and MORE GREEN CHEESE!"

The next day I did nothing but laugh and sing and dream about green cheese. Late that afternoon the two scientists came into the laboratory. They carried me down a long hall, and took me outside. We drove to where the rocket was. When I saw the rocket, my eyes popped. How big it was! Before long, they put me inside. I was very happy when I saw my new home. It was so big and beautiful and shiny. "If only my friends in the laboratory could see me now," I said to myself. "I guess I must be just about the most important mouse in the whole world!"

Suddenly there was a roar that was louder than any noise I had ever heard. I put my paws over my ears and huddled in the corner. The rocket was moving! "I'm on my way to the moon!" I shouted. I crawled out of the corner and explored my new home. Soon I discovered a tiny window. I looked out, and to my surprise, there were hundreds of bright little lights sparkling in the sky. I stood for a long time with my nose pressed against the window pane, looking at them. "How beautiful," I said to myself. "I wonder what they are?"

After a long time, I felt a jolt that sent me flying to the other side of the rocket. I ran to the window. I had landed! But surely this couldn't be the moon! I couldn't see any green cheese at all. Wherever I looked, there was nothing but rocks and sand and more rocks, making criss-crossing shadows. But I was eager to explore this place called the moon, so I jumped to the ground and scampered across the sand. Maybe somewhere I could find the green cheese I had heard about. I climbed up one rock and down the other, but there was no green cheese! "Maybe it is under the sand," I thought. I began to dig excitedly, scratching as fast as my little paws could go, but I couldn't find even a tiny piece of cheese.

I was very disappointed that there was no green cheese on the moon, but went on anyway, exploring to see what the moon was like. After a while it became very cold. As I stood shivering, I thought about my nice warm house and all my friends in the laboratory. "Oh, well," I thought, "I'll hurry back to the rocket where it is warm." As I bounded off, I glanced back to take one last look. Something was chasing me! Goodness, could it be the man in the moon? Maybe he didn't like visitors on his moon. I ran faster, but when I looked, the thing was still right at my tail. I zig-zagged between the rocks, hoping he would get lost, but when I zigged, he zigged, and when I zagged, he zagged.

I ran lickety-split until I reached the rocket, jumped through the open window and pulled it closed. I was safe! I looked out to see if it really was the man in the moon who had been chasing me, but there was nothing in sight— nothing at all. Then I laughed. "Why, you silly little mouse," I sighed. "It was only your shadow." Then I sat in my corner, waiting for the rocket to take me back to the laboratory where the woman in the white jacket would bring me a slice of cheese every single day. I thought about how happy I would be to see all my friends again and to be back in my nice warm glass house. Still, it had been very interesting to visit the moon.

Soon I heard the roaring noise again. I was on my way back home! Hooray!

The Great Egg Hunt

Listen, children, listen, my dears,
And a marvelous, magical tale you'll hear;
A tale that will have you shouting "Hooray!"
For the great egg hunt held on Easter Day.

It happened not so long ago,
On an Easter morning full of woe,
The girls and boys awoke to find,
Empty Easter baskets, oh, how unkind!

"Oh me, A my! Oh my, Oh me!
What is this dreadful sight I see!"
Exclaimed an excited Barnaby Easter Bunny.
"Something here is really quite funny!"

"Last night I filled these baskets, I know.
What could have happened to empty them so?"
Then, without warning, a little bunny appeared;
He had a mischievous smile and very big ears.

"Hi! I'm Butch!" he said with a grin,
"And I've planned a game I know you can win.
The great egg hunt is the game we will play,
And find all the eggs I've hidden away!"

The children looked high and they looked low;
Some were quite fast and others were slow.
They looked and they looked and they looked some more.
They found one egg, then two, then three, and then four.

They jumped up high and they crawled on their knees;
Five, six, seven, and eight were found under the trees.
Nine, ten, and eleven were found in the tulip bed;
Twelve, thirteen, and fourteen were hidden inside the shed.

"Keep looking, keep looking!" Butch shouted with glee;
Fifteen, sixteen, and seventeen weren't so easy to see.
Eighteen and nineteen were hidden down in the grass,
And twenty was found by a sweet little lass.

"Look harder, now!" said Butch, while dancing around;
Twenty-one, two, and three were in a hole in the ground.
Twenty-four and twenty-five were found under a rose,
By one little person that followed his nose.

"Hooray!" cried Butch. 'You found every last one!
Wasn't that great egg hunt lots of good fun?"
"Now, let's share all the eggs," said Barnaby Bunny,
And that Easter Day turned out to be happy and sunny!

(Turn "The Great Egg Hunt" into a flannel board story. Enlarge the patterns on this page.)

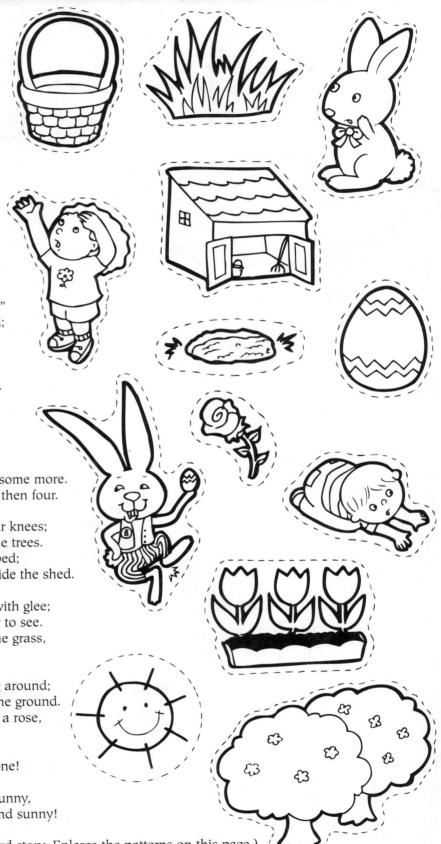

Somebunny Loves You

This activity makes a darling Easter card for the children to send their parents. Take a picture of each of the children in your room or ask each child to bring a picture of him/herself to school. Fold an 8½" x 11" piece of construction paper into four sections. Follow the diagram at the left. Insert the child's picture so that it shows through the bunny's face.

(Mrs. James F. Miller, Concord, North Carolina)

Easter Egg Divider

This room divider is quick and easy to construct, as well as being colorful to view. It is appropriate for a unit on Easter or eggs, and can allow for participation by the children.

Let the children decorate the Easter egg cut-outs with crayons, sponge painting, or by gluing on ribbons and other decorations. Glue the eggs to strips of crepe paper with one egg on each side of the strip so the eggs are back-to-back. Attach to the ceiling with string by folding over the top edge of each strip and gluing or stapling to form a casing through which the string may go. Hang several strips in a straight line to form a divider. Strips could also be taped to the ceiling if it has a smooth surface.

Try using this idea for other holidays, such as decorated tree cut-outs for Christmas, jack-o'-lanterns for Halloween, shamrocks for St. Patrick's Day, hearts for Valentine's Day, etc.

Baby Chick

Dip a ball of cotton into dry yellow tempera paint. Make the chick's eyes with a black felt pen. The beak can be made from a piece of black construction paper cut in a triangle shape and glued on the cotton. Glue the cotton chick into half an eggshell.

Bunny Baskets

This is a fun project for creating an Easter basket for the kids in your class. Using a white paper bag, cut out bunny ears at the top, open end of the sack. Draw, color, or paste on the features of the bunny's face. Pipe cleaners make cute whiskers for the bunny. After the facial features are completed, open the sack and staple the top of the ears shut. Fill the bunny baskets with green grass. On the day of your spring or Easter party, you can fill the baskets with treats for the children.

Bunny Puppet

The children color a picture of a bunny that the teacher has prepared ahead of time. Those children who are able may cut out their bunnies. Tape a drinking straw to the back of each bunny so it can be used as a puppet.

Color a Rainbow

Demonstrate to the children how to color a rainbow. Leave your example up for them. Then let the children use their crayons and color rainbows of their own. Afterwards each child might like to use his/her blue crayon on its side and color lightly all over the paper, for the sky.

April Showers

Give each of the children a picture of an umbrella. The children can finish the pictures by drawing someone under the umbrella.

Cats

Make the cat's body by cutting a pie-shaped wedge out of a circle of construction paper and forming a cone shape by joining the edges of the remaining piece with tape or paste. Make the head by cutting a circle of construction paper and pasting it on the cone. Cut the paws out of construction paper and paste or tape them on the cone. Cut the ears out of construction paper and paste them on the back of the head. Glue a piece of yarn on the bottom of the cone for the tail. Add features with a felt pen or crayons.

Hanging Fish

Using construction paper or paper plates, give each child a large circle and two crescents, one small and one large. Cut a V in the circle for the mouth. Tape the smaller crescent to the circle for a tail, the larger one through the middle for fins. Add an eye by pasting on a button, a small piece of construction paper, or by drawing it on.

Hang the fish in the windows of your classroom. Decorate the windows so they look like an aquarium.

Our Classroom Pet Dragon

This activity ends the unit on house pets. What a great time to create a classroom pet that needs very little care! The children will each need to bring to school a small, individual-serving size cereal box. The teacher can provide a large cereal box for the head and one for the tail.

Cut off the narrow sides and top of one large cereal box. Flatten the front, back, and bottom. Draw the shape of a flower pot on the front and back and make teeth. Draw eyes and nostrils on one flower pot only. Fold front and back. Bend teeth down. Trace a tail, punch a hole, and tie a string to it. Then thread the string through all the small cereal boxes, through a straw, through the back of the head, through the bottom, and finally through the top of the front of the head. Allow enough extra string with which to pull the dragon.

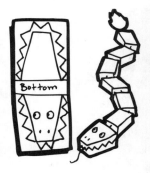

A Rocket and Space Suits

The rocket is formed using three hoola hoops taped to the floor in upright position, about 3' apart. Cut two tagboard circles as large as the hoops. Tape one circle on the front hoop. Fasten the other to the last hoop with tape hinges so it can be lifted for the children to get in and out of the rocket. Cut a semi-circle of heavy wrapping paper to form a cone. Tape it to the first hoop. Cover the hula hoops with strips of heavy wrapping paper, ending a little above the floor. Cut out a hole for a window on each side. Cover holes with acetate—one red and one blue—and decorate with gummed stars. On the inside, on the front tagboard circle, glue foil circles for controls. Add triangular wings and a tail.

The space suits are paper bags with holes cut out for the faces. Add pipe cleaner antennae and yarn for apparatus.

Putting Baby to Bed

On a white piece of paper, have the children draw a picture of a baby. If the children are having a difficult time drawing a picture of a baby, have them cut one out of a magazine, and paste it on a piece of white paper.

When the picture of the baby is completed, have the children paste some felt or fabric (scrap material) over the baby for a blanket. The children may also wish to draw a stuffed animal or find a picture of a stuffed animal in a magazine. Now the baby is all ready for bed.

Rolled Paper Rabbit

You will need to prepare for the children strips of paper for the heads and bodies of the rabbits. (Body: 6" x 24" construction paper. Head: 6" x 18" construction paper.) Follow the illustration.

Each child can decorate the body of his/her rabbit so it looks like it is wearing clothes. Facial features can be drawn on the face. Roll the strips of construction paper and staple them together.

Cut out feet and staple them to the bottom of the rabbit and it will stand up. Glue on a ball of cotton for its tail.

Easter Baskets

All teachers seem to save egg cartons. If by chance you do not have enough on hand, ask each child in your classroom to bring an egg carton to school.

From the ends of a colored plastic egg carton, cut two 4-cup sections. Put a pipe cleaner handle through the center. Around the edge of the section, add a fringed strip of crepe paper or tissue paper.

Rabbit Headband

Each child will need a 2" x 24" strip of construction paper. Staple the strip of paper to fit the child's head.

Each headband will need ears. The white outer ear should be 12" x 3", and the pink inner ear should be 10" x 2". Cut each to a point. Paste the pink ear on the white ear. Fold the sides to the center. Staple the ears on the back of the head band. Cover all staples with tape, so they will not get caught in the child's hair.

My Easter Egg

Give each child a large construction paper cut-out of an egg. Provide the children with glue, glitter, sequins, scrap fabric, foil, buttons, crayons, markers, and anything else that you might have in your art scrap box. Let them go to town and decorate the fanciest Easter eggs ever!

Pussywillow Pictures

The children can make pussywillow pictures by using construction paper strips and cotton. They may color in the background (sky, ground, flowers) with color crayons.

Crayons and Paint

Using color crayons, the children should draw pictures of "spring" on white paper. Encourage the children to make flowers, trees, grass, and birds. When the children have finished coloring their pictures, have them paint over the entire picture with light blue water colors. The paint will not cover the crayon, and it will give the sky an interesting texture.

Weather Chart

Name_____

SUNSHINE

RAIN

o

- -
Cutting Line

Attach arrow to o with brad

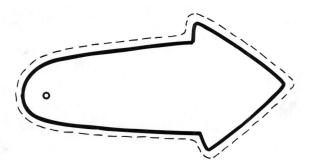

Color arrow
before cutting.

Baby Chick and Egg

Directions:
Color and cut out the baby chick and egg. Attach at the X's to show the chick hatching from the egg.

TSD1896-4 *The Preschool Calendar*

Hopping

For Older Children:

The teacher instructs the student to hop on the right foot, taking off and landing on the same foot. The arms should be lifted up, head held high, and knee bent. The inactive leg is bent and should make no contact with the floor.

1. Hop in one place; the child should be told to take his/her time hopping.
2. Hop and turn at the same time, turning in various patterns.
3. Hop high in the air, then hop low.
4. Hop backward, forward, sideways, make a square, etc.
5. Hop trying to cover a long distance.
6. Hop over a line.
7. Hop backwards over a line.
8. Hop with a partner.
9. Hop to different rhythms (clap hands, use a drum, recorded music, etc.)

For Younger Children:

Younger children can do the same activities that are listed above, but instead of hopping on one foot, they can hop on two feet.

Mrs. Hen's Eggs

Use leftover Easter basket and paper eggs. One child is Mrs. Hen carrying a basket of colored eggs. He/she passes them out to the children. One child is Mr. Fox. He/she goes to Mrs. Hen to buy some eggs. "What color do you want?" Mrs. Hen asks. If the fox says "red," all those holding red eggs will run around the room. The fox may catch some and put them in his/her "den."

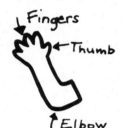

Naming Our Body Parts

The children sit or stand facing the teacher, who asks them to name body parts as he/she touches them—head, neck, arms, elbows, wrists, thumbs, fingers, trunk, hips, legs, thighs, knees, ankles, feet, toes, hair, eyes, ears, nose, mouth, lips, cheeks, chin, eyebrows, eyelashes, etc. Pair the children; one child may act as the teacher and the partner as the responder. Alternate partners in these roles.

Scoops

You will need scoops and bean bags, fleece balls, or tennis balls.

Individual Activities:

1. The child tosses the ball into the air and catches it in a scoop.
2. The child throws the ball upward with the scoop and catches it in the scoop.
3. The child assumes different positions such as sitting or lying. He/she catches the ball with the scoop, first tossing the ball into the air, then throwing it into the air with the scoop.
4. The child tosses the ball at targets such as hoops or wall targets.

Partner Activities:

1. One child rolls the ball to the other child, who catches it in a scoop and returns the ball by rolling it back.
2. One child bounces the ball to the other child, who catches it in the scoop and returns the ball by bouncing it back.
3. One child tosses the ball to the other child, who catches it in the scoop and returns the ball by tossing it back.
4. Both children have scoops and play catch using rolling, bouncing, and throwing methods.

Puddles

There are two versions of this game.

Version 1: Prepare the same number of puddles as the number of children in your class. The puddles can be made from blue construction paper or foil. Place them in a circle on the floor. Sing a song about rain. The children march in a circle, stepping only on the puddles. When the music stops, the children stop on his/her puddles. You can also play this game like "Musical Chairs."

Version 2: Each child has his/her own puddles. When the music is on, the children walk in a circle around their puddles. When the music stops, the children jump onto their puddles.

We Do As the Animals Do

Have the children move like the more common house pets—cat, dog, rabbit, fish, guinea pig, hamster. You can also have the children imitate other animals which are not usually house pets—horse, pig, cow, lion, elephant, giraffe, snake, alligator, etc.

While the children are participating in the movement activity, discuss which pets live in people's homes and which places the non-house pet animals may live.

Jumping on the Moon

All the children practice saying the poem below and clapping in rhythm. Then, while all the children recite the poem, a few are chosen to do the jumping. On every clap, the jumpers jump. This can be varied by having them pretend they are wearing parachutes and jumping from the rocket (chairs). Let all the children have a turn to jump.

One jump, we jump to the moon,
Two jumps, we jump to a star,

Three and four and maybe more,
We don't know where we are!

Fly Around in Space

The children form a circle, which is the landing field. One child is chosen to "fly" around the inside of the circle while the others sing the poem below. Use the name of the child who is the flyer in the poem. When the flyer goes "boom" in the last line, he or she should squat down to the floor. The others squat down too. The last one down joins the child who is already in the center. One child can be in the "control tower" (standing on a chair) to watch for the last one down. When about half the children are in the "landing field," the flyers in the center can be "grounded" and watch while the others have a turn.

Johnny go 'round the stars,
Johnny go 'round the moon,

Johnny can fly up in the sky,
And land with a big boom.

Walking in Space

The concept of weightlessness and the loss of gravity is very difficult for a preschooler to understand. A fun way to help them "see" this concept is to give each of the children a blown-up balloon. Have the children draw a picture of an astronaut on the balloon. Now let the children enjoy batting the balloons. Their weightless spacepeople are floating in space.

The Countdown

The countdown and the launching of a rocket lends itself to a good rhythm activity. Individual rugs or resting mats make good launching pads. One child is chosen to do the countdown. The child counts "10, 9, 8, 7, 6, 5, 4, 3, 2, 1, Blast off! Zoom!" They all take off into "space."

The music can be varied so the children can go fast, slow, up, down, and around, depending on their imaginations and interpretations of the music. Then the children return to the launching pads. This rhythm activity can be done with a few at a time or with the whole group, depending on the play space available.

Baby Games

Tell the children, "It is so much fun to remember all the fun you had when you were a baby. Babies play lots of games and have lots of people to play with. Can you remember some of the games that you played when you were a baby?"

The children may or may not remember. Remind them of the games "Ring Around the Rosey" and "London Bridge Is Falling Down." The most mature four-year-old will still enjoy playing these games. Play any other games that the children are able to remember.

Balloon Catch

You will need inflated balloons and funnels. If you do not have funnels, roll tagboard into a funnel shape and tape it to a tongue depressor.

Place the balloon on the funnel. Push the funnel up to toss the balloon into the air. As the balloon comes down, try to catch it. The children will have fun with this activity and it is very good for eye-hand coordination and muscular control. As the children become more adept, the class can count aloud each successful catch.

Hopping Races

Children naturally love to hop and jump. Utilize this natural energy by providing the children with a variety of hopping races.

- Burlap sack races
- Three-legged races. (Pre-schoolers are not very good at this race, but they surely have fun trying!)
- Hopping backward race.
- One-foot hopping race.
- Big hopping/little hopping races.
- Quiet, tip-toe hopping races. (End the races with this one.)

Little Birds

The birds are returning home from the south. Have the children be the birds. They should do what the rhymes tell them to do. Make up other rhymes to fit your location.

1. Little birds, little birds
   Fly to the door.
   Little birds, little birds
   Sit on the floor.

2. Little birds, little birds
   Jump up and down.
   Little birds, little birds
   Don't make a sound.

3. Little birds, little birds
   Tip-toe to me.
   Little birds, little birds
   Sit down on your knees

4. Little birds, little birds
   Creep, creep, creep.
   Little birds, little birds
   Sleep, Sleep, Sleep.

Go

You will need a whistle, bell, or some type of device to signal the children. Tell the children that they can move in any way that they would like: skip, run, walk, crawl, gallop, hop. When the teacher says "go" the children should begin to move. When the children hear the signal (whistle, bell, etc.), they should freeze in whatever position they stopped. The teacher will count to 10. The children must hold their positions until the teacher reaches the number ten and then says "go."

The Duck Family

The children should dramatize the following story as the teacher reads it. They will probably want to dramatize this story several times.

THE STORY: A mother duck and three baby ducks were taking a nap. (You may use the entire class instead of three baby ducks.) One duck woke and tripped away—then another—then another. Mother woke up. She quacked loudly. The babies answered their mother and the mother duck found them by their sound. (The babies must quack softly until they are found.)

Space Fun

Draw lines to match the spaceships.

My Pet Fish

Name_____

✂ out the 🐟

🍯 the 🐟

in the 🐠

🖍 the picture.

ᐱᐱᐱ Language Activities ᐱᐱᐱ

Weatherperson

Each day, let one child have a turn being the "Weatherperson." This is a wonderful opportunity for children to learn to use descriptive words appropriately. It is also a nice means of introducing children to speaking before a group, and besides, it is always fun to be the "star."

Let's Fly a Kite

Fold a piece of colored construction paper, 9" x 9". Tape on some yarn for a tail. Add paper pieces to the tail, and a string for pulling at the top. Decorate the kite with an animal picture or a pretty flower. Run and pull the kite.

While the children are flying their kites, use this as an opportunity to discuss which kites are high and which are low, which are going fast and which are going slow, etc. Use as many basic concepts as you can when your children are having this experience.

Sky Ceiling

This "sky" dropped ceiling is appropriate for use during a unit on "Weather" or the sky's features such as "Stars, Moon, and Sun." It could be used over the science area or dramatic play area.

Drape a parachute or sheet which has been dyed blue in billows from the ceiling. Wire or string can be used to tie it to the ceiling. Cut out from poster board various sizes of stars, a moon, and a sun. Suspend these shapes from the parachute or sheet with string or wire.

This prop not only looks great in a preschool classroom, but also helps encourage dramatic play and language development. The children can pretend that they are camping out under the stars, that they are on some new unexplored planet, etc.

What Do You Do on a Rainy Day?

So many children complain that there is nothing to do on a rainy day, and we all know that the month of April gives us our fair share of rainy days.

Tell your children that you never know what to do on a rainy day. Ask them to come up with a list of things to do to help you.

Things That Are Wet/Things That Are Dry

Show your children pictures of things that are wet and things that are dry and have them label each picture accordingly. Examples: a boy in a raincoat, a pond, an ice cube, a piece of bread, rubber boots, etc.

Now Hear This!

You will need a series of paper bags containing such items as paper to crush, a glass and a pencil, two blocks to clap, a tin can filled with pebbles, a bottle to blow into, etc.

One child is chosen to be "it" and must close or cover his/her eyes. Another child is then invited to select one of the bags, and at a signal, manipulates its contents. If "it" can guess what made the noise, he/she may have the next turn.

Variation: Use musical instruments, or movements such as clapping hands, snapping fingers, stamping feet, walking, running, etc.

Family Pets

Have a discussion with the children in your class about the responsibilities of caring for a pet. Here are some guideline questions:

Who feeds the pet?
Who makes sure water is available?
Who walks (cleans up after) the pet?
Who takes the pet to the vet when it gets sick?
Can you touch this pet?
Does he/she like it?
Should you wake up your pet if he/she is asleep?

The children who have pets should be encouraged to talk about what things they do at home to help in the caring of their pet.

Mother and Baby Animals

Discuss with the class the fun that can be gained from having a pet. Talk about the animals that are suitable for farm pets. Lead the group into giving ideas on why these same animals would be hard to care for in the city. Let each child give his/her observations of the care and type of food required by each kind of animal.

Give the names for animals and their babies: Cow—Calf, Dog—Puppy, Horse—Colt, Duck—Duckling, Hen—Chick. Don't burden the children with the names of too many animals. Talk about those the children are familiar with.

Distribute magazines to the members of the class and have them cut out pictures of various animals. Mount these on tagboard. They can be used in the following ways:

1. Set up a pocket chart in one of the learning centers. Place the pictures in the chart. The children can take turns choosing a mother and then her baby.
2. Hand out pictures of baby animals. Place a picture of a mother pet in the pocket. The child with the picture of the correct baby puts it in the pocket.
3. Hold up a picture of the baby or the mother animal. Choose someone to give the characteristic sound.

In another interest center, children can make illustrations of their favorite mother pet and her baby. These can be cut out and mounted on tagboard.

Where Is the Spaceship?

Prepare cut-outs of the moon, spaceship, planets, sun, and a star for use on the flannel board. Move the spaceship around the flannel board. Have the children describe where the spaceship is, i.e. under the sun, over the moon, next to the planet.

What Do You See?

The children pretend they are at Cape Canaveral. As each child has a turn sitting in the rocket, the others pretend they are asking questions from the control center as they do on real flights.

It is fun for the child who is asking the questions to say, "Control center to Astronaut Jones (give child's last name). What do you see?" The astronaut answers, "I see different countries," "I see a beautiful rainbow," "I see the moon with rocks and sand," etc.

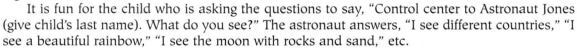

Going on a Spaceship

Start the game by saying, "I am going on a spaceship. I have my space bag here. What do you think I should pack to bring on my spaceship?" Have each child think up something that you might need on the voyage.

ᜃᜃᜃ Language Activities ᜃᜃᜃ

Let's Learn about Babies

Tell the children that they will be spending the next couple of weeks learning about babies. Show the children some pictures of babies in books and in magazines.

Guide the children through a discussion about babies. Find out how much the children understand and some of their own ideas about taking care of babies.

- Can new babies walk or crawl? How do they get around?
- What kinds of food do you think the babies should eat?
- How do babies tell us what they want? Do they talk?
- Babies cry! Why do you think that babies cry? What are they trying to tell us?
- What kinds of toys are good for very little babies?
- Do you remember when you were a baby? What kinds of things did you like when you were a baby?
- Do any of you have a baby brother or sister at home? Can you tell us about the baby in your house?

What Do Babies Need?

Prepare a box filled with some of the things that are used in caring for a baby. If you are not a parent, and do not have easy access to baby things, ask some of the parents to help provide you with the following objects:

Bottle	Baby Powder	Stuffed Animal	Rubber Tipped Spoon
Pacifier	Infant Seat	Rubber Pants	Baby Wipes
Diaper	Baby Food Jar	Newborn Outfit	Rattle
Blanket	Formula	Baby Washcloth	Music Box
Stroller	Diaper Bag	Crib Mobile	Baby Booties

Show the children the objects one at a time. Ask the children what the object is and why it is needed. Also talk about high chairs, cribs, playpens, mechanical swings, and car seats. It is astounding all the equipment that a tiny baby needs. A preschooler's response to the equipment can be even more astounding!

Caring for Baby

After the first two language lessons, the children should have a pretty good idea of all the things that are needed to take care of a baby. Not only do babies need a lot of equipment, but they also need a lot of time. Have the children role-play ways that they would care for a baby. Use dolls for the role-playing—bathing, feeding, rocking, and playing with baby.

As a group, have the children name the body parts of the doll. Play "This Little Piggy" with the dolls. The children may also wish to sing "Rock-A-Bye Baby."

I Am Getting Bigger

Have the children share baby pictures of themselves. They will enjoy seeing what their friends looked like as babies. Talk to the children about how much they have grown. What things can they do now, that they could not do when they were babies? Talk about how physically small babies are. Weigh and measure the children. Mark the children's heights on the wall. Mark how tall a newborn baby would be. The children will be impressed when they see how much they have grown since they were born.

Bunny Puzzle

Directions:
Have the children cut out the bunny parts.
Arrange them on a large piece of construction
paper and glue them in place.

 and =

My Handprints

These are my little handprints
Because I am still small.
But soon my hands will grow,
And I will be very tall.

Name _____

Clouds

The clouds are floating through the sky.   *(hold hands up high and move them in floating motion)*
They seem to wave as they go by.   *(wave hands)*
Some shaped like animals I know,   *(make odd shapes with arms and hands)*
Some look like pretty drifts of snow.   *(move hands across front, in drifting motion)*

The Rain

Pitter-patter, raindrops,
Failing from the sky.   *(wiggle fingers to imitate falling rain)*
Here is my umbrella
To keep me safe and dry!   *(hands over head)*
When the rain is over,
And the sun begins to glow,   *(make a large circle with arms)*
Little flowers start to bud
And grow and grow and grow.   *(spread hands apart slowly)*

Two Little Rabbits

Two little rabbits hopped to the gate.   *(make two fingers "hop")*
Two little rabbits ate and ate.   *(make eating motions)*
Soon they heard a noise
That sounded like thunder,   *(clap hands)*
And when they reached that gate,
They hopped right under!   *(make two fingers dive downward)*

The Wind

The wind came out to play one day.   *(make sweeping motions with arms)*
He (she) swept the clouds out of his (her) way.   *(make fluttering motions with fingers)*
He (she) blew the leaves and away they flew.   *(lift arms and lower them)*
The trees bent low and their branches did, too.   *(repeat sweeping motions)*
The wind blew the great big ships at sea;
The wind blew my kite away from me.

Fun in the Rain

When rain comes down,
Drip, drop, drip, drop.   *(flutter fingers)*
Windshield wipers
Flip, flop, flip, flop.   *(move forearm back and forth)*
And boots in puddles,
Plip, plop, plip, plop.   *(pretend to splash in puddle)*
I wish the rain would never stop.
Drip, drop, drip,   *(repeat all motions)*
Flip, flop, flip,
Plip, plop, plip, plop, PLOP!   *(jump with both feet on final "PLOP")*

Hop and Stop

The first little rabbit went hop, hop, hop.
I said to the first rabbit, "Stop, stop, stop!"
The second little rabbit went run, run, run.
I said to the second rabbit, "Fun, fun, fun!"
The third little rabbit went thump, thump, thump.
I said to the third rabbit, "Jump, jump, jump!"
The fourth little rabbit went sniff, sniff, snuff.
I said to the fourth rabbit, "That is enough!"
The fifth little rabbit went creep, creep, creep.
I said to the fifth rabbit, "It's time to sleep!"
*(Since there is repetition of words, the children should
be able to say the entire rhyme with you the second time.)*

Rocket Ship

Our rocket ship is standing by,	*(hold up one finger)*
And very, very soon,	
We'll have a countdown, then we'll blast	
Ourselves up to the moon.	
Begin to count: ten, nine, eight,	*(hold up ten fingers, then count backward, bending down each finger)*
Be on time, don't be late.	
Seven, six, five, and four,	
There aren't many seconds more.	
Three, two, one! Zero! Zip!	
The rocket is off on its first moon trip.	

Who Is Smiling at Me?

I'm looking out my window,	*(open window)*
You'll never guess what I see.	*(poke head out of window)*
That funny Man in the Moon,	*(point to moon)*
Is smiling at me!	*(smile)*

Stars

At night I see the twinkling stars,	*(open and shut hands)*
And a great big smiling moon;	*(make circle with arms over head)*
My mommy (daddy) tucks me into bed,	*(lay finger in cupped hand)*
And sings a good-night tune.	*(make rocking motion with hands)*

Turtles

One little turtle, feeling so blue;	*(hold up 1 finger)*
Along came another. Now there are two.	*(hold up 2 fingers)*
Two little turtles, on their way to tea;	
Along came another. Now there are three.	*(hold up 3 fingers)*
Three little turtles, going to the store;	
Along came another. Now there are four.	*(hold up 4 fingers)*
Four little turtles, going for a drive;	
Along came another. Now there are five.	*(hold up 5 fingers)*

Goldfish Pets

One little goldfish lived in a bowl.
Two little goldfish eat their food whole.
Three little goldfish swim all around.
Although they move, they don't make a sound.
Four little goldfish have swishy tails.
Five little goldfish have pretty scales.
(Suggest that children cut fish from yellow construction paper and lay them on the flannel board. If the board is slanted slightly backward, the fish will cling. Children may add one "fish" at a time and count as they do so.)

My Pets

There are lots of pets in my house.	
I have one gerbil and one white mouse.	*(hold up one finger on each hand)*
I have two kittens and two green frogs,	*(hold up two fingers on each hand)*
I have three goldfish and three big dogs.	*(hold up three fingers on each hand)*
Some folks say that is a lot!	
Can you tell how many pets I've got?	*(twelve)*

Five Little Puppies

Five little puppies were playing in the sun;	*(hold up hand, fingers extended)*
This one saw a rabbit, and he began to run;	*(bend down first finger)*
This one saw a butterfly, and she began to race;	*(bend down second finger)*
This one saw a pussy cat, and he began to chase;	*(bend down third finger)*
This one tried to catch her tail, and she went round and round;	*(bend down fourth finger)*
This one was so quiet, he never made a sound.	*(bend down thumb)*

For Baby

Little fingers,
Little toes,
Little mouth,
Little nose.
Little ears,
With which to hear,
Little baby,
So precious and dear.
(Have the children point to the body parts on a doll. The children may also wish to choose partners. One child can be the baby, the other child can be the parent.)

It's Raining

It's raining, it's raining,   *(move finger up and down)*
It's pouring from the sky.
Let's find a big, leafy tree
And it will keep us dry.   *(hands over head)*

Little Baby

Here is a baby so soft and small   *(put up piece for baby)*
His legs can't walk, so he must crawl.
He drinks from a bottle and naps in a crib.   *(put up bottle)*
He dribbles his food, so he wears a bib.   *(put up bib)*
When his pants are wet, he starts to cry.
His mom will change them, so he'll be dry.   *(put up diaper)*
(The teacher repeats the rhyme and encourages the children to join him/her. For an alternate version, substitute "she" and "her" for "he" and "his, " and "dad" for "mom." Use this as a flannel board activity.)

Mud

Squish, squash says the mud,
When I go out to play.
It oozes up between my toes,
After a rainy day.
(The children should take high, steps and walk around the room.)

The Rabbit

I have a little rabbit   *(make fist, thumb on top)*
He lives in a tree
When the sun comes out
So does he!   *(pop thumb up)*

All about Me

Here are my ears, and here is my nose
Here are my fingers, and here are my toes.
Here are my eyes, both open wide.
Here is my mouth with my teeth inside,
And my busy tongue that helps me speak.
Here is my chin, and here are my cheeks.
Here are my hands that help me play,
And my feet that run about all day.
(Touch each part of the body as mentioned.)

Rabbits

A family of rabbits lived under a tree;   *(close right hand and hide it under left arm)*
A father, a mother, and babies three.   *(hold up thumb, then fingers in succession)*
Sometimes the bunnies would sleep all day;   *(make a fist)*
But when night came they liked to play.   *(wiggle fingers)*
Out of the hole they'd go creep, creep, creep,   *(move fingers in creeping motion)*
While the birds in the trees were all asleep.   *(rest face on hands, place palms together)*
Then the bunnies would scamper about and run . . .   *(wiggle fingers)*
Uphill, downhill! Oh, what fun!   *(move fingers vigorously)*
But when Mother said, "It's time to rest."   *(hold up first finger)*
Pop! They would hurry   *(clap hands after "Pop!")*
Right back to their nest!   *(hide, hand under arm)*

Five Young Rabbits

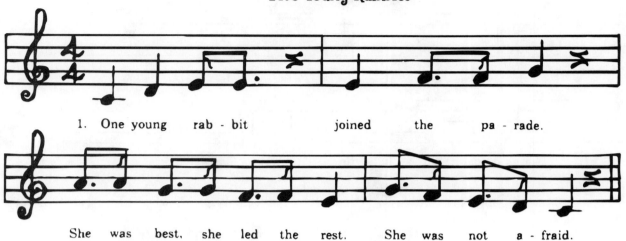

1. One young rab - bit joined the pa - rade.

She was best, she led the rest. She was not a - fraid.

2. Two young rabbits dressed up so fine,
   Marched along and sang a song,
   Keeping perfect time.
3. Three young rabbits feeling very proud,
   Stepping high as they went by,
   Waving at the crowd.

4. Four young rabbits looking very grand,
   Pink and white, left and right,
   Marching with the band.
5. Five young rabbits, this is what they said,
   "Parades are fun, but when we're done
   We're glad to be in bed."

The children take turns being rabbits, pantomiming the action as the class sings.

Spring Puddles

Days of melting snow and rainy days are good days for puddles and rubber boots. To walk right into the middle of a big puddle without getting wet is great fun, because puddles never last very long. What does the child do in the last part of the song?

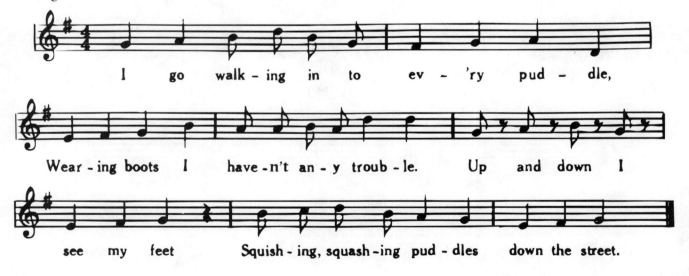

I go walk - ing in to ev - 'ry pud - dle,

Wear - ing boots I have - n't an - y troub - le. Up and down I

see my feet Squish - ing, squash - ing pud - dles down the street.

Suggestion: Make your hands go up and down when you sing the "up and down" part.

Puppies

1. I like one friend-ly pup-py be - cause She
   has four soft lit - tle fur - ry paws.

2. The reason I like two puppies is that
   Their bodies are little and round and fat.

3. I like three puppies because they're fun.
   They play with me as they jump and run.

4. My four puppies bark when I say, "Hello!"
   They follow me wherever I go.

5. Five puppies are sleepy and new and small,
   They are so friendly—I love them all.

The Man in the Moon

We're going to outer space, to meet the man in the moon.

We'll bring back some green cheese, on an afternoon.

Where is the Man in the Moon? He is not here to-

day. He must have gone a - way.

A Rocket in Space

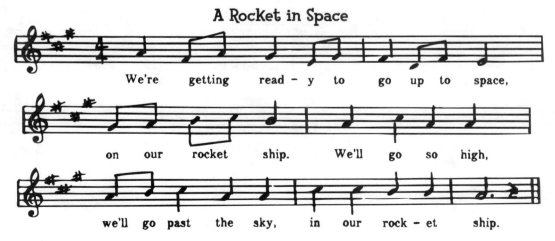

We're getting read - y to go up to space,

on our rocket ship. We'll go so high,

we'll go past the sky, in our rock - et ship.

 TSD1896-4 *The Preschool Calendar*

Rock-a-Bye, Baby

Rock-a-bye, ba-by, On a tree top. When the wind blows, the cra-dle will rock,

When the bough breaks the cra-dle will fall, And down will come ba-by, Cra-dle and all.

Hop, Little Rabbit

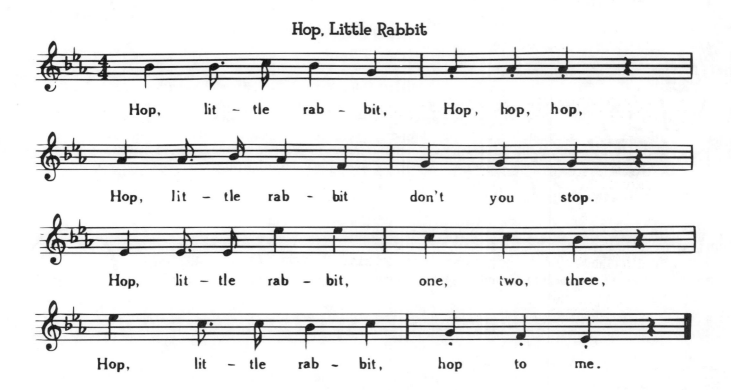

Hop, lit – tle rab – bit, Hop, hop, hop,

Hop, lit – tle rab – bit don't you stop.

Hop, lit – tle rab – bit, one, two, three,

Hop, lit – tle rab – bit, hop to me.

The Farmer Plants the Grain
Sing to the tune of "Farmer in the Dell."

The farmer plants the grain,
The farmer plants the grain,
Hi-ho in springtime, the farmer plants the grain.
   *(The farmer goes around planting, and
   those in the circle all stoop to ground.)*
The sun begins to shine, the sun begins to shine.
Hi-ho at planting time, the sun begins to shine.
   *(One child, who is the sun, spreads his/her arms
   overhead and runs around the circle.)*

The rain begins to fall, the rain begins to fall,
   (Another child is "rain.")
Hi-ho at planting time, the rain begins to fall.

Continue with "The plants begin to grow,"
"The farmer cuts the grain,"
"The farmer stacks the grain," etc.

Hard-Boil Eggs and Decorate

Hard-boiling eggs and decorating them is always a wonderful experience for children. After you have completed decorating the eggs, you can leave them in the children's Bunny Baskets for their party.

Weather Calendar

Copy a calendar each month on a large sheet of tagboard. Each day allow one child to draw a picture of the sun, wind, rain, clouds, or snow in the space by the day's date.

This is also a great tool for teaching the four seasons, and can encourage discussions on how plants change with the seasons, the different types of clothing needed in different seasons, and how the activities of people and animals change with the seasons and weather.

Wind and Air

When explaining the wind and air to preschoolers, it is always easier to use a visual example. Sailboat experiments are a very good way to show preschoolers what the wind and air can do.

Construct simple sailboats. Some examples are shown in the pictures at the left. Float the sailboats in a container of water. The children may play the part of the wind, discovering how the moving air pushes the sail and thus moves the boat across the water. To make waves, the children may blow on the water like the wind, or blow through a straw.

Prism

Talking about rainbows naturally lends itself to the discussion of colors. Bring in a prism and show the children the colors of the rainbow as the sunlight penetrates it. Identify the colors and follow up with some artwork.

Water and Rain

Be sure you use identical glass containers. (Glass is often easier to see through than plastic.) Try dissolving salt, sugar, and sand. Stir thoroughly and let settle. Salt and sugar will dissolve. The sand will not.

Try to dissolve some other things: bread (it disintegrates), sponge (it absorbs water), dye (it colors water), etc.

Let's Make Rain

Heat water in a teakettle. Hold a glass jar over the spout of the kettle to collect steam. The steam may be compared to fog or rain clouds. The air outside the jar is colder, so droplets will form inside the jar and fall down like real raindrops.

This is a science concept that is very difficult for preschoolers. Even if they do not understand any of the scientific principles, they will enjoy the fun of really making rain in their classroom.

Field Trip to a Pet Store or Pet Day at School

If you have a nice pet store near your school, a field trip there can be a lot of fun. Many pet stores welcome the opportunity to show children their animals and talk about some of the animals' needs. After you visit the pet store, the children can draw pictures of their favorite animals or find pictures of the animals seen at the pet store in books or magazines.

If you are brave enough, a pet day at school is also great fun. Arrange this day with the parents, so the parents will be able to bring in the pets, stay while the pets are on display, and take the pets home again. It is advisable to have cats and dogs come on separate days.

The Pets' Game

Prepare the mistake cards in the following fashion: Cut out pictures of animals. On each card, glue five animals, for example, four dogs and one cat, or four birds and one fish. Cover with clear contact paper. With a wax crayon, the child should mark the animal that does not belong with the others.

The Sun Is a Star

Have a discussion with the children about stars. Tell them: The sun is a star. There are many other stars, some larger, some smaller than the sun. They all look like the sun, but since they are farther away they look smaller and not so bright to us.

Here is a fun beginning science activity for helping children see why stars appear to twinkle. In a darkened room, light a candle. The candlelight will flicker and look similar to the twinkling of stars.

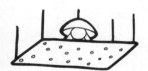

Starlight in the Classroom

This project will create an interesting light pattern in your classroom. It is fun to pretend that you are in outer space and that the light pattern is the stars.

Select a piece of sturdy cardboard large enough to cover an area of ceiling, and paint it black. Randomly punch holes in the cardboard. A paper punch, ice pick, or nail can be used to make the holes. Suspend the cardboard below a ceiling light fixture so the light will filter through the holes.

Why Do Rockets Fly?

If the weather is nice, this activity is probably best done outside. This will allow for more running room. This activity can also get very noisy.

Blow up a long balloon, release it, and watch it travel. This is how rockets push into space. The children will probably want to chase the rocket. Have several balloons available.

Man in the Moon

The teacher prepares the cookies:

1 chocolate cake mix	1 teaspoon vanilla
2 eggs	chocolate chips or nuts
⅔ cup liquid shortening	

Mix all ingredients together. Drop by small spoonfuls onto a cookie sheet. Bake at 375° for about 10 minutes. Remove from oven when bottoms of cookies just begin to brown.

The teacher wraps each of the cookies in clear plastic wrap, and hides them in various places around the room. The children should pretend that they are walking on the moon and are searching for the surprise that the Man in the Moon made for them. Be sure to hide the cookies in very obvious places.

Baby Food Snacks

Have mashed bananas or baby food for snack time. Baby food applesauce or bananas will probably be the most appealing to preschool children. Ask the children if they can remember eating baby food. Add a small amount of cinnamon to the applesauce.

Let the children crawl around and pretend they are babies. It is a lot of fun to reflect on "the good old days"!

Bunny's Fried Egg Rounds

You will need a slice of bread and an egg for each child in your class. Cut a hole in the middle of the bread with a biscuit cutter. Melt butter in an electric skillet. Place the bread in the skillet. Crack an egg and pour it into the hole in the bread. Fry until the white is slightly set. Turn and fry the other side of the egg. With a glass of orange juice and a glass of milk, this makes an excellent and healthy breakfast.

Flower Petal Bingo

You will need to make a variety of colored construction paper petals, six of each color, craft stick stems, and a spinner. (Follow the illustration on the left.)

Each child decides before the game begins what color flower he/she would like to grow. The children take turns spinning the spinner. Each time the spinner stops on the color that the child has chosen, he/she may take a petal. Play the game until all the children have had the fun of finishing their flowers.

Baby Animals Are Born

Spring is the time that many animals are born. Show the children pictures of baby animals and adult animals. The children can match the baby animals to the parent animal.

Discuss with the children the names of the baby animals, (lamb, colt, chick, etc.). What things do the mother animals do for their babies? How are the babies different from their mothers?

A Magic Plant

In the spring many farmers and gardeners begin to prepare for the planting season. Here is an exciting activity for preschool children. You are going to grow a pineapple plant.

Bring a pineapple to school. Let the children watch you cut it and share the fun of eating it. Cut off the top of the pineapple, leaving about one inch of the fruit. Put it in water, leaving the leaves exposed to the air. When the roots appear, transfer the plant to a pot of dirt and cover with a plastic bag for three weeks. After everyone has waited "patiently" for the three weeks to pass, remove the cover and you will discover a pretty cactus-like plant. Uncovering the plant and viewing how it has grown is like magic to young children.

Water and Beans

Let the children experiment with pouring activities. Use water or beans. Provide the children with a wide variety of containers and objects for pouring. As the children are playing, talk about the concepts of empty and full.

If you are not brave enough to use water for the pouring activities, you can just use the beans. The children won't get wet and they are easier to clean up than water. They also make really interesting sounds when they are being poured from container to container.

Spring and Planting

Spring and "planting" go hand in hand. The children will be able to experiment with a wide variety of planting and sprouting techniques. Many of the planting activities teach about various foods that are grown to eat. It is equally important to stress to young children that they should NEVER eat a plant without knowing what type of plant it is, and showing an adult the plant first.

For your reference I have included a list of toxic plants. You may be surprised at how many plants are poisonous. You have permission to copy this list and send home the toxic plant information to the children's parents.

Toxic Plants

The following plants are considered toxic (poisonous, possibly dangerous). These plants contain a wide variety of poisons, and symptoms may vary, from a mild stomachache, skin rash, or swelling of the mouth and throat to involvement of the heart, kidneys, or other organs.

Acorn	Delphinium	Jonquil	Philodendron
Anemone	Devil's Ivy	Lantana Camara	Poinsettia
Angel Trumpet Tree	Dieffenbachia	Larkspur	Poison Ivy
Apple Seeds	Elderberry	Laurel	Poison Oak
Apricot Pit—Kernels	Elephant Ear	Lily-of-the-Valley	Poppy (Calif. Poppy excepted)
Arrowhead	English Ivy	Lobelia	Pokeweed
Avocado—Leaves	Four O'Clock	Marijuana	Potato—Sprouts
Azalea	Foxglove	Mayapple	Primrose
Betel Nut Palm	Hemlock, Poison	Mescal (Peyote)	Ranunculus
Bittersweet	Holly Berries	Mistletoe	Rhododendron
Buckeye	Horsetail Reed	Moonseed	Rhubarb—Blade
Buttercup	Hyacinth—Bulbs	Monkshood	Rosary Pea
Caladium	Hydrangea	Morning Glory	Star-of-Bethlehem
Calla Lily	Iris	Mushroom	Sweet Pea
Castor Bean	Ivy (Boston, English)	Narcissus	Tobacco
Chinese Lantern	Jack-in-the-Pulpit	Nephthytis	Tomato—Vines
Creeping Charlie (Ground Ivy)	Jequirity Bean or Pea	Nightshade	Tulip
Crocus, Autumn	Jerusalem Cherry	Oleander	Water Hemlock
Daffodil	Jessamine (Jasmine)	Peach Seeds	Wisteria
Daphne	Jimson Weed (Thorn Apple)	Periwinkle	Yew

Source: American Association of Poison Control Centers

Reference Material

About Ants

Ants are insects. They live in organized communities called "colonies," which may have millions of members. There are 10,000 different kinds of ants.

Ants are very strong. Most ants can lift objects ten times the weight of their bodies, and some can even lift fifty times the weight of their bodies. The ant's antennae help the ant to smell, touch, taste, and hear. The ant has two compound eyes.

In most colonies, ants are in three classes: queens, workers, and males. The queen lays eggs. The workers care for the queen, enlarge the colony, repair and defend the nest, care for the young, and gather food. The males do not do any work in the colony.

Ants communicate by tapping out messages on the walls of the nest. They also give off chemical signals. Different chemicals provide different information.

About Birds

All birds have feathers, they all have wings, they all hatch from eggs, and they do not have teeth. The smallest bird is a bee hummingbird. It is two inches long. The largest bird is an ostrich, which is around eight feet tall.

Birds communicate through their songs and calls. A call is a single sound, and a song is a series of notes. Birds may also communicate by drumming with their beaks, or by flapping their wings.

Birds have different kinds of beaks and feet. The shape of their beaks is determined by how or what they eat. Sharp pointed bills are used for drilling and these birds eat insects out of the bark of trees. Wide flat beaks, such as those ducks have, are used for scooping up water and filtering the food from it. The fish-eating birds have long pointed beaks for spearing the fish. Birds of prey have hooked beaks. The seed eaters' beaks have a longer top beak than bottom beak to help them crack nuts and seeds.

Most birds have four toes. Perching birds have three toes in the front and one in the back to help them balance on a limb. Climbing birds like woodpeckers have two forward toes and two back toes. Most running birds have only three toes on each foot. The ostrich is the only two-toed bird. Swimming birds have webs of skin between each of their toes.

Think Spring

Older children may be able to draw pictures of things that they do in the springtime. Younger children may prefer looking through magazines to find pictures of people playing games or doing things outside. This is a good activity to stress the concepts "inside" and "outside."

You can make frames for the pictures by bending the corners of colored construction paper. This will make the pictures take on a 3-D effect on your bulletin board.

All This Comes from Farms

Ask the children to bring in empty containers of products that were either grown or produced on a farm. Examples are illustrated in the above drawing. The children will probably be very surprised to see how many of the foods that they eat come from a farm.

Spring Collage

Paint a background the size of the bulletin board. Place a colored strip around the edge for a decorative border.

The children may paint a variety of flowers and leaves, and then cut them out. Arrange them on the board, overlapping some to make an attractive collage. Pin or paste in place.

Beautiful Butterflies

Cut butterflies from 12" by 18" colored paper. Cut half of the butterflies slightly smaller than the others. Paste a smaller butterfly on top of each larger one. Decorate the butterflies with colored foil, keeping both sides identical.

Place two pipe cleaners on each butterfly to form antennae. Paste one on each side of the fold, twisting the ends.

Pin to a "sky" background, adding tissue paper flowers at the bottom of the board.

Where Do the Animals Live?

Divide the background of the bulletin board into three sections: a jungle, a farm, and a forest. Let the children color the background paper, and design what they think each environment should look like.

Ask the children to draw some pictures of animals and cut them out. The children may tape their animals in the proper environments.

What Do Plants Need?

Use light blue background paper for the sky, green paper at the bottom for the grass, and cotton or quilt batting for the clouds.

The teacher should make a large yellow sun, highlighted with gold or yellow glitter. The children can cut out rain drops from foil and make construction paper flowers.

A caption can be added to the bulletin board that says "Plants need sun and water to grow."

A Day at the Farm

"Good morning, Gail," said Aunt Gretchen. "Are you ready for breakfast?"

Gail had ridden all yesterday to get to the farm. She was going to spend a week with her Uncle George and Aunt Gretchen. Now the first morning had finally arrived and she was ready to help her uncle and her aunt with the chores.

"You had better eat a good breakfast so you won't get hungry today," said Uncle George.

"How would you like some nice fresh eggs?" asked Aunt Gretchen. "These came from the chickens on the farm and the sausage is some that Uncle George and I made from one of the pigs. Did you know sausage was made from pigs?"

"No, I didn't know that," said Gail. "What do farmers like you and Uncle George do all day?" she asked.

Uncle George said, "We always say 'Good Morning' to the animals, and then we start working. You can help us today and see for yourself. Maybe by the end of the day you'll be ready to be a farmer. Let's go check G.G. first."

Gail was glad her uncle suggested that. "I remember G.G. from last summer. She is the pretty brown horse that I rode after the chores were finished."

They gave G.G. some fresh oats and water, and then Gail went to help Aunt Gretchen feed the chickens. They were waiting at the chicken coop. Gail threw some feed to them and it wasn't long before the chickens knew they had a new friend. While the chickens ate, Aunt Gretchen showed Gail how to check for eggs. They went up and down the rows of nests. That morning they found six fresh eggs, just enough for everyone to have two for breakfast tomorrow morning.

"Can I see the cows next?" asked Gail.

"I milked the cows before breakfast," said Uncle George, "but you can help me put them in the pasture."

Gail held the gate to the pasture open until all the cows went through. She closed the gate so that the cows wouldn't get out, then she stood on the fence and watched the cows graze.

"Do you want to sit on the tractor while I plow?" asked Uncle George.

"This is fun," said Gail as she and her uncle rode up and down the rows on the tractor.

"This is where the wheat will soon be planted," Uncle George explained.

All day Gail helped Uncle George and Aunt Gretchen. They fed the pigs and sheep. They pulled weeds from the garden and even picked some fresh vegetables for supper.

At the end of a long day, Gail knew that farmers work hard, even if they don't go to the office every day.

Story Activities

1. As a class, make a list of all the chores that Gail, Uncle George, and Aunt Gretchen did on the farm. How many chores can the children remember? Can they put the chores in sequence?

2. Let the children draw pictures of their favorite farm animals. Ask each child to tell the class about his/her picture.

3. Find out how many children either have been on a farm or live on a farm. Has anyone ever done any of these types of chores?

Exploring Spring

"Wake up, wake up!" said Mother Bear to her cubs Stinky and Winky. "Spring has arrived."

The two fuzzy black cubs stretched their legs and rubbed their eyes. They had been asleep all winter. When they were wide awake, they followed Mother Bear outside into the warm sunshine.

Mother Bear was glad to be able to stretch her legs. She sniffed the sweet smells of spring.

"Spring is my favorite time of year," she said to her twin cubs.

The cubs were scampering about in the warm sunshine. Mother Bear could tell they were enjoying spring also. "Stay close beside me," Mother Bear instructed her cubs. "We'll walk through the woods and enjoy springtime."

Mother Bear took Stinky and Winky down to the stream. "Watch how I catch a fish," Mother Bear said.

Mother Bear scooped her paws into the cool stream. When she brought her paws out of the water, she held a fish. "That looks easy!" said Stinky.

The two cubs walked into the water and leaned over to look for a fish. Suddenly Stinky splashed Winky with water and the battle began. Mother Bear watched her cubs playfully splash one another. Pretty soon the cubs grew tired of their play and wanted something to eat. They tried over and over again to catch a fish, but it was very hard to do. The bear cubs didn't catch any fish.

"Come," said Mother Bear, "I'll show you something else good to eat."

Stinky and Winky followed their mother to a green bush covered with red berries.

"Each spring this bush is covered with delicious berries," said Mother Bear.

The cubs nibbled on the berries until their tummies were full. They were sleepy, so they curled up on a soft patch of clover and went to sleep.

Stinky and Winky woke up after a while, eager to find out more about spring. Mother Bear showed them beautiful pink and yellow flowers and colorful butterflies.

"I like springtime," said Winky.

"Springtime is a beautiful season," said Mother Bear.

All too soon, the sun began to hide its face. Mother Bear led her cubs back to their den.

"Do we have to go in?" asked Stinky.

"Yes," said Mother Bear. "We'll enjoy spring again tomorrow."

The Dog and the Bumblebee

A little dog set out one day, adventuring was he—
When what did he meet upon the way, but a great big bumblebee!
"Bzzz, bzzz, bzzz," said the bumblebee.
"Little dog—stay away from me."
The little dog laughed, "Silly fly—you can't give me a scare.
Afraid of no little bug am I, and I will bite you . . . there!"
"Bzzz, bzzz, bzzz," said the bumblebee.
"I'm warning you—stay away from me."
But the little dog opened his mouth up wide—and just as you'd suppose,
"Very well," the bee replied, and stung the little dog's nose!
The little dog yelped, "Oh-oh-oh," and the bee replied, "I told you so."
So the little dog turned and ran did he—as fast as he could go.
Now he won't ever again bite a bumblebee! Absolutely no!
(Turn this story into a flannel board story. Make the dog and the bee.)

The Peaceable Kingdom

This is the story of a kingdom where many different kinds of animals live together in harmony. There is a legend that tells the story of how the animals left their old home where there was much war and much fighting, to look for a new home where they could live in peace.

The story begins:

They came to live on the mountaintop, many years ago.
The legend says they came in peace, looking for a home where love could grow.

And so they all came together—the giraffe, the lion, the bear, the lamb, the chipmunk, the cow, the monkey, the dog, the cat, and the deer. They were led by the beautiful unicorn to the green and growing mountaintop. This is where they made their home.

The animals believed it was important to learn to live together in happiness and peace. They cared for each other and worked together and created a beautiful new home.

They learned that feelings are important and decided that each animal would have the responsibility of teaching a special feeling to the younger animals so that the young ones would learn to respect feelings as they grew up.

The giraffe was given sadness.
The lion was given bravery.
The bear was given thoughtfulness.
The lamb was given peace.
The chipmunk was given fear.
The cow was given acceptance.

The monkey was given anger.
The dog was given happiness.
The cat was given jealousy.
The deer was given tenderness.
The unicorn was given love.

The animals taught all the different feelings so that the young ones would not be frightened of any of their feelings, but would learn to accept all of their feelings as a part of life. The unicorn helped the young ones to understand the importance of love, and the bear taught the young ones that their loving, tender, peaceful feelings were the most special ones.

So all the different kinds of animals lived in harmony on their mountaintop. Their story was a happy one.

They came to live on the mountaintop, many years ago.
The legend says they came in peace, looking for a home where love could grow.

A discussion of feelings is a good accompaniment to this story. Use pictures of people expressing a variety of feelings to help children identify feelings they have experienced.

(Turn "The Peaceable Kingdom" into a flannel board story. Make a giraffe, lion, bear, lamb, chipmunk, cow, monkey, dog, cat, deer, and unicorn.)

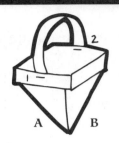

May Baskets

Make these May baskets in the same way that a small "soldier hat" is made. Use colored construction paper. Press sides A and B together, then spread apart again. Staple the handle on sides 1 and 2.

Clothespin Butterflies

Use clamp clothespins for the body. The clothespins can be painted or you can leave the wood plain. Slip tissue paper or crepe paper into the clothespin. These butterflies make wonderful mobiles. Even the very youngest of preschoolers will have success with this project.

Pin Cushion

This pin cushion can be used as a gift for Mother's Day. Use the lid from a peanut butter jar and fill it with cotton. Cover the lid and cotton with a circle of scrap material and tie it with a small ribbon or piece of yarn.

What mother wouldn't appreciate this wonderful gift?

Mother's Day Card

To accompany the pin cushion for Mother's Day, it would be nice to also include a card. Reproduce copies of the following poem so it is ready for the children to paste inside construction paper cards. The children can then decorate the covers of the cards and sign their names.

Mother, my darling,
Mother, my dear,
I love you, I love you,
Each day of the year.

Spring Flowers

Make spring flowers by using pastel colored cupcake papers for the blossoms. Color in green stems and leaves or cut them from green construction paper. Use a pretty pastel paper as a background.

Paper Garden

Color the bottom of a Styrofoam meat tray brown. Let the children cut vegetables from construction paper, or they can cut out pictures of vegetables from magazines. Glue the vegetables to pipe cleaners or toothpicks and stick them into the tray in rows.

Clothespin Farm Animals

This art project will last two days. You will need the type of clothespins that clamp, along with cut-outs of animal shapes that do not have legs. The clothespins will be the animals' legs. When the animals are completed, they will stand up.

On Day 1, the children will paint one side of the clothespins and the animal shapes. On Day 2, the children will finish painting the animals and the clothespins.

It is fun to have each child in your room create a different animal. When all the farm animals are completed, you or your class can make a barn and fences and actually arrange the animals in a farm scene.

Colored Chalk Drawings

Colored chalk is a wonderful medium for young children. It can be used in a wide variety of ways. Drawing on construction paper is a lot of fun. Spray the chalk drawings with hair spray and they won't smear so much.

In the spring and summer, drawing on sidewalks with chalk is exciting, too. Decorate the outside of your preschool with sidewalk drawings. Be sure to tell the children that their pictures will disappear when it rains.

Notepad for Mom

Mother's Day is the second Sunday in May. Children love to make their moms presents. Here is a fun and easy idea.

Have the children paint a design on the shiny surface of a plastic tile. Provide each of the children with a small notepad or small sheets of paper cut to fit the plastic tile. The paper can be attached to the tile with a wooden clothespin. Paint the clothespin to make it look more attractive. Mom will love it!

Mom's Wrapping Paper

After the children have made the notepad gifts for their mothers, they will want to wrap them. Here is a fun way the children can make their own wrapping paper.

Peel the paper jackets off short lengths of crayons and rub their edges on drawing or construction paper to make pictures or designs with interesting effects. If the crayon colors are applied to the paper lightly, the colors can be applied over one another to create transparent effects.

Cereal Mosaics

There are many dry breakfast cereals at the grocery store which are filled with artificial coloring. They are amazingly colorful! I personally think that they are better for art projects than they are for breakfast.

Give each child a piece of construction paper or poster board with the outline of a flower on it. Fill the inside of the flower with glue. Have the children place the cereal inside their flowers.

Flowerpot

Small children love parties. Save the extra napkins, paper cups, and straws from all your parties to use in art projects.

Fill a cup with clay and sand to make the flowerpot. Cut flowers from brightly colored poster paper. In the center, on both sides of each flower, paste a small circle of construction paper in a contrasting color. Staple the flowers to green pipe cleaner stems. Attach green paper leaves. Stick two flowers in each pot for an attractive arrangement.

Twin Wings

Give each child a cut-out of a butterfly. Children with good fine motor skills may wish to cut out their own. The children should splatter or drop paint on one of the butterfly's wings. Fold the butterfly in half, pull it apart, and you should see an identical pattern on each of the butterfly's wings.

Add antennae and hang the butterflies from the ceiling.

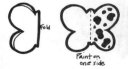

May Basket

Here is an easy May basket for the children to make. Paste or staple two paper plate halves together. Decorate both sides of the basket with crayons or paint. Paste a strip of colored construction paper to the ends for a handle.

Potato Print Jungle

Cut potatoes in half. Paint the ends of the potato and print them on paper. Use greens and browns for the background of the jungle picture. When the paint is dry, the children can draw or color pictures of jungle animals on their potato print jungle paintings.

Farm Picture

Provide each of the children with a piece of paper that has a picture of a barn, a chicken coop, a pond, and a fence. Children can color the pictures their appropriate colors and cut them out. Give each child a large sheet of newsprint. Have each glue the barn in place, leaving the door open. Ask each child to draw a picture of an animal that lives in the barn. Next paste the fence near the barn. Ask the children to draw a picture of an animal that they might see in the pasture. Let the children paste their chicken coops onto the newsprint. Encourage the children to draw the hen family around the coop. Paste the ponds in place and suggest the children draw a bird which likes to swim in the pond. The children can be encouraged to finish their pictures by drawing other things that they might see on the farm.

Sponge Painted Forest

The teacher should cut sponges into triangle shapes. Dip the sponges in green paint to create pine trees. These are the trees in the forest. When the paint is dry, the children can color in brown tree trunks and add pictures or drawings of forest animals.

Window KnickKnack for Mother's Day

You will need a cereal box for each child in your room, scissors, clay, and dried flowers or weeds.

This knickknack can be made from a small, individual box or a medium-sized box, depending on what size you want your gift to be. Sit the box upright and cut off part of the front leaving enough at the bottom for a flower box. Cut 8 little blocks from the back resembling panes in a window. Paint the box. Put a clump of clay on the bottom of the box toward the front. Stick dried flowers into the clay so that they come forward and stick out the window.

Have the children make small gift cards to go with their window knickknacks. All the moms will love this Mother's Day gift.

Seed Plaque

Help the children to collect a wide variety of seeds—dried weeds, leaves, branches, acorns, buds, nuts, etc. Ask the parents to send some of these things to school with their children.

Have each child arrange and glue all the above mentioned specimens to a section of chipboard or plywood. Coat with a clear varnish and attach a hanger to the back.

Farm Animal Match

Draw lines to connect the matching animals.

TSD1896-4 *The Preschool Calendar*

Name_____

 and

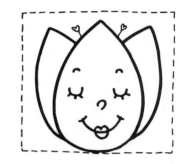

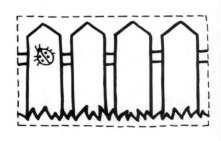

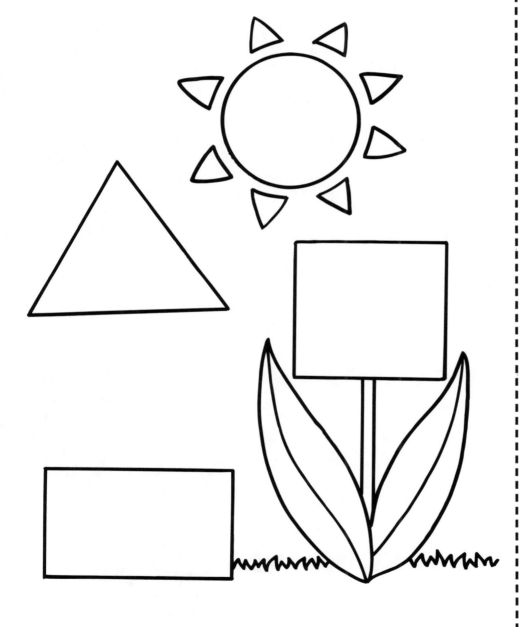

Balance Beam

You will need a balance beam (this can be a 10' plank that is 4" wide), or you can use tape on the floor. Many children can participate if you tape many straight lines on the floor, each 8-10' long and 4" wide. If your children have never had the experience of using a balance beam, be sure to do the tape exercises first.

Exercises:
1. Walk forward, toes pointed straight ahead, eyes looking down, heel in front of the toe.
2. Walk the same style as above, but eyes looking straight ahead.
3. Walk forward to the middle, turn, and walk back.
4. Walk backwards, arms used as balancing rods.
5. Hop on one foot.
6. Jump on beam, landing with one foot in front of the other each time.
7. Stand on one leg, swing other leg back and forth.
8. Sit on the beam, feet straight out.
9. Sit with knees bent, then knees straight.
10. Walk with weight on all fours (animal walk); first walk forward with hands while keeping feet stationary, then walk feet up to meet hands.
11. Bounce the ball while walking; then try bouncing two balls.
12. Throw the ball into the air and catch while walking.

Stone Putting

You will need a small stone or rock. Tape a 2' x 2' square on the floor. Have the child stand approximately 20' away. The child kicks the small stone or rock. After kicking it toward the square, he/she follows it and kicks it again until the rock lands in the square. This is a great outside game.

Whenever you are allowing children to do kicking activities or activities using rocks, be sure to be nearby to provide close supervision.

Tee Ball

Now that it is baseball season, even the youngest of children want to play baseball. The motor skills in baseball are very difficult for young children. To satisfy their desire to play baseball and to offer the children a successful experience, teach them how to play Tee Ball. You can explain to the children that this is an activity that the "real baseball players" do to get better at their baseball playing.

You will need a rubber traffic cone, a wiffle ball bat, and a wiffle ball. The child places the ball on the rubber cone. Depending on the size of the child, a number of cones may have to be placed on top of one another. The child proceeds to bat the ball held stationary on the cone. Have the child bat from a preferred side. After success, the child may alternate batting between the right and left sides.

A Simple Maze

This maze is constructed for crawling. Use blocks, chairs, or any handy classroom materials that can be used to make a simple maze. Instruct the child that he/she is to go through the maze on hands and knees without bumping into any objects.

Skip in Time

Skipping is always a fun activity, even if you are a preschooler and really don't know how to skip the right way yet. Have your children skip in time to music. When the music stops, the children must stop in their positions. If they move, they must sit down.

Call Ball

Have the children stand in a circle with one child in the center. The child in the center tosses the ball high above his or her head while calling the name of another child in the circle. The child whose name was called tries to catch the ball before it hits the ground. (It could also be allowed to bounce once or twice before being caught.) The child who is successful in catching the ball becomes the next one in the center.

Flower Relay Races

Relay races are done in teams. The players of each team must race to a vase full of artificial or paper flowers, pick a flower out of the vase, and race back to their teams. The next person races down to the flowers, picks one, and so on. The first team to finish is the winner.

Yardstick Crawl

This game is similar to the "limbo." The teacher and a child hold a yardstick. Each child takes a turn crawling under the yardstick. After all the children have had a turn, the yardstick is lowered. The children must be careful not to touch the yardstick.

Walking

The weather is beautiful now! It is warm and dry. Be sure to take your children on lots of walks. Make your walks "adventures." Choose special things of which the children should be aware and for which they should look. Collect nature things along the way.

The Bugs Go Marching

The bugs go marching one by one.
The little one stopped to wiggle its thumb.
They all go marching once again,   *(refrain)*
Go marching to escape the rain.
The bugs go marching two by two.
The little one stopped to tie its shoe.
They all go marching once again,   *(refrain)*
Go marching to escape the rain.
Continue with:
The bugs go marching three by three.
The little one stopped to disagree.
The bugs go marching four by four.
The little one stopped to shut the door.

The bugs go marching five by five.
The little one stopped to learn to drive.
The bugs go marching six by six.
The little one stopped to do some tricks
The bugs go marching seven by seven.
The little one stopped to point to heaven.
The bugs go marching eight by eight.
The little one stopped to shut the gate.
The bugs go marching nine by nine.
The little one stopped to walk a line.
The bugs go marching ten by ten.
The little one stopped to say, "The End."

Start with two children, adding two more each time until there are "ten by ten." The one at the end of a line stops for the action and all then stop. They begin again as the lines are repeated and new "bugs" are added. The class may choose one "bug" to perform the action. One can be chosen to say, "The End."

Old King Lion

The child chosen to be Old King Lion wears a paper lion mask, while the rest of the children sit in a circle with their chairs facing outward, each child holding a picture card. Old King Lion walks around the outside of the circle of chairs, calling the names of different animals. As he/she calls each animal the child who has that animal on his/her picture card leaves his/her seat and walks behind Old King Lion. When all children have been called, Old King Lion calls "I am hungry!" and breaks into a run with the children behind him/her. As soon as he/she sits down, the rest of the children must find seats. The child left without a seat becomes the new king and the game proceeds as before.

Start

Stop

We're Lost in the Forest

After a discussion of forest animals, have the children play the game "Lost in the Forest." The children must follow a maze pattern to get successfully out of the forest. The maze can be made by using masking tape on the floor.

Following a maze can help with the overall development of a child's body control, and help to increase physical coordination.

1. Have each child walk through the entire maze, following the lines.
2. When each child can successfully walk through, then add another activity, such as arm signals, hopping, etc., until he/she can do all of the suggested activities in the maze.
3. Innovate with dribbling, skipping, traffic games, etc. Have the children create other variations.

Going Places

Animals not only live in different kinds of environments, but they also move in a wide variety of ways. Here is a fun action rhyme that combines movement, creativity, and listening skills. The children can pretend to be any animals that they wish.

Hippity, hoppity,	Dusty and dirty
Skippity, skoppity,	And scratchy and hurty,
Jumpity, jumpity, **jump.**	Lumpity, lumpity, **lump.**
Slipping and crawling	Up on your feet again.
And tripping and falling	Start down the street again
Bumpity, bumpity, **bump.**	Hippity, hoppity, **hump.**

This is a skipping rhythm. Children should stop at the last word of every third line, ready to take off again.

Everyone Dance

Movement and music both enchant and delight young children. Provide the children with the opportunity of dancing. Choose a wide variety of music: rock and roll, jazz, and don't forget classical music.

Make your own cassette tape of the music so it can be used again. Use a variety of tempos and rhythms so the children can be creative with the movement. (A word of advice: End the tape with a soft, slow song. This will help the children to relax after the excitement of all the dancing.)

Using Mental Images

Very young children sometimes have difficulty imitating or performing gross motor movements. Here are some images that you can use that will help assist children with gross motor activities. Have all the children perform these movements. Think of others they could imitate.

1. Bouncing: bouncing on a trampoline, bouncing a basketball.
2. Bending: Raggedy Ann doll.
3. Balancing: person on the edge of a cliff, tightrope walker in a circus

Name_____

I Know These Birds

We have learned about these birds.
I know their names and what they look like.
I have colored them.
Ask me about the birds.

My State Bird , the _____

Cardinal

Robin

Blue Jay

Woodpecker

Little Bugs Finger Puppets

Directions:

Have children color and cut out the finger puppets. Help them fold and paste to fit their fingers. Have each tell a story about his/her bugs.

Near and Far

When the children are sitting, the teacher will demonstrate the relation of objects to their positions by telling them when the object is near and when the object is far. After the children are able to identify the concepts of near and far, the teacher can move an object "near" and "far" to/from a fixed object, such as a chair.

You can also emphasize the concepts of near and far by:

1. Setting objects at various locations in the room; the child will determine if they are near or far.
2. Using pictures with many objects.
3. Drawing pictures of something "near" and "far."
4. Having the children make up sentences using the terms "near" and "far."

Let's Remember

"Let's Remember" is a game which helps children recall a list of several items.

Have the children pretend that they are packing a suitcase. Have one child name an item he/she would include in a suitcase. The next child repeats that item and adds his/her own to the list. Continue letting each child take a turn until there are about four or five items on the list. You may continue by using different opening statements, such as "I went to the grocery store and bought . . ."

Happy Face

The children draw their own large happy faces on 9" x 12" pieces of manila paper. Those children who are able may cut out their happy face; you may need to cut out the happy faces if you have younger children. On the back, each child can draw something that has made him/her sad (broken toy, lost puppy, etc.). Have the children tell the class about their pictures and then ask them what made them feel happy again like the happy face side of the pictures.

Animal Sounds

This game will help children identify and locate the source of an animal sound. Have the children make and identify several different animal sounds (i.e. dog, cat, cow, pig, horse, sheep, etc.). Make sure that the sounds are recognizable to the children.

Have one child stand blindfolded in the middle of the room. The rest of the children make a circle around him/her. Ask one child at a time to make a different animal sound, and have the child in the center identify the animal sound and point to the direction from which it came. Children really enjoy this game.

Old MacDonald

You will need to have pictures of animals for this activity.

Teach the children the song "Old MacDonald Had a Farm," using the sounds associated with the animals mentioned in the song (cow—moo, dog—bowwow, cat—meow, pig—oink, duck—quack, sheep—baa, etc.).

Present pictures of the animals and ask the children to describe them, tell what they look like, what they do, etc.

Flower Petals

Have ready petals cut from colored paper and backed with sandpaper that will stick to flannel. Place a brown circle on the flannel board to make the center of the flower. Have a child choose a petal and name its color. If the color of the petal is named correctly, the child can place it near the circle. If he or she does not call it by the correct name, the petal is returned to the box and the next child gets a turn.

After a flower is completed with eight petals, put up another circle and have the children start the next flower.

When two or three flowers are made, the game can be changed. The teacher names a color and each child must take that particular petal off the board, until all the petals are picked.

This is also a nice activity for teaching the children more than just "petals" and "centers" of a flower.

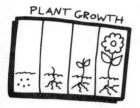

Plant Growth

Draw or find pictures that will show the children the sequence of plant growth (refer to the pictures at the left). Discuss the sequence of plant growth with the children. Let them take turns sequencing the pictures.

You could also make copies of the page of the pictures. Have the children cut them out and paste them in sequence on sheets of construction paper.

You Tell the Story

Place a picture behind a roll-up window shade attached to the wall or bulletin board. Use the type of shade brackets that are intended for black-out shades.

One child each day gets to raise the shade and tell a story about the picture that is hidden behind it. The children should be encouraged to use expressive language to formulate their stories.

Learn Five Birds

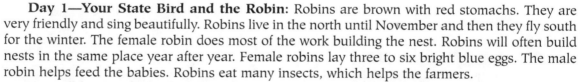

The goal for the children is to learn to name five birds and be able to tell something about each bird. This activity will take four days. Here is the agenda and a paragraph about each of the birds.

Day 1—Your State Bird and the Robin: Robins are brown with red stomachs. They are very friendly and sing beautifully. Robins live in the north until November and then they fly south for the winter. The female robin does most of the work building the nest. Robins will often build nests in the same place year after year. Female robins lay three to six bright blue eggs. The male robin helps feed the babies. Robins eat many insects, which helps the farmers.

You will have to find information on your own about your state bird.

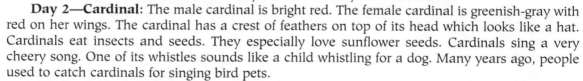

Day 2—Cardinal: The male cardinal is bright red. The female cardinal is greenish-gray with red on her wings. The cardinal has a crest of feathers on top of its head which looks like a hat. Cardinals eat insects and seeds. They especially love sunflower seeds. Cardinals sing a very cheery song. One of its whistles sounds like a child whistling for a dog. Many years ago, people used to catch cardinals for singing bird pets.

Day 3—Blue Jay: Blue jays are blue, of course! They are related to crows. They have loud and harsh voices, and sometimes they sound like they are yelling, "Thief, Thief!" This bird sometimes bothers other birds by wanting to take their eggs. Blue jays build very untidy nests in large trees. The blue jay is so beautiful that its noisy ways and bad habits can be forgiven.

Day 4—Woodpecker: The woodpecker uses its strong bill to make holes in trees to search for insects. The toes of a woodpecker are arranged so that they can cling to the side of a tree, and even climb up and down the trunk. Two of the toes are pointed forward and two are pointed backwards. Woodpeckers make holes in trees for their nests also, and they leave little wood chips on the bottom of the holes as pillows for their eggs.

Jungle Animals

For the next three days the children are going to be learning the names of the animals (jungle, farm, and forest), and the names of the environments in which they live. Review the jungle animals. Which ones live on the ground? Do we have jungle animals living in the United States? If so, where do they live?

Farm Animals

Present picture cards of the farm animals. Have the children name the farm animals. Are farm animals "wild" like the jungle animals? In what kinds of buildings or environments do the farm animals live (barn, coop, pond, etc)? Farm animals live on farms because they are needed by farmers. What kinds of jobs do the animals do on the farm? How are jungle animals and farm animals the same? How are they different?

Forest Animals

Present picture cards of some of the forest animals (raccoon, squirrel, skunk, deer, beaver, moose, otter, bear, etc.). Are these animals "wild" or would they make good pets? Why wouldn't they make good pets? How are they similar to farm/jungle animals? How are they different? Where do some of these animals live in the forest? Which ones live in the trees? Which ones live in caves? Which ones live in the water?

Plants Grow from Seeds

Recruit help in making a large collection of seeds. Ask the parents to send seeds with their children to school. Use the seeds to provide several different learning experiences for the children.

Magnifying Glass: Let the children observe how the seeds differ in size, shape, and the type of plant into which they grow.

There are many different kinds of seeds:
Seeds that grow inside fruits
Seeds we can eat (corn, nuts, rice, wheat)
Seeds animals eat (acorns, pine nuts, etc.)
Seeds that grow into flowers
Seeds that grow into trees and shrubs
Seeds that grow into foods we eat

Seeds travel in many ways:
Carried by birds or animals
Blown by wind
Washed away by rain
Shot out of pods
Float through the air

If I Could Buy an Animal

Have each child describe the animal he/she would buy if he/she had a hundred dollars. The other children must guess the animal. It is a good idea for the teacher to describe the first animal for the children to guess.

Sequencing Gardening

Read the following paragraphs about the farmer's garden (children may wish to pantomime the story as you read it.) Provide the children with three pictures of the story, in the correct sequence. Follow the illustration next to this activity.

The Farmer's Story

Farmer Brown plants seeds in his garden. He plants carrots, lettuce, and beans. When the vegetables are ripe, he pulls them out of the ground and off the vines. He loads them into his truck and takes them to the grocery store where he sells them.

Our mother buys these good foods at the store and brings them home. She washes them, cooks them, and serves them to us. "Yum, yum," we say, "these are good!"

Help Us Find Our Homes!

Name_____

- -

Cut out the animals.
Paste them on their correct homes.
Color the picture.

Look at My Garden!

Name_____

I'm a Little Flowerpot

I'm a little flowerpot Mom (Dad) put out.	*(point to self)*
If you take care of me, I will sprout.	*(nod head, point to self)*
When you water me, I will grow	*(make sprinkling motions with right hand)*
Into a pretty flower, don't you know.	*(raise left hand slowly up from floor, make wide circle with hands)*

(This poem can also be sung to the tune "I'm a Little Teapot.")

Farm Animals (response)

Listen to the riddle and you can name
A farm animal when you play this game.
At night my home's a stable. It keeps out the rain.
My baby is a foal. I eat lots of grass and grain. *(horse)*
I live in a coop and have two legs.
I have feathers. You eat my eggs. *(chicken)*
I live on a farm. I have four feet.
My baby is a calf. I provide milk and meat. *(cow)*

I help the farmer by catching mice.
I have fur. The farmer treats me nice. *(cat)*
I stay in a fold at night on the farm.
My coat will keep you very warm. *(sheep)*
I help the farmer bring in the cows.
Sometimes the farmer takes me into her house. *(dog)*
On the farm I stay in a pen.
My meat gives you sausage and bacon. *(pig)*

Six Little Ducks

Six little ducks went out to play, over the hill and far away.
When the mother duck went "Quack, quack, quack,"
Five little ducks came waddling back.
Five little ducks went out to play, over the hill and far away.
When the mother duck went "Quack, quack, quack,"
Four little ducks came waddling back.
Four little ducks went out to play, over the hill and far away.
When the mother duck went "Quack, quack, quack,"
Three little ducks came waddling back.
Three little ducks went out to play, over the hill and far away.
When the mother duck went "Quack, quack, quack,"
Two little ducks came waddling back.
Two little ducks went out to play, over the hill and far away.
When the mother duck went "Quack, quack, quack,"
One little duck came waddling back.
One little duck went out to play, over the hill and far away.
When the mother duck went "Quack, quack, quack,"
All the little ducks came home.
(Use this poem with the flannel board. Make one mother duck and six baby ducks.)

Robin

Little Robin Redbreast sat upon a rail.
Niddle, noddle went his head,
And wiggle, waggle went his tail.

A May Basket

Up the steps,
One, two, three, four.
I will ring the bell on your front door.
I'll leave a May basket just for fun,
I'll turn around and I'll run, run, run!
(Most preschools and kindergartens have stairs which the children can climb as they act out this rhyme.)

A Farmer

If I were a farmer	*(point to self)*
With flour, milk, and meat,	
I'd sell you these and other things	
That you would like to eat.	*(make eating motion)*

(Make a chart with your class listing all the foods that are grown on a farm.)

∿∿∿ Finger Plays/Poetry ∿∿∿

Mother's Day

Five flower baskets sitting on the floor.
One will go to _____'s mom,
Then there will be four.
Four flower baskets, pretty as can be.
One will go to _____'s mom,
Then there will be three.
Three flower baskets with flowers red and blue.
One will go to _____'s mom,
Then there will be two.
Two flower baskets, bright as the sun.
One will go to _____'s mom,
Then there will be one.
One flower basket, oh, it's sure to go
To your very own mother, who is the
Nicest one you know.
(Make five flower baskets for the flannel board to use with this poem.)

Birds and Spring

I am a bird, all dressed in black.
I flew away, but now I've come back.
I am a bird, all dressed in blue.
I like to fly and I like to sing, too.
I am a bird, all dressed in green.
I am the smallest bird ever seen.
I am a bird, I am in orange, you know.
Whenever I fly, you can see me glow.
Four birds fly and four birds sing.
They all seem to know that now it is spring.
(Show pictures of the birds the children have learned.)

The Little Bird

Once I saw a little bird,	*(extend left arm and forefinger)*
Go hop, hop, hop.	*(extend middle finger of right hand, make fingers "hop")*
So I said, "Little bird,	
Will you stop, stop, stop?"	*(hold palm up like police officer)*
I went to the window,	
To say how-do-you-do.	
But she shook her head,	*(shake head "no")*
And away she flew.	*(make hands "fly" to sides)*

Hoppity Toad

I am a funny hoppity toad,	*(squat down)*
Trying to jump across the road.	*(jump in squatting position)*
Winking, blinking my big eyes,	*(blink eyes)*
Snapping at some bugs and flies.	*(open and close mouth quickly)*

Bees

Here is the beehive.	*(make fist)*
Where are the bees?	*(hold out hands, palms up)*
Hidden away,	
Where nobody sees.	
Soon they'll be coming,	
Out of the hive.	
One, two, three,	*(hold up fingers one by one)*
Four, and five.	

Taking a Walk

Taking a walk	*(make fingers walk)*
Was so much fun,	
We didn't hurry,	*(move fingers faster)*
We didn't run.	
We watched for birds,	*(move hand in flying motion)*
We watched for bees.	*(wiggle fingers)*
We looked at all	
The lovely trees.	*(hold fingers upright)*

Birds

Here is a tall, straight tree.	*(stand)*
Here are five birds, you can see.	*(wiggle five fingers)*
One, two, three, four, five to arrive!	*(bend down fingers)*
Now—let's count again to five.	*(repeat action)*

ᴧᴧᴧᴧ Finger Plays/Poetry ᴧᴧᴧᴧ

Pets in Our Classroom

One white rabbit came to our classroom.
And she stayed only one day.
We fed her lettuce and carrots.
It's too bad she couldn't stay.

Two hamsters came to our classroom.
They filled their little cheeks
With vegetables and lots of fruit,
And they made sharp little squeaks.

Three caterpillars came to our classroom.
They stayed, but by and by,
One day we went to look at them,
Each was a butterfly!

Four canaries came to our classroom.
And for us they did sing.
They made great entertainment,
As we watched them swing.

Five fish came to our classroom.
They were quite a lively brood.
We liked to watch them swim around
And dart up for their food.

Six turtles came to our classroom,
In a terrarium.
It had warm water and a rock.
Good pets they did become.

Seven lizards came to our classroom.
They needed a terrarium, too.
They ate all kinds of insects,
And gave us quite a view.

Eight red ants came to our classroom,
In a box of glass.
We fed them drops of honey.
They were fun to have in class.

So we have had some visitors,
And each one was a pet.
If you could have a choice of them,
Now which one would you get?

(Use as a finger play. Children hold up the designated number of fingers. Pause for a discussion of each animal, bird, or insect.)

What the Animals Do

We'll hop, hop, hop like a bunny.
And run, run, run like a dog.
We'll walk, walk, walk, like an elephant,
And jump, jump, jump like a frog.
We'll swim, swim, swim like a goldfish,
And fly, fly, fly like a bird.
We'll sit right down and fold our hands
And not say a single word.

There Was a Little Turtle

There was a little turtle,
    (make small circle with hands)
He lived in a box,
    (make a box with hands)
He swam in a puddle,
    (wiggle hands)
He climbed on the rocks.
    (climb fingers of one hand up over other)
He snapped at a mosquito;
    (clap hands)
He snapped at a flea,
    (clap hands)
He snapped at a minnow,
    (clap hands)
He snapped at me.
    (point to self)
He caught a mosquito,
    (hold fingers up, snapping the fingers shut)
He caught the flea,
    (repeat above)
He caught the minnow,
    (repeat above)
But he didn't catch me.
    (bend fingers only halfway shut)

Flower

I'd like to be a flower,   *(cup hands together)*
With petals for my head.
When nighttime comes,
I'd fold up   *(fold hands together)*
And never go to bed.   *(shake head "no")*

Five May Baskets

Five May baskets are waiting by the door.
One will go to _____, and that will leave _____.
Four May baskets, they were made by me.
One will go to _____, and that will leave _____.
Three May baskets (I hope one is for you.)

One will go to _____, and that will leave just _____.
Two May baskets for children having fun.
One will go to _____, and that will leave just _____.
One May basket, it is sure to go
To my friend, _____, the nicest person that I know.

(Substitute names of children or people. The class or individuals supply the missing number.)

Five Little Mice

2. Four little mice ran out to the farm,
   Out to the farm one day.
   One little mouse heard a mew-mew-mew!
   And she scampered away, away!

3. Three little mice ran out to the farm,
   Out to the farm one day.
   One little mouse heard a quack, quack, quack!
   And he scampered away, away!

4. Two little mice ran out to the farm,
   Out to the farm one day.
   One little mouse heard a baa-baa-baa!
   And he scampered away, away!

5. One little mouse ran out to the farm,
   Out to the farm one day.
   That little mouse heard a cock-a-doodle-doo!
   And scampered away, away.

6. No little mice are out on the farm,
   Out on the farm today.
   Let's bring them all back. 1, 2, 3, 4, 5.
   And we hope that the mice will stay.

One child at a time runs away; all children return for the sixth verse.

Mother Hen

Suggestion: Walk and sing the song. Follow a leader, who will be Mother Hen.

My Mother

Every day is Mother's Day, but each year we set aside one very special day in which to honor our mothers. That day is the second Sunday in May. It is fun to plan something special on the day to honor our mothers and make them happy. What does this song say about someone's mother?

Suggestion: This song could be about your mother. Sing it to me that way. Sing proudly!

Hush-A-By Swing

High up in a tree, far out on a branch, a beautiful brown and red bird builds her nest. She fastens it securely to the branch, a cradle that swings in the breeze and is out of reach of cats. The mother bird doesn't worry about her eggs or babies when she leaves the nest. They are perfectly safe in their soft little cradle. My song tells you who the bird is and what she is doing.

Suggestion: Make a nest with your hands and swing it very gently as you sing. Put the baby robins to sleep with your smooth singing and swinging.

The Maypole Dance

This action play may be sung to the tune of "Go in and out the Window."

Walk around the Maypole   *(walk around*
Walk around the Maypole   *in wide circle)*
Walk around the Maypole,
On the First of May!

Pick a colored streamer   *(hold hand out*
Pick a colored streamer   *as if holding*
Pick a colored streamer   *a streamer)*
Hearts are light and gay!

Skip around the Maypole   *(holding out*
Skip around the Maypole   *hand—skip*
Skip around the Maypole,   *around in wide*
Joyfully we sing!   *circle)*

Dance around the Maypole   *(holding out*
Dance around the Maypole   *hand—in small*
Dance around the Maypole,   *dancing steps,*
To welcome happy spring!   *dance around in wide circle)*

Rhythm Instruments

Place the rhythm instruments within easy reach of the children. Each child may select an instrument that would best describe one of the following situations:

> A summer rain
> Soldiers marching
> A buzzing bee
> Church bells
> Sweeping the floor
> Building a house
> The rumble of thunder

Tell a story. Then have the children retell it using various instruments for the sound effects.

Off to the Garden Patch

"Cock-a-doodle-doo!"

The farmer hears the call of the big rooster and he knows it is time to get out of bed. There are the chores and the planting to do. So the farmer eats his breakfast after chores, and away he goes to the garden patch. The ground is soft from the rain and all ready for planting. This day he will spend in the garden so his family will have fresh vegetables all summer.

What does he take with him to the garden?

Suggestion: March around the room singing this song. Play that you are carrying garden tools over your shoulder.

May Day

The first day of May is called "May Day." People have always been very happy to have the cold weather end and sunny days begin. In England, everyone—even the king and queen—would get up early on the first day of May and gather flowers. In the afternoon, a Maypole, decorated with flowers, was set up in the village and everyone danced around it. Then they chose one of the girls in the village to be "Queen of the May."

Today, boys and girls still like to celebrate May Day. Usually they make pretty little baskets and fill them with candy and flowers. They hang one on the door of a friend's house, ring the bell, and then run away before the friend can discover who left the lovely basket.

Let your children make a Maypole and celebrate the first day of May by dancing around the Maypole and delivering May baskets. (See *May Baskets—Fine Motor/Art Activities,* page 254.)

A Bouquet

Place a colorful bouquet of flowers in front of your class. Point out the different heights of the flowers. The children then move the flowers into a second vase, moving the tallest flower first, then the next tallest, etc. When the smallest flower is finally moved, find a place in the room for the bouquet.

Planting

The experience of planting something, caring for it, and watching it grow is a delightful experience for a young child. If you have space in the grounds outside your school, planting a real garden can be great fun. The children can really see their work from beginning to end. (Radishes and beans grow especially well!)

If you do not have space for a real garden, then planting seeds in paper cups can be a lot of fun, too.

Make Butter

You will need baby food jars or small plastic containers with lids, a spoon, and a larger container (for buttermilk).

The ingredients you will need are whipping cream and salt.

Shake the whipping cream by hand in the containers. As the cream thickens, add a small amount of salt. As the butter forms, pour off the milk.

Bring in crackers or bread and let the children sample their butter.

Milk Carton Match

You will need two half-pint milk or cream cartons, a brad, butcher paper, clear adhesive paper, and two identical sets of picture stickers. This will provide children with the experience of matching two like pictures.

Cut the tops off the milk cartons. Cover each carton with butcher paper. Place milk cartons bottom to bottom and secure (in the center) with the brad. Place one set of stickers on the sides of each milk carton. Do **not** place the stickers in the same order on both cartons. Cover with clear adhesive paper.

Animal Crackers

You will need a box of animal crackers. Spread the animal crackers on a sheet of 12" x 18" construction paper. The children can sort the animal crackers onto paper plates by matching animals.

For Younger Children: After the animals are sorted, the children may want to practice naming the animals, and making the animal sounds. Then they can eat the animals.

For Older Children: After the animals are sorted onto the paper plates, the children can talk about the animals as sets. How many are on each plate? They can then order the sets from smallest to largest.

Sewing Cards

Make four 6" by 6" poster board cards, each with a geometric shape on it. Cover with acetate. Tape all sides. Punch holes at regular intervals on the lines of the shape. Knot a shoelace and put it through a hole from the back. On the acetate, color a picture or design, using the geometric shape.

To use the card, the child "sews" the shape with the shoelace by going in and out of the punched holes.

Match the Flowers

You will need two identical seed catalogs. Cut out flower pictures, two of each. Mount one set of pictures on a card that has been divided into sections. Cover with clear adhesive paper. Glue the second set to tagboard. Cover with clear adhesive paper and cut out. Have the children match the flowers.

Spring Ice Cream

Spring is a wonderful time of year to make ice cream. This recipe is good for a group. Have fun!

      3 pasteurized eggs
    1½ cups sugar
         pinch of salt
      5 cups light cream (2½ cups half-and-half and 2½ cups whipping cream)
      1 teaspoon peppermint extract
      1 small package of peppermint candy, crushed
      1 tablespoon vanilla

Beat eggs. Mix all ingredients well. Cut off a half gallon milk carton for each child. Place a small metal juice can inside each milk carton. Pack ice and rock salt around the can. Caution the children to keep the salt and ice outside the metal cans. Fill each metal juice can half full. Have the children stir their ice cream mixtures with spoons or craft sticks until frozen. Makes 25 servings.

Ant Farm

You will need one one-gallon jar, soil, dark paper, cotton, and cheesecloth. Fill the jar with soil about halfway to the top. Find an ant hill. Use a shovel to lift the ant hill and the surrounding dirt and debris into the jar. Cover the jar with dark paper to encourage the ants to make tunnels. Place some cotton on top of the dirt and pour a little water on it every few days. Cover the top of the jar with cheesecloth, then punch holes in the lid for air, and screw on the lid. Feed the ants crumbs of bread, honey, or sugar water.

Critter Cage

This critter cage is very easy to make. If you are ambitious, each child in your class could make one; you could also have one cage for each 4 or 5 children. Roll copper wire screen to fit aluminum cake pans. Join the edges of the screen by sewing them together with a single strand of copper wire removed from the cut edge.

Bird Nest Bag

Help your children collect brightly colored items that birds could use to build their nests, for example, yarn, thread, ribbons, strips of plastic or fabric, hair, and feathers.

Hang all the items in a mesh onion bag and tie it at the top. Hang the bag in a nearby tree and watch the contents slowly disappear. In a few weeks, go on a nature walk with your children. See if you can spot any bird nests with colorful items tucked in between the grass, twigs, and mud.

Where Should I Live?

The children have talked much about jungle, farm, and forest animals. Divide your classroom into four environments: the jungle, the farm, the forest, and a home.

Variation 1: Whisper the name of an animal to each child. Have the children run to where their animals should live.

Variation 2: Give each child a picture of an animal. Have each child take his/her animal picture, and put it in the animal's home.

Variation 3: Let each child choose where he/she would like to go and live: the jungle, the farm, the forest, or home. Once the children are all standing in the environments that they have chosen, have the children tell you what animals they are pretending to be.

Fruit Seeds

Have the children plant lemon, orange, tangerine, and grapefruit seeds in small pots of potting soil. Show the children where to place the pots and how to water them. If successful, these plants will sprout quickly.

Plants We Eat

Explain to the children that people plant gardens to grow some of the foods that we eat. Can the children name some vegetables that we grow to eat?

Teach the children some of the vocabulary words about plants: flower, stem, leaves, root, seed. Make a chart to visualize the parts of a plant. Connect the pictures of the vegetables with yarn. *(See illustration)*

Can the children name some of the vegetables we eat?

Flowers (e.g., cauliflower, broccoli, etc.)   Roots (radish, carrot, beets)
Stems (celery, chives)   Seeds (corn, nuts)
Leaves (spinach, chard, lettuce)

Sprouting Seeds

Use many different receptacles to make your sprouting experiments interesting: tin cans, milk cartons, wax cups, eggshells in egg cartons, orange or grapefruit shells cut in half, muffin tins, jars, glasses. An inverted Pyrex bowl may be used as a cover at first.

Here are some interesting methods for sprouting:

Jar Method: Line a round jar or glass with blotting paper. Slip seeds between glass and paper. Add ½ inch water.

Sponge Method: Place sponge in any flat shallow pan. Arrange seeds. Cover with second sponge until sprouting is quite developed. Large seeds, like lima beans, pumpkins, or nasturtiums, are easily observed. However, try birdseed or mixed wildflower seed for interesting results.

Garden Stew

Gardens grow so many wonderful vegetables that we can use in the following recipe. So, let the kids make lunch today! Here is a healthy, good tasting, and easy recipe.

2 pounds ground beef	1 15-ounce can tomato sauce
1 onion, diced (optional)	4 cups water
6 potatoes, peeled and diced	1 teaspoon salt
6 carrots, peeled and diced	½ teaspoon pepper
1 can green beans (or ½ pound fresh)	dash of oregano
1 can whole-kernel corn (or fresh from 3 ears of corn)	

Brown ground beef and onions; drain. Add remaining ingredients. Cook on medium heat for 20 minutes and simmer for 30 additional minutes. (Increase time if fresh green beans are used.) Makes 12 servings.

Storytelling

One of the most special times of the day to a young child is "Storytime." The summer section of *The Preschool Calendar* provides an increased number of stories and story-related activities. You can make your classroom's storytime educational, creative, and lots of fun. Here are some helpful suggestions.

Benefits of Storytelling

1. It can be the child's first introduction to the world of books.
2. It can help teach an appreciation of literature.
3. Storytelling can help increase language development, both receptive and expressive.
4. The child's listening and "paying attention" skills can be increased.
5. Cultural traditions of people can be taught through storytelling.
6. Storytelling can also be used to teach reading, math, science, etc.
7. . . . And of course, storytelling will entertain, amuse, and delight children.

The "How to Prepare" for Storytelling or "The Do's"

1. Read the story through once—just for the enjoyment.
2. Read it again for the sequence of events, the outline of the plot.
3. Choose some "high" words—colorful words—to give flavor to your story.
4. Find some "key phrases" like—"Fee-fi-fo-fum," "Mirror, mirror on the wall," "I'll huff and I'll puff."
5. Practice telling the story. Read it over several times.
6. The ending is very important. It should be final and happy. Strive to retain the mood of your story. If it is joyous, use a lifting voice; if it is serious, use a sober tone.
7. Help the children to visualize the story as you go along, and bring the characters to life for them. If a child misbehaves or is inattentive, look him/her right in the eye and you will bring his/her attention back to you. Look at each child as you speak, and try to include all of them.

Some "Do Not's"

1. Speaking too fast.
2. Being overly dramatic.
3. Talking down to children.
4. Explaining in too much detail.
5. Forcing attention, with "Now, children," "Listen, children," "Pay attention," etc. Never do that.
6. Holding the children's attention too long or telling too many stories. No matter how much they beg for more, leave them wanting more.

The Fourth of July

Our Fourth of July national holiday lends itself to a discussion of America. Learn the Pledge of Allegiance. Talk about the history of our flag—13 stripes for the original colonies and 50 stars, one for each state. Show pictures of the Statue of Liberty. Discuss the renovation of the statue. Explain that it is a symbol of freedom and that it was a gift to us from France. Bring in a globe and show the children where our country and other countries are located. Sing "America the Beautiful."

When you begin discussing "Other Lands," show a picture of the flag of the country for that day. Tell what language the people speak. Explain some of the more colorful customs. Read a story about a child living in that country. Talk about the kinds of clothes the people wear. Explain any interesting features of the country—for example, Holland has tulips and windmills, and Mexico and Canada are our neighbors.

Make Summer Special

Many children of full-time working parents will attend a day care program all summer long. Change your daily schedule. Everyone gets tired of the same thing. You could even call your daycare program a "summer day camp." Try to plan as many activities as you can that take place outdoors. Set up sprinklers and wading pools. This is a great way for the children to really enjoy summer and to keep cool during those very hot months.

Happiness Is . . .

Ask the children about all the things that make them happy. After this discussion, have the children draw large pictures of some of these things. Post all the pictures on a bulletin board entitled "Happiness is . . ."

Under each picture, staple a small card with the child's name and a description of the picture.

Make Flags

Give each child a piece of white construction paper. Each child should also have red paper strips and a blue paper square. Let the children paste the red strips and the blue square to the piece of white paper to make our American flag.

After the pieces have been glued on, let the children put star stickers on the blue part of the flag. Putting on the star stickers is usually the children's favorite part of this project. Glue each flag to a black strip of construction paper (for the pole).

Our Own Story

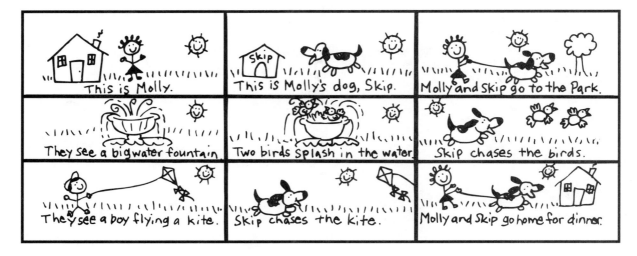

Cover the bulletin board with white paper, and divide it into nine boxes. Have the children make up a story. You will probably have to guide them. Illustrate each part of the story in the boxes. Write a caption under each picture, describing that part of the story. When you are finished, have the children take turns retelling the story that they created as a group. Be sure to title the story and put up a list of the children's names as authors.

Fireworks

Give each child a piece of black paper. Have the children make designs on the paper using white glue from a bottle. Sprinkle glitter over the glue. If you use a variety of colors, this project will look even more spectacular.

When the glue and glitter have dried, staple the pictures on the bulletin board or tape them to a wall. Entitle the display "Fireworks."

Have a discussion with the children about fireworks. They are dangerous. Only adults who are trained should set off fireworks. Talk about why we set off fireworks on the 4th of July.

Summer Bugs

Collecting bugs is a favorite summer activity for many children. Cover the background of this bulletin board with green and blue construction paper, to represent the sky and the grass. Have each of the children make a "bug." The children can color, paint, and glue on scrap fabric or other interesting things to create their bugs. Place all the crawling bugs in the grass and all the flying bugs in the sky.

Wet Chalk Drawings

This is a fun "outside" activity. Give each of the children colored chalk and a wet piece of white construction paper. Let them draw anything they wish. After the pictures are dry, back them with pieces of colored construction paper. Mount them on the bulletin board.

Climbing Koala Bears

The background of this bulletin board should be filled with branches, to resemble the tops of the trees.

Give each of the children two cut-out shapes of a bear. Have the children draw in the facial features. Staple all around each koala bear, leaving an opening so the koala bear can be stuffed with newspaper. Staple the opening shut after stuffing. Display the koala bears on the tree branches.

Get-Together at the Zoo

A whooping crane came walking,
He wanted to have fun.
But he was very lonesome,
For he was only one.

The whooping crane kept walking,
Till he came to the zoo,
And there he met a camel,
And she, of course, made two.

The camel and the whooping crane,
They stood beneath a tree.
A huge baboon then came along,
And he, of course, made three.

They talked about the friendly zoo.
They heard an awful roar.
A lion with a yellow mane
Came by and there were four.

A great big lumbering animal
Was the next one to arrive.
She said, "I am an elephant,"
And she, of course, made five.

Next was a monkey-doodle
All full of funny tricks.
He said to them, "Why, howdy-do,"
And he, of course, made six.

And then there came the tall giraffe,
Her neck stretched up to heaven.
She bowed and smiled at everyone,
So she, of course, made seven.

A polar bear came lumbering by.
She said, "I'm very late.
If I can stay and play with you,
Of course, we will be eight."

A great huge hippopotamus
Thought it was time to dine.
He stayed and ate a bale of hay,
And he, of course, made nine.

A moose with antlers on his head
Was kept inside a pen.
But he got loose, the daring moose,
And he, of course, made ten.

The animals all danced around.
They played some zoo games, too.
They were so happy they were friends,
And had their own fine zoo.

(If the children can read, duplicate the poem for each child. Children not acting out the rhyme can indicate the numbers on their fingers.)

The Treasure Hunt

"We're going on a treasure hunt today, boys and girls," said Mr. Johnson.

The boys and girls in the kindergarten class jumped up and down with excitement.

"Where's the treasure hidden?" asked Johnny.

"On the beach," said Mr. Johnson. "Let me show you where it's located."

He unfolded a yellowed piece of paper about the size of a newspaper and tacked it on the bulletin board. The children gathered around Mr. Johnson as he began explaining the map.

"This is a map of the area where the treasure is hidden," he began. "If you look carefully, you will find clues." The room buzzed with excitement as the children examined the map.

"This is a sand dune," said Janie.

"Here's the picnic tables," said Jeff, pointing to the spot on the map where the tables were drawn.

"Is the 'X' the place where the treasure is hidden?" asked Mark.

"That's right!" said their teacher. "The treasure is hidden there. After everyone has made a copy of the treasure map, we'll drive to the beach and see who can find the treasure."

After the children drew their maps, they boarded the bus that was to take them to the beach.

"Everyone will line up outside the bus," said Mr. Johnson when they arrived at the beach. "When I say 'go,' you follow your map and see if you can locate the treasure."

What fun the children had looking for the treasure!

"I found it," shouted Jeff a few minutes later. All the children ran to the spot where Jeff stood. Underneath a weather-beaten log was a treasure chest.

"Open it! Open it!" yelled the children.

Jeff pulled the chest out, lifted the rusty latch, and opened the lid.

"Oh!" sighed the children. Inside the chest were tiny objects wrapped in gold paper.

"They look like gold pieces," said Timmy.

"Many years ago when pirates ruled the oceans, they often hid their money chests in inlets along the bay," said their teacher.

Each of the children took a surprise from the chest and opened it. Wrapped inside the shiny gold paper was candy. "We'll eat the candy after we have our picnic lunch," said Mr. Johnson.

What a nice way to end a treasure hunt!

The Elephant and the Monkey (A Tale from India)

Once upon a time, an elephant and a monkey had a quarrel. The elephant was proud because she was so strong. "See how big and strong I am!" she said. "Can you pull a tree down?"

Now the monkey was proud because he was so quick. "See how fast I can run and climb!" he said. "Can you climb a tree? Can you hang by your tail from a branch?"

At last they went to a wise old owl. "We can't agree," they said. "Tell us what you think. Which is better—to be strong, or to be quick?"

The owl said to them, "Do just as I tell you, so that I can find out which is better. Do you see that big fruit tree across the river? Go and pick the fruit and bring it to me."

So the monkey and the elephant went to the river, but the water was so swift that the monkey was afraid. "Get on my back," said the elephant proudly. "I am big and strong. I am not afraid to swim across a swift river."

The monkey got on the elephant's back, and they soon got across the river. On they went until they came to the tree. It was so tall that the fruit hung high above them. The elephant tried to reach the fruit with her trunk, but it was too high.

"Wait a minute," said the monkey proudly. "I can climb." He ran quickly up the tree, and threw down the rich, ripe fruit. The elephant put it into her big mouth. Then they crossed the stream and gave the fruit to the owl.

"Now," they said, "which is better—to be strong, or to be quick?"

"Neither one of you is better," said the owl. "You had to work together to get the fruit. It took the elephant's strength and the monkey's quickness. One crossed the stream; the other gathered the fruit. So you can see that it is best when we work together."

(Use as a flannel board story. Make an elephant, a monkey, an owl, some fruit, a stream, and a tree.)

Gilly Guppy

Gilly Guppy was slowly **gliding** through her home, an aquarium tank, using only her tail to swim, **moving it back and forth.** She loved to swim! Gilly **moved faster now, turning at the middle, using her side fins to balance.** Suddenly, she noticed something in the water. Gilly **stopped** and **looked up.** Food! A person was dropping fish food flakes on the water. With a quick **flick** of her tail, she **darted** upward and **gulped** at the flakes.

Then a black molly and a swordtail decided to play a game of tag. The swordtail **glided** at Gilly with a **flick** of his tail and **moved his side fins back and forth.** He **touched** Gilly, who **turned around quickly** and joined in the fun. She **chased** another guppy, then a rosy barb, but had no luck.

Gilly **swam** up to the big angelfish and **tagged** him. The angelfish **turned quickly.** He was angry. He was not playing and did not like being disturbed. Gilly slowly began **swimming backward, moving her side fins in circles**, trying to get out of his way. The angelfish **darted** at Gilly, hoping to nip her and teach her a lesson—he was ruler of the aquarium.

Poor Gilly **turned** quickly, **bending at the middle,** and **dashed** to the back of the tank where the seaweed would hide her. Gilly **stopped** for a second to catch her breath; she **opened and closed her mouth** to swallow air in the water, and she **moved her gills.** The angelfish got tired of chasing Gilly, **turned,** and **swam away.** Gilly **relaxed.** She was safe!

(The children can pretend to be Gilly Guppy, making motions with their legs and using their arms as side fins. After trying the actions, the children can repeat this verse whenever the name "Gilly" is said:
   "Glup, glup, gloop, gloop, gobble, gobble, good
   I swim all day, I swim all night, to find a little food."
Some children can be the other fish.)

The Bear Cub and the Hollow Tree

Once there was a bear cub,
A hungry bear was she!
She looked up at the hollow,
In an old oak tree.

She stared at that hollow.
She sniffed at the air.
Thought bear cub, "Now I wonder,
Could there be some honey there?"

Up climbed bear cub,
Carefully as could be,
Up—Up—Up,
towards the hollow in that tree.

(Use as a flannel board story.
Make a tree and a bear cub.)

In front of the hollow,
Bear cub stopped for just a minute.
She licked her hungry lips,
Then she reached her paws down in it!

Next she poked her head in,
And—What do you suppose?
"Yow!" shouted bear cub.
"Something pinched me on the nose!"

Down scrambled bear cub,
Down towards the ground.
Bump!—Went bear cub,
As she landed in one bound.

Away hurried bear cub—
"There's no honey there for me!"
"Hoot," called out the hollow,
Of that old oak tree!

Off I Go A-Fishing

Off I go a-fishing, a-fishing, a-fishing,
Off I go a-fishing,
To the sparkling brook.

I hope there is a big one, a big one, a big one,
I hope there is a big one,
To nibble on my hook.

First I cast my line in, my line in, my line in,
First I cast my line in,
And hold the pole so tight.

Watch the bobber go under, go under, go under,
Watch the bobber go under—
I think I've got a bite!

Now I start a-reeling, a-reeling, a-reeling,
Now I start a-reeling,
This fish must weigh a lot!

Here it comes a-wriggling, a-wriggling, a-wriggling,
Here it comes a-wriggling—
Just see what I have caught!

(Have the children pantomime the actions of this rhyme.)

Summer Days

It was a hot, sunny day in the summer. Mother Duck and her fluffy little ducklings were taking a walk. Mother quacked, "Today the pond is warm and you will have your first swimming lesson. All little ducks must learn to swim."

All the ducklings waddled into the water, except for David Duck. He said, "I don't want a swimming lesson. I want to watch today."

The other ducks splashed and popped under the water to look for bugs. They paddled their feet and played tag. What fun!

Cathy Caterpillar crawled by and asked David why he wasn't swimming. "I don't like to get water in my eyes," said the little duck.

Francis Frog hopped over and said, "Jump in the water!" David Duck said, "It's too deep for me."

Terry Turtle crawled along and said, "I'll show you how to swim." "No, thank you, I just want to watch," said David.

Kevin Crow flew by and laughed. "I bet you're afraid to get in the water!" he cawed. "Can you imagine, a duck afraid of water?"

Just then, Mother Duck swam over to David and said that it was okay to watch sometimes. Maybe tomorrow he might want to try swimming.

(Use as a flannel board story. Make a mother duck, three ducklings, a pond, flowers, a caterpillar, a frog, a turtle, a crow, and a sun. You could also use this story to encourage discussion about possible "scary" situations, such as swimming lessons, a high slide, dark rooms, getting lost, etc.)

The Shadowy, Shady Tree
(A Quiet Action Story)

Once there was a sleepy, sleepy place under a shadowy, shady tree. In that sleepy, sleepy place lay a small brown puppy. The puppy stood up. *(Children stand.)* She stretched and yawned, and she stretched and stretched some more. *(Children stretch and yawn.)* Then she went to look for something to nibble and gnaw. She took a bone to her doghouse, but she couldn't keep her eyes open. So she went back to the shadowy, shady tree and went to sleep. *(Children sit down and clasp hands beside their heads.)*

Once there was a furry, purry, little gray ball of a kitten. He said in a wee sleepy voice, "Oh, dear! I am so sleepy." So he yawned and yawned and yawned. *(Children yawn.)* He found a basket on the back porch and climbed inside, but he couldn't sleep. So he went to the shadowy, shady tree and under it he curled up like kittens do, and went to sleep. *(Whisper.)*

There was a baby chick who looked for something to eat. The mother hen knew that her baby chick was hungry, so she found some yellow meal for him. She knew that her baby chick was tired, so she led him to the shadowy, shady tree and spread out her warm feathers so that he could creep under them. And he went to sleep. *(Whisper.)*

There was a duckling, quack, quack, quack.
She had soft feathers on her back.
She was tired of swimming and everything,
So she put her head underneath her wing.   *(Put arm over head.)*
And there under the shadowy, shady tree,
She slept until it was half past three.

A butterfly, blue, green, and red,
Sat with her wings above her head,   *(Raise arms over head and*
On a branch of the shadowy, shady tree,   *place palms together.)*
Oh, what a sleepy place to be!

The children saw all of those marvelous sleepy things. They lay down on their backs under the shadowy, shady tree, just as you are lying now in your very own quiet, sleepy, sleepy place. *(Children lie down.)* And what did they do, boys and girls?

(This story can be told in installments. Other animals may be added.)

The Three Wishes
(Traditional)

Long, long ago a man and his wife lived in a little house.

One day the man went into the woods. He wanted a tree for his fire. He looked at all the trees. He saw a big, big tree. The man looked at the big tree. "I will cut you down," he said. "I will put you in my fire. You will burn and burn."

A little fairy heard the man. The fairy said, "Do not cut down my tree. Do not cut down my big tree."

The man looked at the little fairy. He looked at the big tree. "I will not cut down your tree," he said.

"Thank you," said the fairy. "I will give you three wishes. You and your wife make three wishes." Then away went the fairy into the woods.

"Three wishes, three wishes!" said the man. "We will make three wishes. How happy my wife will be!" The man ran to tell his wife. The man saw his wife at the door. "Oh, wife!" he called. "We may make three wishes. I met a fairy in the woods. She gave me three wishes."

The man and his wife sat down by the fire. They had three wishes to make.

"I will wish for a big house," thought the man. "I will wish for a magic fire. It will burn and burn. I will wish for a magic cupboard. Then we shall never be hungry."

The man and his wife thought and thought by the fire.

"Now I will have a big house," thought the wife. "I will have a cat. I will have a dog."

"Wife, wife," said the man. "We cannot sit by the fire all day."

"Come, come, wife," said the man. "Where is my dinner? I have had nothing to eat. I am hungry."

"I wish we had some porridge," said the wife. "I wish we had a pot of porridge."

And at once a pot of porridge was on the fire.

"Oh, wife, wife!" called the man. "You made a wish. Oh, why did you wish for porridge? You foolish woman! I wish you had the porridge on your nose."

And at once the porridge was out of the pot. It was on his wife's nose.

"Oh, oh!" called the wife. "The porridge is on my nose. What can I do? How can I get the porridge off my nose?" The wife pulled and pulled. She could not get the porridge off her nose.

The man pulled and pulled. He could not get the porridge off her nose. The man looked at his wife. He looked at the porridge on her nose.

"I know what I will do," he said. "We still have one wish. I will wish the porridge off your nose." Then the man said, "I wish the porridge were off my wife's nose."

And at once—the porridge was off her nose.

The man looked at his wife. Then he said, "We have made the three wishes. But we have no big house. No magic fire! No magic cupboard! No porridge! All we have is a pot on the fire."

Father's Day Project

The children can make paperweights for their fathers. You will need to have a photo of each child, clear plastic caster cups, white glue, plaster of paris, and felt.

This is how you make the paperweight:

1. Trim the photo to fit inside the cup.
2. Squeeze glue into the cup.
3. Place the photo on top of the glue, face side down.
4. Let dry overnight, or until the glue turns clear.
5. Fill the cup with plaster; let dry.
6. Cut felt to fit.
7. Glue the felt to the plaster.

Father's Day Card

Have a copy of the verse below for each child. Fold the paper into the shape of a greeting card so that the verse is on the inside. Let the children decorate the covers of the cards and sign their names.

Here is the verse for the card:

Though I'm just a little one,
I am so very glad
To tell you that I love you so,
My very special dad.

Template Coloring

Using templates (shapes cut from cardboard), you can make any number of interesting drawings. Use templates of butterflies, bugs, boats, the sun, etc. Slip these under a piece of newsprint, and color over the top with a crayon used on its side. These really make very pretty pictures.

The Sky

Let the children cut pictures out of magazines of things that they would see in the sky (clouds, the sun, rain, airplanes, rockets, bugs, spaceships, planets, birds, etc.). When each child has a good collection of pictures, let him/her paste the pictures on blue construction paper for a daytime sky picture, or on black paper for a nighttime sky picture.

Turtle

Glue or tape a cardboard or paper circle to the back of a spoon. The spoon can be wood or plastic. Yarn can be looped for legs and glued to the circle. Tiny circles can be drawn or glued on for eyes.

Starfish

Draw a starfish on blue paper. Apply glue to the inside of the starfish shape, and then sprinkle on cornmeal. Let dry and remove the excess meal.

You can also get a realistic starfish by cutting one out of sandpaper, but these are not as much fun or as messy.

Butterflies

Talk about the brilliant colors of butterflies and bugs. Trace around the feet of each child on brightly colored construction paper to make butterfly shapes. Draw a body shape between the two "butterfly wings." Cut out the butterfly. Paste narrow strips of black paper in place for the antennae. Decorate the butterflies with bits of bright fabric or construction paper. Hang them from overhead light fixtures or from the top of the chalkboard with colored yarn.

Red Riding Hood's Basket

Read or tell the story of Red Riding Hood to the children. (This story is often a favorite because it is just a little bit scary. When I tell it, I usually have Grandmother hide in the closet instead of being eaten by the wolf.)

After you have told the story, give each child a brown construction paper cut-out of Red Riding Hood's basket. Have the children cut out pictures of food from old magazines and paste the pictures in the basket.

Abstract Painting

Cut black tagboard in 8" x 12" pieces. Put red, blue, yellow, and green enamel in plastic squeeze bottles. Have the child squeeze the enamel onto the tagboard, one time across for each color, keeping the hand in motion constantly. Sprinkle the tagboard with gold glitter.

Let the paintings dry thoroughly, then mount them on a white background.

Liquid Starch Finger Paint

This art activity may be a little messy, but it is a lot of fun. After all, being little and finger painting just seem to go together.

Put various colors of dry tempera paint in salt shakers or small jars with holes in the lids. Pour a small amount of liquid laundry starch on non-absorbent paper, such as shelf paper. Let the children shake the tempera paint onto the starch.

Paint Blowing

Another fun painting technique is paint blowing. Give each child a sheet of construction paper. Put a small amount of paint on the paper. (If you use several colors, the paintings will more exciting.) Have the children blow the paint with straws to create abstract designs.

Crayon Creations

Use old broken crayons to create new ones. The children will love to use these new crayons, and it is a great way to use crayons that usually end up in the trash.

First, collect old crayons and peel off the paper. Next, you will need to melt the crayons. Muffin tins work well for this. Line the compartments with foil, so that the tins will not be permanently covered with melted crayon (melted crayons will stick to metal pans). You can melt a lot of different colors at once if you use muffin tins. You can also use an old double-boiler.

Pour the melted crayons into ice cube trays. Make solid colors, or layer different colors for a rainbow effect. If you are layering the colors, be sure to wait a few minutes for the crayon to solidify before adding the next color.

You can also pour the melted crayons into plastic candy molds to get numbers, shapes, etc. This will make fancier crayons.

(Sue Lewis, Wauwatosa, WI)

Watermelon

Have a watermelon party at snack time on a hot June day and save the seeds. Soak them in soapy water, rinse well, and set them out to dry on paper towels overnight.

From construction paper, cut 3 half-oval shapes for each child: a large one from green, a medium one from white, and a small one from pink or red (see illustration at left).

Have the children line up the straight edges and glue the paper together to form a slice of watermelon. Use a squeeze bottle of white or clear glue to dot glue all over the pink or red paper, and then place a dried watermelon seed on each dot of glue.

(Joyce Cini, Garden City, NY)

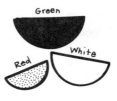

Father's Day Gift

Have each of the children draw a picture of his/her father, or the significant male in his/her life. Back the picture with colored construction paper. Fold the corners of the construction paper to "frame" the picture. Each child should also make a gift card, and wrap the picture of his/her father.

Ladybugs

You will need to purchase Styrofoam balls. Cut the Styrofoam balls in half. Each child should receive one half. Paint each Styrofoam ball red. When the paint dries, black construction paper "dots" can be glued on. Add pipe cleaner legs. The children may either paint on the eyes, or make eyes out of construction paper and glue them on.

Stone Painting

The children should collect smooth stones of various shapes and sizes. With thick tempera paint, have the children paint imaginary faces or animals on the stones. When the paint is dry, the stones can be sprayed with lacquer or varnish.

Twig Painting

This is a fun "outside" painting activity. Instead of using paintbrushes, have the children find twigs with which they would like to paint. When painting with the twigs, you should use thick tempera paint and heavy paper. Using the twigs will give the children's painting an interesting texture and effect.

Oatmeal Carton Dolls

You will need: oatmeal cartons, glue, scissors, scraps of fabric, construction paper, buttons, cotton, or any other scraps that can be used for decorating.

Use the top third of the carton for the head, and the bottom two-thirds of the carton for the body. Decorate the body by using a band of color, ribbon or yarn to differentiate the head from the body. Decorate the head by using yarn, cotton, or fringe for the hair.

These dolls can also be made from the tubes of toilet paper rolls.

Fish

Provide each of the children with a piece of paper with the shape of a fish drawn on it. Have the children tear small pieces of paper, to be glued on the fish to represent scales.

It will be easier for the children to tear all the paper first. With a paintbrush, paint the glue onto the fish shape. The children can then place the "scales" on the fish. Facial features can be added when the scales are dry.

Butterflies

Use a pipe cleaner for the body and variegated tissue paper for the wings. Sheer fabric, dipped in liquid starch and dried, can also be used for the wings. The starch will give the wings body.

Bug Puzzle

Name_____

 and PASTE and =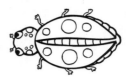

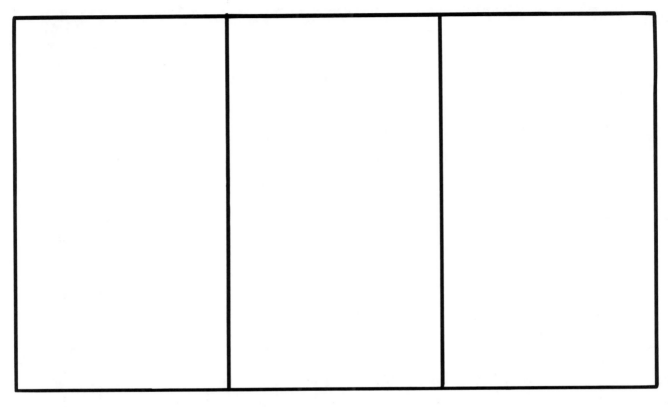

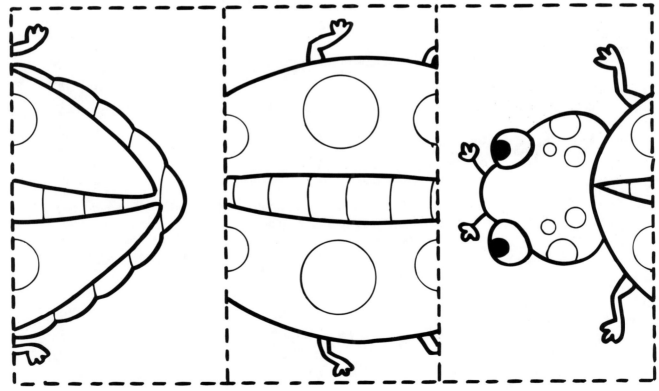

TSD1896-4 *The Preschool Calendar*

Happy Birthday, America!

Connect the dots and color the picture. You may add candles if you would like.

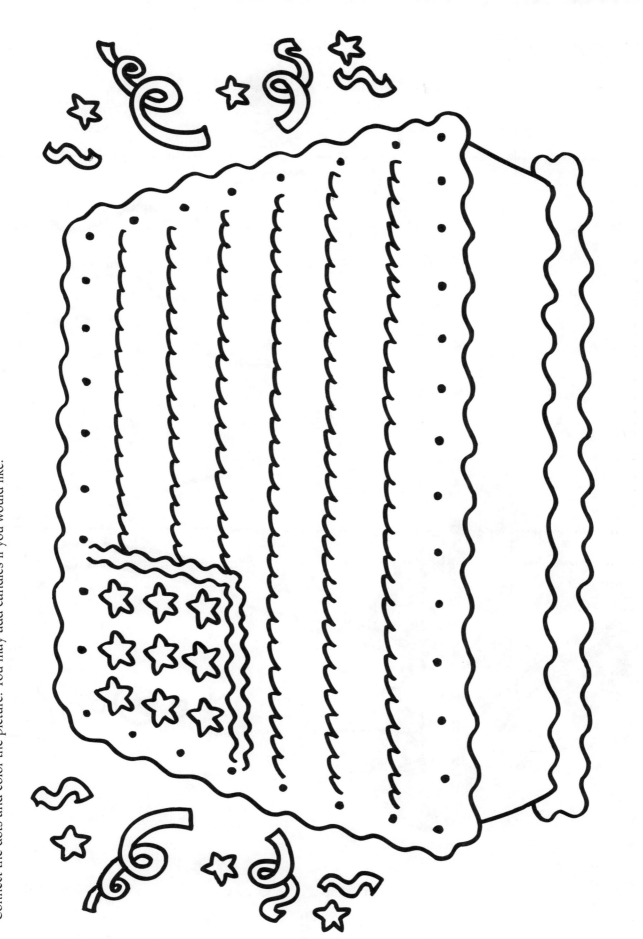

Name _____

Finish the Zebra

Name _____

TSD1896-4 *The Preschool Calendar*

Follow the Leader

The teacher has the children line up directly behind him/her. They should stand at least an arms length apart. The teacher begins to walk around the room, moving in different patterns and assuming various body positions. Equipment can be added if you wish.

Examples:

1. Arms straight over head.
2. Arms straight out like an airplane, then down at sides.
3. Right arm out, then back to side.
4. Left arm out, then back to side.
5. Right arm over head, then down.
6. Left arm over head, then down.
7. Hop on right foot.
8. Hop on left foot.
9. Hop on both feet like a bunny.
10. Clap hands over head.
11. Clap hands in front of body.

Using Equipment:

12. Walk across a balance beam.
13. Crawl through hoops.
14. Roll like a log across a mat.
15. Leap forward in giant leaps across many mats.

Go Find Your Partner

Pin a picture of a zoo animal on each child. If you have ten children in your class, you should use five different animals—each child should have a match.

One child skips around the room until he/she hears the words "Go find your partner." He/she stops by the child who is wearing the same animal picture, then takes the partner's hand and they skip around the room together. When they have finished their turn, another child is chosen.

Jumping the Brook

You will need to make X's on the floor with tape. Place them in random sequence, varying the distance apart. These X's are the "rocks" in the "brook."

1. Have the child jump, feet together, from "rock" to "rock," landing on each X with both feet together.
2. Next, have the child jump and straddle the X with both feet.
3. Have the child jump from X to X, alternating take-off with the right foot, then the left foot.

Roll-a-Ball

Use chalk to draw a large circle on the floor. Draw a line several feet from the circle. The children stand behind the line and take turns trying to roll a ball into the circle. If the ball does not roll into the circle or if it rolls out, the child must sit down.

Tug-of-War

It is so much fun to be outside in the summer. A natural summer activity is "Tug-of-War." Divide the children into two teams and let them "tug-of-war." The children will feel that they are playing a very grown-up game.

Playground Maps

Draw large mazes or "maps" on the playground with chalk. Have the children follow the mazes by walking, skipping, hopping, etc.

It is also fun to draw in houses along the roads. Let each child draw his/her own house. The children can visit each other in their houses by following the roads.

Streamers

Streamers that wave in the wind are a lot of fun for children and they are very easy to make.

Cut party crepe paper into 18" lengths. Attach the crepe paper to tongue depressors so the children have handles to grasp.

Let the children move their streamers in any way they wish. Go outside and let the wind blow the streamers. If you use them inside, play the piano or put on a tape or CD. The children will love moving their streamers to the rhythm of music.

Hansel and Gretel Lost in the Woods

Read or tell the children the story of Hansel and Gretel. Then, as a fun movement activity, have the children act out the part of the story where Hansel and Gretel are lost in the woods.

Make a path for the children to follow using bread crumbs, or let the children make the path themselves. Ask the children to pretend that they are the characters. Are they scared? Are they brave? To make this activity even more exciting, the teacher can play the part of the witch.

Jack-in-the-Box

Have the children curl up on the floor like Jack-in-the-boxes with closed lids. Then have them chant:

> "There's old Jack down in his box,
> He's as crafty as a fox.
> Will he jump or will he stay?
> Listen now and you can play."

Say "jump" or make a sharp sound to signal to the children that they should jump up out of their imaginary "boxes." This activity is even more fun if the teacher varies the length of the pause before saying "jump."

Sprinklers

Summer is the time for water fun. Children who spend full days at a day care program should also have the opportunity to play in water. Sprinklers are always tons of fun. Wading pools and even water balloons (if you are brave enough) can be a delightful and refreshing experience on a hot summer day. Be creative with water ideas, and let the kids get wet!

Duck, Duck, Gray Duck

The classic game, "Duck, Duck, Gray Duck," has enchanted children for years. I'll bet you remember playing it as a child. Take the kids outside and let them enjoy running around the circle playing "Duck, Duck, Gray Duck."

ᨒᨒ Gross Motor/Movement Activities ᨒᨒ

Water Play

During the summer months, provide the children with many opportunities to play with water. Use sprinklers, wading pools (closely supervised), water tables, pails of water for sinking and floating activities, etc. It is a great way to cool off during the summer months, and will provide the children with wonderful exercise and excitement.

1-2-3-4-5

This is a fun rhyme for exercising. When practicing for the "Preschool Olympics Track and Field Day," this rhyme can provide a good warm-up activity.

Hands on shoulders,	Hands on nose,	Hands in front,
Hands on knees,	Hands on ears,	Hands to the side,
Hands on head,	Hands on the floor,	Hands in the sky,
1-2-3.	1-2-3-4.	1-2-3-4-5.

Where Am I?

Children sit on the floor in a circle. "It" is blindfolded and stands in the center of the circle. Children chant:

Sometimes I'm way up high,
Sometimes I'm way down low.
Now I'm up—now I'm down,
Guess where I am now!

While chanting, the children stand on tiptoe and stretch their arms high for "up" and stoop low for "down." At the end of the chant, a child selected to be the subject sings out alone, "Where am I?" "It" must guess either "up" or "down" by location of the child's voice. If he/she is correct, the child he/she catches becomes the new "it."

How Do You Do?

The children stand in a circle, preferably one painted on the floor or ground. One child is chosen as "it" and walks around inside of the circle, stops before the selected child and offers his/her hand, saying, "How do you do?" The other child responds, "How do you do?" Then the one who is "it" says "Goodbye" and drops his/her hand. He/she races around the inside of the circle while the other child goes around outside. The one who gets back to the empty place first is the winner.

Variation: The children are paired, and in turn go through this ritual; or they race in different directions around the outside of the circle (though this often leads to collisions).

Hide-and-Seek

What is more fun than playing hide-and-seek? Have the children play this game outside during the warm summer months. Be sure to establish boundaries, so the children do not decide to hide in a place that may not be safe. Teach the children that when the teacher whistles (or some type of signal) that the game is over and all the children must come out of hiding.

Drop the Bean Bag

Have all the children sit in a circle. Choose one child to be "it." "It" is given the bean bag and is instructed to walk around the circle very quietly. "It" drops the bean bag behind a child of his/her choice. That child picks up the bean bag and chases "it" around the circle. "It" must sit in the child's place first. The child who was given the bean bag is the next child to be "it." Make sure that each child is given a turn to be "it."

The "Preschool Olympics" is a wonderful track and field experience for young children. Everyone has fun and everyone wins!

The following will provide you with complete directions for a very successful Olympics day.

Organization

Divide your playground into seven stations where the events will be held. (Description of the stations is below.) One adult should stay at each station, and be in charge of conducting that event.

The children should be divided into small groups (5 to 10 children). Each of the groups of children should have one adult (or coach) assigned to them. This adult will rotate with his/her group of children to each of the stations.

Each group of children will begin at a different station and rotate every five to fifteen minutes. (You will have to determine how long the events will take.) Using a rotation method, all the children begin at the same time, and will end at the same time. No waiting!

Extra Help

To have a successful Olympics day, you will need lots of help. If you do not have enough staff members, ask the parents to volunteer some time. I am sure that you will find parents who are willing to assist.

Awards

Every child should receive an award at every station. The children could have ribbons pinned onto them at each station, or the children could wear 5" x 7" index cards. At each station, a sticker could be added to their index cards. Be creative with the awards!

Conclusion

End your Preschool Olympics day with a picnic lunch. After an entire morning of physical activity and lunch outside, everyone will probably be really ready for a rest time.

Practice ahead of Time

Prepare to hold your Preschool Olympics on a Friday. Spend the four days prior to the Olympics practicing. Let all the children become familiar with the skills required for each event.

A note of caution: When practicing, use a golf ball on a spoon for the "Egg on a Spoon Race," and a ball for the "Water Balloon Toss."

The Seven Stations

25 YARD DASH: (or less) This may be too great a distance for many young children. This should simply be a running race.

FRISBEE THROW: Each child should try to throw the frisbee as far as he/she can.

LONG JUMP: Draw a measurement system on the pavement. Mark with chalk how far each child was able to jump.

TRICYCLE RACES: Arrange a course around which the children may ride the tricycles. It is extra fun to decorate the tricycles with crepe paper.

EGG ON A SPOON RACE: Each child should run from one point to another carrying an egg on a spoon. (Plan this race in an area that won't mind becoming covered in egg.)

WATER BALLOON TOSS: The children should throw the water balloons at a specified target. They are not to throw the balloons at each other.

WALKING BACKWARDS RACE: This should be a short course, without barriers into which the children might bump.

Name _____

Inside Toys/Outside Toys

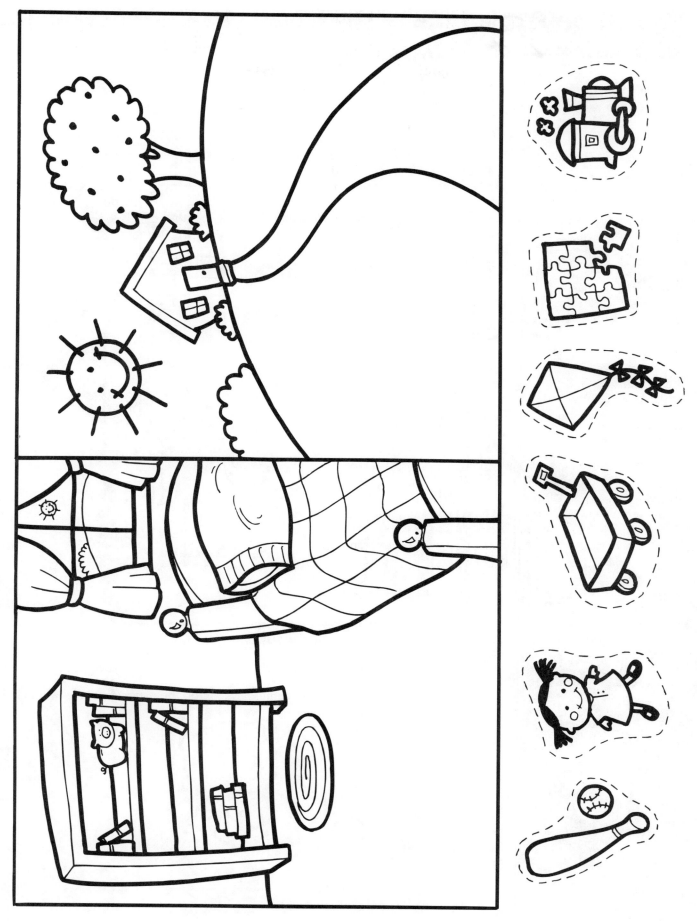

The Three Little Pigs
and the Big, Bad Wolf

Name_____

- -

Cut out the three little pigs and the wolf. Paste each pig by his house. Color the picture.

TSD1896-4 *The Preschool Calendar*

Match Flags

Draw lines to match the flags.

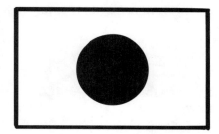

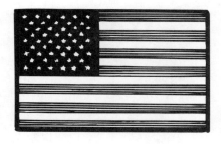

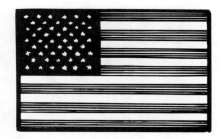

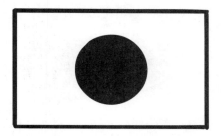

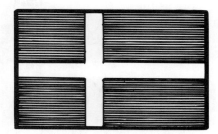

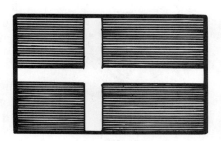

Zoo Animal Sounds

Help the children make a tape recording of the sounds the many different zoo animals make. The children will have a lot of fun making the tape, and probably even more fun listening to it.

Opposites

The concept of things that are opposites is very difficult for young children. To help teach this concept, bring in real objects that the children can see and touch. While the children watch, set up a display at the front of the room depicting things that are opposites. Show the children:

- a big ball and a little one
- a clean jar and a dirty one
- a box with a cover and one that is not covered
- a doll that is asleep and a doll that is awake
- two cups from the playhouse (one cup should be empty; the other cup should be filled with water)
- a wooden block and a bit of fluffy cotton (to show hard and soft)

Nonsense

Ask the following kind of questions, and have the children decide which answer is correct.

- If your dog is sick, do you need: a chair, a cow, a flag, or an animal doctor?
- If you are tired and sleepy, do you need: a kite, an egg, a bed, or a duck?
- If you are very cold, do you need: a fan, a boat, a doll, or a sweater?
- If you are hungry, do you need: a sandwich, a hat, a book, or a clock?

Because children love nonsense, the older preschoolers will enjoy making up their own questions.

Billy Goats Gruff

Read the story of "The Billy Goats Gruff' to the children. Then have the children take turns retelling parts of the story.

Encourage them to dramatize the story. With your help, one child can retell the story as the other members of the class act it out. Horns and tails of the goats can be made from construction paper and attached with rubber bands. Use chairs for the bridge over which the goats must cross. The troll will find his/her hiding place under one of the chairs. The children will have a great deal of fun acting this story out.

Bottom of the Ocean

The teacher starts this game by saying, "We are all at the bottom of the ocean. I am a big clock fish. All the other fish will look at me when they want to know what time it is." Then give each child a turn to name any object that can be seen in the classroom, and to describe the type of fish he/she wants to be. Any kind of fish can be named, but it must be an object found in the schoolroom (i.e. blackboard, crayons, dolls, blocks, etc.). It is important that the child tells what the other fish will do with him or her. For example: "I am a chair fish. The other fish will sit on me."

Comment favorably if a child names something that requires a little thought and imagination. When the game is finished, the children may want to draw pictures of the funny fish about which they talked.

Order by Phone

Play "store" with the children, using a toy phone. Have the child pretend to be the store employee, while you pretend to be the customer. Call the "store" and place an order. Have the child repeat the order for you. Begin by "ordering" only a couple of items, then increase the number of items as the child is able to remember the list.

Three Billy Goats Gruff

Read or tell the story of "The Three Billy Goats Gruff." This is a fun story to tell using a flannel board.

After you have told the story, discuss the concepts of little, medium-sized, and big. Give the children pictures or objects at which to look and describe what the size of each is. The children can also work on matching things that are the same size.

The story of "The Three Bears" works well for this activity, too.

Coupon Book for Dad

Father's Day is just around the corner. Fun Father's Day gifts for the children to bring home are coupon books filled with loving deeds that they can do for their fathers. Have the children help you think up ideas for the coupons. Here are some suggestions:

Bring Dad the newspaper.

Help Dad with household tasks like doing the dishes or raking the yard.

Give Dad a back rub.

Duplicate copies of the ideas and make them into books for the children. Then have the children decorate the books.

You'll enjoy hearing the children's ideas of what they think is helpful to their parents.

My Name Is . . .

Have each child in your classroom tell the class what his/her full name is—first, middle, and last. Ask the children if they like their names. If they could change their names, what would they like to be called? Ask the children to think up "funny" or "silly" names.

What Are You Wearing?

Have the children describe what they are wearing. "Look at the colors you are wearing. Are they plain or plaid? Are they striped? Are the colors light or dark?" Have the children look in a mirror while they are answering these questions.

We Are Different

Discuss the ways in which people are the same or different. Talk about the colors of skin, the languages they speak, the customs they have, the clothes they wear, the colors of eyes and hair, and their sizes.

Make a graph to put up on the wall, indicating eye color, hair color, and height. How many children have brown eyes? How many children have red hair? Who is the tallest? Who is the shortest?

Discuss how differences make us special. The world would not be a very interesting place if we were all alike.

Treasure Hunt

Ask the children, if they were to go on a treasure hunt, what kinds of treasures would they like to find? Where would they find these treasures? Who left the treasures there? What are they going to do with all the treasures that they found?

Let each of the children make a small treasure box. One method is to glue toothpicks to a toothpick box. Paint or spray the box. Add some "treasures." You may also cover any small box with brown construction paper. Use a felt pen to draw lines on the paper to give it the appearance of wood. Paper handles can be glued to the ends.

My Pet Rock

Have each of the children find a rock. Tell the children that these rocks are going to be their new pets. Have each child tell the group about his/her new pet. What is the pet's name? What does the pet like to eat? What types of games does the pet play? Where does the pet sleep? What makes his/her pet rock so special? The children will think that this game is very funny!

Neighborhood Walk

Take the children for a walk around the neighborhood. Plans for the outing in the immediate vicinity of the school need not be elaborate and need not be made far in advance.

Divide the class into groups of three and go for a nature study walk. Give the children time for observation and communication as they develop curiosity about plants, bugs, birds, rocks, and other exciting findings. Take back to the schoolroom any treasures of special interest to be examined under a magnifying glass. These could include:

Rocks	Butterflies	Seeds	Leaves
Bugs	Worms	Flowers	Shells

Help the children decide where they wish to display the rocks they collect, and encourage them to bring others to add to the collection. Appoint several children to see that the rocks are properly displayed.

Magazine Pictures

Give each child a magazine from which to cut pictures of the following types of objects—of course, the categories are unlimited.

Cars	Insects	Zoo Animals	Fish
Farm Animals	Toys	Flowers	Homes
Birds	Clothes		

Paste the cut-outs on 4" x 4" tagboard cards. Set up a pocket chart at the front of the room. Begin by using only two categories. Place one picture from each of these in different pockets.

Divide the cut-out cards among the children. Each child matches his/her card to the corresponding category and places it in the correct pocket.

This game has many variations. Place four pictures in the pocket. Three of the objects will be in the same category and one will be different. The child must pick the one that does not belong.

Learning Roles of Family Members

This takes place as a picture of each family member is placed on the flannel board and the children are led to identify the member and discover what he/she does in the home and for the family. Be sure that the children know the name of each person—mother, father, sister, brother, baby, grandmother, grandfather, etc. Be sensitive to gender roles and stereotypes.

Arrange several family characters on the flannel board, and review their names. Turn or cover the board and remove a character. Return the board and invite the children to identify the missing member. Clues can be given by describing what the missing person does in the family. Continue until all family members can be identified. Keep this activity very open-ended.

These Animals Live in Australia

Color the animals.

Emu

Wallaby

Kangaroo

Banded Anteater

Koala

Platypus

Name _____

Running
Through the Mazes

∿∿⋀∿ Finger Plays/Poetry ∿∿⋀∿

At the Zoo

One, two, three. What did I see at the zoo?
One, two, three. Guess when I give you a clue.
I saw an animal with a long neck. *(giraffe)*
I saw the king of beasts that gives a loud roar. *(lion)*
I saw a large animal with a long trunk. *(elephant)*
I saw a big cat with yellow and black stripes. *(tiger)*
I saw a big, furry animal that hibernates in winter. *(bear)*
One, two, three. What do you see at the zoo?
One, two, three. Give us a clue. We'll guess who.
(Give each child the opportunity to give a clue.)

A Seashell

One day a little shell washed up   *(hold shell)*
Out of the waves at sea.
I held the shell up to my ear,   *(hold shell to ear)*
And I heard it sing to me.
Sh . . . sh . . . sh . . . sh.   *(children repeat)*
A little shell washed up one day,
And lay upon the sand.   *(hold shell in hand)*
It sang a song about the sea,
As I held it in my hand.
Sh . . . sh . . . sh . . . sh.   *(children repeat)*
(This is excellent for practice on the "sh" speech sound. Bring in a conch shell and let the children take turns holding it to their ears to hear the sound of the sea.)

Our Flag

As red as a fire,
As blue as the sky,
As white as the snow—
See our flag fly!
Three pretty colors
Wave at the sky.
Red, white and blue
On the Fourth of July!
Red, white, and blue,
Those colors are.
And every state
Has its very own star.
Hold up the flag,
Hold it up high.
And then say, "Hurrah,
For the Fourth of July!"
(Discuss states in the union. Ask: "How many stars are there? What do the stars stand for? Can you draw a flag?")

Five Little Ducks

Five little ducks, swimming on the lake.
First one said, "Watch the waves I make."
Second little duck said, "Swimming is such fun."
Third little duck said, "I would rather sit in the sun."
Fourth little duck said, "Let's swim away."
Fifth little duck said, "Oh, let's stay."
Then along came a motorboat with a pop, pop, pop. *(clap hands together 3 times)*
And five little ducks swam away from the spot.

Mud

Mud is very nice to feel
All squishy between the toes!
I'd rather wade in wiggly mud
Than smell a yellow rose.

Monkey See, Monkey Do

A little monkey likes to do
Just the same as you and you.
When you sit up very tall,
Monkey sits up very tall.
When you pretend to throw a ball,
Monkey pretends to throw a ball.
When you try to touch your toes,
Monkey tries to touch his(her) toes.
When you move your little nose,
Monkey moves his (her) little nose.
When you jump up in the air,
Monkey jumps up in the air.
When you sit down in a chair,
Monkey sits down in a chair.
(Continue this game using other movements, rhyming or otherwise. Use this action game to precede a rest time or as a readiness activity.)

I Have a Shadow

I have a little shadow   *(point to self)*
He(She) lives with me.   *(shake head "yes")*
When the sun comes out   *(make circle above head with arms)*
So does he(she)!   *(nod head emphatically "yes")*

La Mariposa/The Butterfly

Uno, dos, tres, cuatro, cinco,   *(pop up fingers on right hand as you count)*
Cogi una mariposa de un brinco.
Seis, siete, ocho, nueve, diez,   *(pop up fingers on left hand as you count)*
La solte brincando otra vez.
One, two, three, four, five,   *(pop up fingers on right hand as you count)*
I caught a butterfly.
Six, seven, eight, nine, ten.   *(pop up fingers on left hand as you count)*
I let him go again.

The Fourth of July Parade

We are having a Fourth of July parade,
A parade on the Fourth of July!
Sammy proudly carries the flag,
Straight, and tall, and high.
Sally plays a triangle, ding!
Billy tootles a flute.
Beth bangs two lids with a clang!
And Jack wears a sailor suit.
Elizabeth loudly blows a horn.
Jimmy whistles a tune.
Mary hits a frying pan,
With a big, long, iron spoon.
Hooray, hooray for the Fourth of July!
For the Fourth of July, hooray!
We will march along and sing a song,
For the good old U. S. A.
(Select eight children to dramatize the rhyme. Use a triangle, flute, lids, horns, frying pan, and spoon for a "real" Fourth of July band. Substitute names of children in the class.)

One, Two, How Do You Do?

1, 2, how do you do?
1, 2, 3, clap with me;
1, 2, 3, 4, jump on the floor;
1, 2, 3, 4, 5, look bright and alive;
1, 2, 3, 4, 5, 6, your shoe to fix;
1, 2, 3, 4, 5, 6, 7, look up to heaven;
1, 2, 3, 4, 5, 6, 7, 8, draw a round plate;
1, 2, 3, 4, 5, 6, 7, 8, 9, get in line!
(This is a good action poem which can be used to precede getting children in line to go out to recess. It also can be used to help children "let off steam" on a rainy day. The poem could also be used with the flannel board. Make cards with the numbers 1 to 9 printed on them.)

Exercise

I can reach high, I can reach low,
I'll touch my head and then my toes.
I'll wiggle my fingers and touch them, too.
I am having fun and so are you.
We stretch up to the ceiling,
And reach out to the wall.
We bend to touch our knees and toes,
Then stand up straight and tall.
(Use appropriate movements.)

My Garden

This is my garden;   *(extend one hand, palm up)*
I'll rake it with care,   *("rake" with three fingers of other hand)*
And then some flower seeds,   *(make planting motion with fingers)*
I'll plant in there.
The sun will shine,   *(make circle above head with hands)*
And the rain will fall,   *(flutter fingers for "rain")*
And my garden will blossom,   *(cup hands together, extend upward)*
And grow straight and tall.

A Japanese Game

Hana, hana, hana, kuchi;
Kuchi, kuchi, kuchi, mimi;
Mimi, mimi, mimi, me.

Nose, nose, nose, mouth;
Mouth, mouth, mouth, ear;
Ear, ear, ear, eye.
— *Traditional*

At the Seashore

Down at the seashore,
Isn't it grand?
Wiggling my toes   *(wiggle toes)*
In the soft warm sand.
Building a tall sand castle   *(make building motions)*
Where the King and Queen can stay,
But when the tide comes rushing in   *(one arm sweeps inward)*
They will have to move away!   *(arm makes leveling motion)*
Splashing in the water   *(hands make splashing motions)*
Of the cool blue sea,
Playing wave tag —in and out,   *(run forward with small steps)*
You can't catch me!   *(run quickly backwards)*
Holding up a seashell   *(hold fist tightly to ear)*
Tightly to my ear.
Shh! It's telling me a secret   *(other hand holds finger to lips)*
That only I can hear!

Frog

Croak said the frog,   *(make croaking sound)*
With his golden eyes.   *(fists up to eyes)*
Sitting on a lily pad,
Catching flies.   *(grab air with hand)*
I have a sticky tongue,   *(with index finger make*
It's as fast as can be.   *darting motion)*
I catch the mosquitoes,
1-2-3.
(Use as a flannel board rhyme.)

Five Little Koala Bears

Five little koala bears in a eucalyptus tree,
The first one said, "Hey, look at me!"
The second one said, "I'm a pretty furry bear."
The third one said, "I don't have a care."
The fourth one said, "Australia is my home."
The fifth one said, "I'll never, ever roam!"
Five little koala bears in a eucalyptus tree,
Climbing and playing and happy to be free!

Swimming

I can dive.   *(move hands flattened together)*
I can swim.   *(swimming motion)*
I can float.   *(hands out to side with*
I can fetch.   *head thrown back)*
But dog paddle   *(paddle like a dog)*
Is the stroke
That I do best.

Sea Gulls

I like to watch the sea gulls,   *(fists up to eyes)*
Playing in the sky.
Dipping and soaring,   *(wave arm in air)*
Through the clouds,
I wish that I could fly.

The Clever Pirates

Clever pirates are we.
We live way out at sea.
When the ships come around
We will take all they've found.
And that's why we're rich you see.

To the Zoo

To the cit - y   zoo we go
Ti - gers, ze - bras,   buf - fa - lo,

On a sum - mer   day.
Li - ons in a   den,

There is much for   us to see.
Birds and mon - keys,   el - e - phants,

How we like to   stay,
Let us come a -   gain.

The Singing Mosquito

In fun

A ti - ny mos - qui - to ___ Is

ver - y near.   He

buz - zes and hums And   he

sings in my   ear.

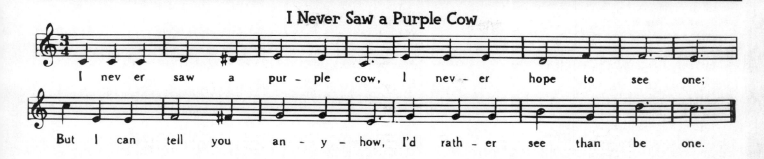

I Never Saw a Purple Cow

I nev-er saw a pur-ple cow, I nev-er hope to see one;

But I can tell you an-y-how, I'd rath-er see than be one.

Wading

A girl and a boy walked o-ver the hill To

wade in the stream, Where there once was a mill, Played in the wa-ter,

splashed on each oth-er. O-ver the hill a-gain Home to their moth-er!

Suggestion. With your hands, make a mill wheel go round and round while you sing the song.

The School Band

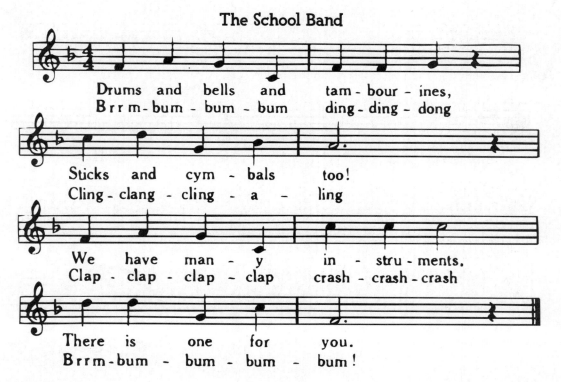

Drums and bells and tam-bour-ines,
Brrm-bum-bum-bum ding-ding-dong

Sticks and cym-bals too!
Cling-clang-cling-a-ling

We have man-y in-stru-ments,
Clap-clap-clap-clap crash-crash-crash

There is one for you.
Brrm-bum-bum-bum-bum!

ᚖᚑᚖ Music Activities ᚖᚑᚖ

Let's Go to the Beach
(tune—"A Hunting We Will Go")
Let's go to the beach
To swim and play and run.
Building castles in the sand
Is ever so much fun.

We'll fix a picnic lunch
And eat it when we like.
And when we all are nice and full
We'll take a nature hike.

Be sure to wear your suit
And bring along your float.
We'll ride so far out in the surf
Pretending it's a boat.

We'll find some pretty shells
And throw the gulls some bread.
Put on a lot of suntan oil
So that we don't turn red.

We'll never want to leave.
Such fun this all has been.
But we'll come back another day
And do it all again!

Birds
(Can be sung to the tune of "Row, Row, Row")

Fly, fly, fly away	*(make hands fly off to each side)*
Happy as can be	*(smile)*
Oh, fly, fly, fly away	*(repeat flying motions)*
Then fly right back to me.	*(beckon them back to you; have hand fly back)*

White Duck

The Little White Duck
(Turn into a flannel board song—enlarge the patterns)

There's a little white duck, sitting in the water.
A little white duck, doing what he oughta!
He took a bite of the lily pad,
Flapped his wings and he said, "I'm glad
I'm a little white duck sitting in the water. Quack, quack, quack."

There's a little green frog, swimming in the water.
A little green frog, doing what he oughta!
He jumped right off the lily pad,
That the little duck bit and he said, "I'm glad
I'm a little green frog swimming in the water. Glub, glub, glub."

There's a little black bug, floating on the water.
A little black bug, doing what he oughta!
He tickled the frog on the lily pad
That the little duck bit and he said, "I'm glad
I'm a little black bug floating on the water. Chirp, chirp, chirp."

There's a little red snake, laying in the water.
A little red snake, doing what he oughta!
He frightened the duck and the frog so bad,
He ate the little bug, and he said, "I'm glad
I'm a little red snake laying in the water. Wriggle, wriggle, wriggle."

Now there's nobody left, sitting in the water.
Nobody left, doing what he oughta!
There's nothing left but the lily pad.
The duck and the frog ran away. I'm sad.
'Cause there's nobody left sitting in the water. Boo, hoo, hoo.

Black Bug

Green Frog

Red Snake

Lily Pad

Sand and Water Activities

Sprinklers

As soon as it is warm enough, set up sprinklers at your center. Children always love running through the sprinklers on a hot summer day. Plan a day or two each week that is "Sprinkler Day" and keep it up all summer long.

Sprinklers can be just as much fun as wading pools, and they are less dangerous.

Sinking and Floating

Use a wading pool or a baby bathtub filled with water. Find many things with which the children may experiment and to examine the concepts of sinking and floating. Have them try to predict ahead of time which things will sink and which things will float.

Celery Action

A fun water experiment (that children often think is magic) is seeing how water travels through celery. Place a stalk of celery in a glass of colored water. The children will be able to see how the water goes through the celery.

A variation of this experiment is to divide one stalk of celery into two sections at the bottom. Place half the stalk in one glass of colored water, and the other half in another glass of a different color of water.

Beach Scene

A fun way to make a beach scene is to fill a baby food jar with sand. Arrange pebbles, shells, and twigs on top of the sand and put on the lid. The lid can be sprayed gold. Pasta shells can be used to represent real shells.

Sand Castle Contest

Plan a day to have a sand castle building contest. Send notes home a day ahead of time asking that the children bring buckets, pails, spoons, etc. from home, so you will be sure to have enough sand castle building tools for everyone.

Before the children begin their castles, give them some ideas of how to build a good sand castle. For example, they can use twigs and leaves as trees around the castles. Sand that has been moistened will be better to build with. The children will really have a lot of fun doing this activity.

Sailboat Races

Have the children make sailboats. They can be made from clay with a stick and paper for a sail. You can also make sailboats from construction paper. Take the construction paper and fold it into a hat. Turn the hat upside down and it will float very well. Or you can make great sailboats from pieces of cork. Use a toothpick with paper attached to it for a sail.

After the sailboats are created, take them outside to a wading pool or baby bathtub for sailboat races. Children love this activity.

Sand Candles

Fill containers such as cake pans, pie tins, etc. with wet sand. Press a hole into the sand for the candle shape. Cut a candlewick.

Melt paraffin wax over low heat until the wax is liquid. Add food coloring to the liquid wax. Pour the wax into the sand, and place the wick in the center of the candle.

The wax will take a day to solidify. When the wax becomes hard, all you need to do is to pull the candle out of the sand.

Wave a Flag

You will need assorted colors of construction paper, craft sticks, small stars, and clear adhesive paper.

Cut at least two 3" x 5" rectangles out of each color of construction paper. Glue one narrow edge of each paper rectangle to a craft stick so that it resembles a flag. Put two or three stars on each flag. Cover each flag with clear adhesive paper.

The children sit around the teacher. Each one is given a flag, while the teacher retains one flag of each color. The teacher holds up a flag. The child with the same color waves his/her flag.

To increase the complexity of the game, you can use different shades of the same color.

Go to the Store

Make a set of cards by pasting cut-outs from catalogs or magazines onto cards about 4" x 5". Pictures of articles of clothing may be mounted on blue, pictures of foods on green, pictures of furniture on brown, pictures of toys on yellow, etc. A spinner with areas of each color should also be made.

To play the game, one child draws from the pile of face-down cards to discover his/her category, and then spins the spinner. If the child spins to the same color as the card, he/she can then try to name the item on the card. If the child names the item correctly, he/she can keep the card. The next child then picks a card and spins. The first child to get a certain predetermined number in a category (such as three or five) wins the game.

Shape Puzzles

Two piece puzzles can easily be made with 5" x 8" cards, or paper cut to that size. Utilizing the paper scrap box, glue small scraps to each piece of the puzzle as illustrated. The children can then fit the two puzzle pieces together.

This is a good activity for an interest center, as it is self-correcting and doesn't need the teacher's assistance. The same kinds of games can be made with letters.

Fishing Game

To make the materials for the fishing game, you will need an 18" dowel stick, string, a magnet, assorted colors of construction paper, workbook pictures or magazine pictures, clear contact paper, and paper clips.

Attach one end of a 24" piece of string to the dowel stick, and attach a magnet to the loose end of the string. This is now a "fishing pole." Cut about a dozen fish out of construction paper. Mount a small picture, depicting a single object, on one side of each fish. Cover both sides of the fish with clear adhesive paper and put several paper clips on each fish. Set an open box on the floor or make a circle on the floor with masking tape. Put the fish inside the box or circle.

To play the game, the children sit around the box or circle, and take turns catching the fish with the fishing pole. The magnet will attract the clips on the fish. As the child catches a fish, he or she tells about the picture on it.

There can be many different variations to this game.

1. You can cut the fish out of various colors and have the children tell what color they have caught with their fishing pole.
2. You can mount different numbers of the same small objects or shapes on the fish. As the child catches a fish, he or she tells how many objects or shapes are on the fish.
3. You can put numerals on the fish and the children tell what numeral is caught.

A Chemical Garden

6 tablespoons salt
6 tablespoons bluing
6 tablespoons water
1 tablespoon ammonia

bits of cotton, wood, cloth, sponge
food coloring
several small pieces of coal or coke

Place coal or coke in a foil pie tin. Mix the salt, bluing, water, and ammonia in a bowl. Pour the mixture over coal or coke. Drop bits of cotton, wood, cloth, or sponge on top. Sprinkle with the food coloring. Place the pan near heat, and watch it grow.

Real Gardens

Real gardens are fun for adults and children. It is like magic to watch something grow.

Easy and fun things to plant are sunflowers, pumpkins, zinnias, marigolds, beans, and radishes. Try to plant both vegetables and flowers. Have the children take turns watering and weeding the gardens. Be sure to supervise the weeding process. My own daughter has been known to weed out all the plants.

The Gingerbread Man

Read or tell the children the story of "The Gingerbread Man." This story has delighted children for many years.

After the children have heard the story, make gingerbread balls. (These are much easier to make than gingerbread man cookies.) Purchase a boxed gingerbread mix. Follow the package directions to make the mix. Roll it into balls, dip in granulated sugar, and bake. This is an easy activity and it is lots of fun.

The Library

During the month of June when you are concentrating on the "Storytelling" unit, take a field trip to your local public library. Check your library's schedule to see if there might be a professional storyteller available, or ask if the children's librarian might be willing to do a special story time for your class. The children will love it.

Show the children all the things that the library has to offer them besides books. Many libraries now have puppets, puzzles, cassettes and read-a-long books, CD's, videos, automatic filmstrip machines, computers with games, etc. This will be a very successful field trip.

Something to Share from Another Country

A couple of days before this lesson is to take place, ask the children's parents to help the children find something to bring from home that is from another country. For families that don't have anything, suggest having the child bring a "word" from another country, or perhaps a recipe. The children could also share a custom that might be a part of their home.

On the day that the lesson is scheduled, have a discussion time where the children all share what they have from another country.

Special Nachos

Nachos come to us from Mexico. Here is an easy recipe:

1 package crisp tortilla chips
1 8-ounce can refried beans
1 cup grated cheddar cheese.

Spread tortilla chips with refried beans. Place on a baking sheet and top with grated cheese. Heat until the cheese melts. Makes about 20 servings.

Toothpick Patterning

This will give the children the experience of duplicating like patterns. You will need: posterboard, wooden toothpicks, and glue.

Cut the posterboard to measure 9" x 12". Divide the posterboard in half. On one side of the posterboard and in a vertical row, glue down patterns made with toothpicks.

The teacher then gives a child a batch of toothpicks. The child places the toothpicks next to those glued down to duplicate the patterns.

Trail Mix

This is an easy recipe that is healthy and good to eat. Mix the following ingredients together and enjoy!

1 package granola cereal
½ box raisins
½ pound banana chips

½ pound carob (or chocolate) chips
½ pound peanuts

Sweet Bars

You will need graham crackers, chocolate sauce, and peanut butter. Mix the peanut butter and chocolate sauce together in a small bowl. Spread the "yummy" mixture on the graham crackers. A quick treat that the children can make all by themselves.

Insect Parade

You will need one baby food jar for each child in your class, a marker, and a punch.

Prepare the baby food jars by punching small holes in the lids. Mark the children's names on the jars. Write a note to parents explaining that they should help their child find an insect, and have the child bring the insect back to school in the jar. Put the notes inside the jars, and send the jars home with the children. When the children bring in their insects, compare the bugs. Identify them if you can, count their legs to make sure they are insects, look at size, color, shape, etc. After analyzing the bugs, have an insect "parade" and show the insects to the children in other classrooms. Then let them go.

Making a Compass

You will need a bar magnet, bowl of water, diagram showing the four cardinal points, cork, and a large needle.

Magnetize the large needle by stroking it on one of the bar magnet's poles (stroke in only one direction). Place the needle on the cork and float the cork in the bowl of water. The needle will point to the magnetic poles of the earth—North and South. Place the diagram showing the four cardinal points under the bowl of water, aligning the directions.

- Have the children think of ways they would find their way home if they were lost.
- Using the compass, have the children find the four cardinal points in the classroom.
- Have the children find things in the room by referring to directions on the compass.
- Set up a campsite in the dramatic play center.

Fruit Puzzle

Use tagboard for the background. Divide it into 16 sections. Cut pictures from a seed catalog and glue them to the cross sections of the squares. Cover the board with plastic and bind the edges with tape. Cut out the squares. The children can mix the pieces and put them back together again.

TSD1896-4 *The Preschool Calendar*

ᴧᴧᴧ Australian Animals ᴧᴧᴧ

Australia is a fascinating continent. It is filled with interesting animals with which most young children are not familiar. The following paragraphs will provide you with information about six Australian animals, along with fun Australian animal activity ideas.

Information about Australian Animals

ANTEATER—The anteater is named after its favorite food—ants! The anteater has no teeth. It will stick its long tongue into the ground and scoop up the ants. Anteaters use their busy tails as a blanket when they sleep. When an anteater is in a tree, its long tail will hold on to the branches so it won't fall off.

KANGAROO—The kangaroo is the largest animal that carries its babies in a pouch. A pouch is like a pocket on the mother's stomach. The kangaroo moves around by jumping. It has very strong legs and a very strong tail. A kangaroo's fur is very soft. Some kangaroos can grow as tall as seven feet. Even though kangaroos are very big, they are really rather shy.

PLATYPUS—A platypus is an unusual animal. It has a soft bill shaped like that of a duck, and fur like a beaver's. The platypus lays eggs like a bird, but is really a mammal. Some people call the platypus "Duckbill."

EMU—The emu is Australia's national bird. It looks somewhat like an ostrich. It cannot fly, but it can run at high speeds on the ground. It is a very large bird.

WALLABY—A wallaby is a little kangaroo. They jump and sit on their strong tails, just like a kangaroo. Some wallabies are brightly colored. Wallabies are usually 2 to 3 feet tall.

KOALA BEAR—A koala bear looks like a small, soft, furry, gray teddy bear. They like to play and hang in the trees. The koala bear's long toes can easily grasp the branches. They love to eat eucalyptus leaves. Mother koala bears carry their babies in their pouches, just like the kangaroo. When the babies grow older, they ride on their mother's backs.

Kangaroo Pouch

Provide each child with a picture of a mother kangaroo (see illustration). The children should color the mother kangaroo. A pocket (pouch), cut from a piece of construction paper, can be stapled onto the mother's stomach. A small baby "joey" kangaroo can be colored, cut out, and placed in the mother's pouch.

Koala Bear Mask

Each child should paint a paper plate the color gray. Gray construction paper ears can be glued on or stapled to the top of the plate. Cut out openings for the eyes. Glue on a large black nose and a mouth. A tagboard stick or tongue depressor can be used as a handle for the mask.

My Australian Animal Book

Reproduce each of the above animal paragraphs on a separate piece of paper for each child. Have the children draw the animal's picture above each paragraph. The reproducible activity sheet, depicting all six animals, can be used as the cover for the *Australian Animal Book*.

Have the children complete one animal a day for six days.

ᴡᴡ Activity Index ᴡᴡ